Inside the Eagle's Head

Contemporary American Indian Studies
J. Anthony Paredes, *Series Editor*

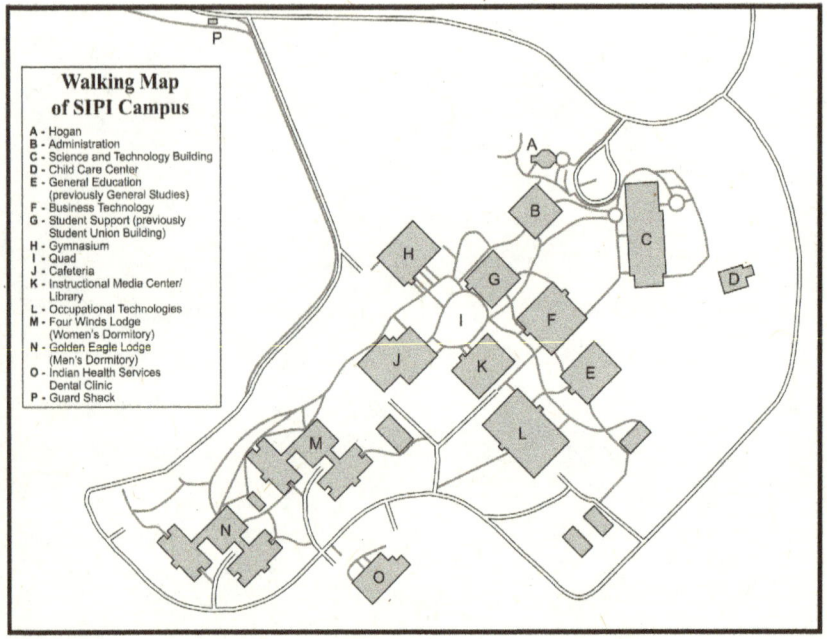

Inside the Eagle's Head

An American Indian College

Angelle A. Khachadoorian

THE UNIVERSITY OF ALABAMA PRESS
Tuscaloosa

Copyright © 2010
The University of Alabama Press
Tuscaloosa, Alabama 35487-0380
All rights reserved
Manufactured in the United States of America

Typeface: ACaslon

∞

The paper on which this book is printed meets the minimum requirements of American National Standard for Information Sciences—Permanence of Paper for Printed Library Materials, ANSI Z39.48-1984.

Library of Congress Cataloging-in-Publication Data

Khachadoorian, Angelle A.
　Inside the eagle's head : an American Indian college / Angelle A. Khachadoorian.
　　p. cm. — (Contemporary American Indian studies)
　Includes bibliographical references and index.
　ISBN 978-0-8173-5614-9 (pbk. : alk. paper) — ISBN 978-0-8173-8353-4 (electronic) 1. Southwestern Indian Polytechnic Institute. 2. Indian universities and colleges—New Mexico—Albuqurque. 3. Indian college students—New Mexico—Albuquerque—Attitudes. 4. Indian college students—United States—Attitudes. 5. Indians of North America—Education (Higher)—New Mexico—Albuquerque. 6. Indians of North America—Education (Higher)—Government policy—United States. I. Title.
　E97.6.S68K43 2010
　378.1′982997—dc22

　　　　　　　　　　　　　　　　　　　　　　　　　　　　2010015560

This book is dedicated to my father, Archie Khachadoorian, a born raconteur who taught me that the best stories are the true ones.

Contents

List of Illustrations   ix

Preface   xi

Acknowledgments   xiii

1. Entering the Turquoise Gates: The Southwestern Indian Polytechnic Institute   1
2. Thinking and Talking About SIPI: Narratives and Metaphors   36
3. "A Standing Army of School Teachers": American Indian Education, Assimilation, and the BIA   50
4. Taking a New Path: The Decision to Attend SIPI   86
5. Life Within the Eagle's Head   107
6. SIPI Is a Reservation: Family, Friends, and Mentors   155
7. SIPI Is What You Make It: Academics, Administration, and Working Around the System   185
8. SIPI Is an Opportunity: Giving Students the Chance to Dream   211

Appendix. Studying the Southwestern Indian Polytechnic Institute   221

Works Cited   227

Index   239

Illustrations

Walking Map of SIPI Campus   frontispiece
1. Campus directions posted at entry   2
2. A view of the Science and Technology Building   30
3. A view of the two-story residential area of the dormitories   110
4. A view of the back of the Hogan, dwarfed by the Science and Technology Building   136

Preface

The setting for this book is the Southwestern Indian Polytechnic Institute (SIPI), a self-described National Indian Community College in Albuquerque, New Mexico. SIPI (pronounced "Sippy") serves registered members of federally recognized American Indian tribes and Alaskan Native villages, and students are drawn from throughout the United States. Yet even with its national reach, it is a school that the vast majority of Americans have never heard of. In fact, many people who live in Albuquerque have either not heard of it, or believe its dilapidated appearance and weedy grounds mean it was shuttered years before. But SIPI is not closed—although the threat of closure has been a steady and worrying theme for most of the school's existence. More important, SIPI is not unknown everywhere—Indian Country knows about SIPI. For almost forty years, grandparents, parents, and their children have chosen to attend this small Bureau of Indian Affairs community college.

There are multiple contradictions to an institution that provides federally funded schooling for a population that has always faced extensive, and at times invasive, oversight by the United States federal government. Complicating that history is that the school also attempts to mesh four conflicting institutional models—federal installation, community college, tribal institution, and successor to historic Bureau of Indian Affairs schools. Underfunded, with conflicting institutional goals, philosophies, and cultures, the contradictions are woven into the very fabric of the school. If this sounds like a setting fraught with conflict and challenges, it is. Students, faculty, and staff cannot help being attuned—even if it is subconsciously—to the inherent contradictions of the institution. Over my years of teaching there, I came to suspect that the students who are best able to recognize the contradictions are the ones who, in turn, overcome them.

Native American young people come to SIPI for all the usual reasons that students everywhere attend college—to get an education, improve their future, move out of the family home. SIPI students have some additional motivations that make the school all the more interesting—they come to learn more about their tribal culture, immerse themselves in a completely Native American peer group, and avoid marginalization or racism as they might have experienced it elsewhere. For all the flaws and contradictions of the school, success and beauty also exist there. Beauty in the student who never knew about her tribe's culture making friends with women who take the time to teach her; beauty in a painfully shy student who finds the voice to share his opinions publically for the first time and refuses to be silent in the future; beauty in the student who stands in front of her justifiably proud extended family to receive her diploma, the first in her family to attend college. Because, in spite of its flaws, and in its own way, SIPI is beautiful.

Acknowledgments

This book is the result of the tremendous generosity of students at the Southwestern Indian Polytechnic Institute who participated in interviews and surveys, and shared their opinions and experiences. While I cannot mention them by name, I am incredibly grateful for their interest in the project and for their willingness to share their stories and their insights.

I want to thank Donald and Alyce Jordan for listening to endless iterations of my research. Thanks to Mark and Laura Khachadoorian and Stu and Anne Merriken for their encouragement. I owe thanks to Stuart A. Merriken II for providing a haven so I could finish this book.

My thanks to Cenita Ettl, who was an incredible sounding board through all phases of the research and writing. I am grateful to Jenny Sanborn for uncountable conversations about the research. Gloria Rutt provided much needed tea and sympathy. I want to thank Louise Lamphere, Les Field, Sylvia Rodriguez, and Anne Nihlen, for their guidance during my research.

This book was greatly improved by the insightful critiques of my reviewers, J. Anthony Paredes, Kendall Blanchard, and an anonymous third reviewer.

I was given the opportunity to participate in two Summer Institutes for Teachers in Tribal Colleges sponsored by the Newberry Library's D'Arcy McNickle Center and the Lannan Summer Institute. These were invaluable experiences to learn from gifted scholars, collaborate with peers, and delve into a treasure trove of historical material that helped shape my understanding of the Bureau of Indian Affairs and its educational mission.

Most important, this book would never have come to be without the amazing support of my husband, James Merriken—I cannot thank him enough for his patience and limitless encouragement

1
Entering the Turquoise Gates
The Southwestern Indian Polytechnic Institute

> [SIPI] gives me an outlook in the world. It's kinda like it helps me prepare to . . . go outside the gates. And know what I'll expect. And [be] ready for it.
> —Dallas Wicke (Sioux)

> SIPI's a great opportunity to pursue your education. It's a great opportunity to establish your academic career. There's a lot of great opportunities here, it's just how you take advantage of them. There's a lot of really good programs at SIPI.
> —Renee Verde (Navajo)

> I'm really, really glad I came here. I'm really glad I took the time to check it out, to see if it was something I could do . . . I knew I'd be able to finish here, be able to do something here. You gotta take advantage of the resources that are available there. If you don't ask questions, if you don't participate, then you really lose out, I think.
> —Clayton Griego (Pueblo)

SIPI: An Origin Story

In 1971, Native American leaders were, after years of effort, able to persuade the Bureau of Indian Affairs (BIA) to fund and build a vocational-technical school in Albuquerque, New Mexico, for Native American students. The new school, the Southwestern Indian Polytechnic Institute, or SIPI (pronounced "Sippy"), resolved a long-standing dilemma. In order for students from the Southwest to attend SIPI's sister school—the venerable Haskell Indian Nations University of Lawrence, Kansas—they had to live far from home, removing them from their communities and the daily life of their tribe. A Bureau of Indian Affairs postsecondary school in Albuquerque meant that students could stay close to home and continue to actively participate in tribal activities. The parcel of land the BIA chose for SIPI's campus is located on the western bank of the Rio Grande River and, the story goes, was once the dairy farm for the Albuquerque Indian School.

1. Campus directions posted at entry. The eagle on the sign is a reference to the layout of the campus road. Photo courtesy of the author.

SIPI was initially designed to provide technical training and job placement services to Native American students who were either not ready for, or not interested in, a standard college education. In 1993, the school underwent a seismic philosophical and curricular shift when it became accredited as a community college with an emphasis on technology. While technology is still a central theme, in recent years most SIPI students have majored in liberal arts or business rather than technical fields.

The Southwestern Indian Polytechnic Institute's genesis was a result of the movement toward Native American educational sovereignty in the 1960s. The 1960s marked a significant shift in attitudes away from assimilationist educational institutions—which had been the norm for Indian education for most of its history—and a move toward putting control of the education of Native American children into the hands of Native American educators and parents. At the same time, postsecondary education was taking a step toward sovereignty as well. The All-Indian Pueblo Council began in 1960 to encourage the Bureau of Indian Affairs to create a federally operated postsecondary institution in the Southwest. It took another ten years before construction began for the new school, the Southwestern Indian Polytechnic

Institute (SIPI 1999:3). By then, tribal colleges and Native American studies programs were being founded all over the United States (Reyhner and Eder 2004:305). The original TCU, Navajo Community College (NCC)—now Diné College—was founded in 1968 in Tsaile, Arizona. Six other tribal colleges quickly followed, with the Southwestern Indian Polytechnic Institute opening only three years after NCC was founded (Reyhner and Eder 2004:305).

During the 1970s, the number of American Indian colleges grew exponentially. Ten years after the founding of Navajo Community College there were sixteen TCUs (Stein 1998:83), and thirty years after the first TCU opened, there were thirty member schools in the umbrella organization for tribal colleges, the American Indian Higher Education Consortium (AIHEC) (Szasz 1999:242–247). When it opened, the Southwestern Indian Polytechnic Institute was an exciting addition to Native American education. The dormitories were filled with amenities not offered in the Bureau of Indian Affairs boarding schools that many of its students graduated from. An older Navajo student described visiting friends at SIPI in its earliest days. She listed the enviable luxuries that SIPI students had that were not available at her boarding school: The entire dormitory was carpeted, there were pay phones and televisions in the common areas, students could bring their own bedding, and best of all, they had lockers instead of the boarding school cubbies where there was always a risk of theft. SIPI, and its peers, represented the beginning of a new era in American Indian education.

For most of its history, SIPI has been operated by the Bureau of Indian Affairs (BIA), a federal agency under the Department of the Interior, through its educational branch the Office of Indian Education Programs (OIEP). The BIA—and now its recently formed offshoot, the Bureau of Indian Education (BIE)—oversees all of the federal government's schools for American Indian children, and its two Native American–serving colleges. The Bureau of Indian Affairs has directed and managed the relationship between the United States government and American Indian tribes for almost two hundred years. The relationship between the BIA, tribal entities, and individual American Indian people is complex and laden with the weight of history; sometimes that history surfaces in unexpected ways at the Southwestern Indian Polytechnic Institute.

Throughout this book I will refer to SIPI as being administered by the Bureau of Indian Affairs or its subsidiary, the Office of Indian Education Programs (OIEP). I do this for two reasons: First, the links between SIPI and historical American Indian educational institutions are derived from the

BIA, and more important, the Bureau of Indian Education (BIE) is so new that it was formed after the research for this book. The school that appears in these pages is a Bureau of Indian Affairs institution, not a BIE one.

SIPI was quite small when it first opened, with 342 students enrolled (Harbert 1996:B2). Its student population in recent years has varied dramatically from around two hundred students during the summer trimester to three or four times that in the fall. Only one year after its highest enrollment—914 students—in the fall of 2003 (SIPI 2004), the school struggled with a severe budget deficit and enrollment fell to 614 students (AIHEC 2005:1). The acceptance rate of applicants is 95 percent, and the average high school grade point average (GPA) is 2.11 (Peterson's 2008). Its student body is neither the largest, nor the smallest, in the tribal college consortium, but falls in the top third. The school has had more than 130 employees but is currently quite a bit smaller (Armijo 2005). When I was hired, there were more than thirty full-time faculty members; now there are fewer than fifteen.

The Southwestern Indian Polytechnic Institute shares membership in several small subsets of postsecondary institutions in the United States. First, SIPI is one of only two federally operated postsecondary institutions for American Indian and Alaskan Native students. Although the Southwestern Indian Polytechnic Institute is the sister school to the far more established, and famous, federally operated Native American college, Haskell Indian Nations University (HINU, or more commonly known simply as Haskell), SIPI is no twin to HINU. HINU is a far less conflicted institution than SIPI. There are, I believe, several reasons for this: Its long history has allowed HINU the time to work out organizational kinks; HINU has a deeply committed and active alumni population, giving students a voice in the institution; HINU has double the budget that SIPI has; HINU operates more like a college and less like a government installation than SIPI. More recently, SIPI adopted a despised, controversial, and ultimately deemed illegal personnel system that has led to multiple lawsuits—and their loss by the institution. HINU rejected the same personnel system from the outset. HINU is not without conflicts. At the time of this writing, the president of the school was being pressured to step down, and the school's endowment organization had folded and given away its funds.

SIPI is also a longtime peer institution to the Institute of American Indian Arts (IAIA). IAIA became a two-year college in 1974 and gained its federal educational charter in 1986 with more than $24 million in an endowment and investments (IAIA 2007:4, 8). Faced with a massive reduction in

Congressional funding, IAIA reshaped itself into an independent institution. IAIA is no longer under the governance of the Bureau of Indian Affairs, but receives its funding directly from the Department of the Interior. Students at all three schools regularly transfer and take classes back and forth among the schools, a trend that is especially common in the case of HINU and SIPI.

Many of their differences are significant to the two schools' (SIPI and HINU) organizational cultures. SIPI is far newer than HINU, which was founded initially as a boarding school in 1884. SIPI offers one-year certificates or two-year associate degrees while Haskell also has bachelor's and master's degree programs. Haskell boasts active alumni associations and famous alumni, and it is far more widely known by non-Natives than SIPI.

SIPI shares unusual characteristics with several types of postsecondary institutions. For example, one quality SIPI and HINU have in common, and that shapes the cultures of these schools, is the composition of their student bodies. These two schools only enroll Native Americans, which stands in surprising contrast to the other set of postsecondary institutions they are usually classed with, the tribally controlled colleges and universities (TCUs). In 2005, for example, only 79 percent of the students at TCUs were Native American (AIHEC 2005:2). Because of its accessibility to people of all federally recognized tribes, and even though it is a small school, at any given time, there may be as many as one hundred different tribes represented in SIPI's student population.

SIPI is one of only seven federally operated postsecondary institutions, a distinction shared by HINU and the five United States service academies, also known as the military academies. These include the United States Military Academy (USMA), commonly referred to by its home city, West Point; the United States Naval Academy (USNA), commonly referred to by its home city as well, Annapolis; the United States Air Force Academy (USAFA); the United States Merchant Marine Academy, and the United States Coast Guard Academy.

In many official contexts, such as research on American Indians and Alaska Natives in higher education (U.S. Dept. of Ed. 1998), SIPI is included with the small group of thirty-six tribal colleges and universities in the United States—again, a group including HINU—which are designed and chartered to serve a primarily Native American student population (IAIA 2007:4). Regardless of how it has been classified, I will show later in this book that SIPI is actually a very different type of institution than the TCUs.

In addition to the characteristics it shares with each of these types of colleges—TCU, federal college, sister to HINU—SIPI is also a fascinatingly hybridized institution that struggles to meld deeply conflicting institutional models, each with their unique corporate cultures, rules, and philosophies. SIPI is a community college, a federal installation, and a Bureau of Indian Affairs educational setting, and at least attempts to be comparable to a tribally controlled college or university. The various models for these types of institutions are all wrestling with each other at the school, with no one system taking the lead. This conflict between institutional models leads to inconsistencies in the rules and attitudes that are applied to students, leading to confusing experiences at the school—sometimes SIPI students are treated like adults attending college, and other times they are as heavily managed as children in a historical Bureau of Indian Affairs boarding school. Students are whipsawed between the two conditions—independent adults and overly managed children—and it leads to frustration and resistance. Many cannot specifically name the source of the frustrations and inconsistencies they encounter at the school. They are, though, very able commentators on the experience of functioning within (or rather, maneuvering around) the school's contradictions. Oftentimes, their analyses of the school take the form of mental or verbal metaphors, which enable them to define the Southwestern Indian Polytechnic Institute by comparing it to another, better understood type of institution.

In its relatively brief history, the Southwestern Indian Polytechnic Institute has experienced a recurrent cycle of dramatic high and low points. Recent high points include earning accreditation as a community college, the funding and construction of the $12 million, 72,540-square-foot Science and Technology Building, and an increase in academic offerings and in student enrollment (Briseno 2003:1). The school's successes are often overshadowed by its near chronic state of crisis and institutional disorder, now near persistent features of the institution. Beginning with the threat to close the school little more than a decade after its doors opened, SIPI's administration has faced, or created, crises requiring significant time, effort, politicking, and legal action to resolve (SIPI 1999:4). The institutional disorder manifests itself in many ways: The high turnover rate of the institution's presidents; perpetual fiscal crises prompted by permanent and severe underfunding from Congress coupled with apparent overspending, like the 2005 budget deficit of $1.06 million that led to massive layoffs and a complete reorganization of the school (Armijo 2005b:1); conflict surrounding the unpopular imposition of a dramatically different personnel system, which faced repeated legal protests and which was subsequently overturned by court order in 2006;

and lastly, but undergirding all the other issues, is the ever-present disorder caused by the lack of a consistent and clear institutional identity. Efforts to mesh incompatible organizational models—college, BIA school, TCU, and federal office installation—necessarily fail when there seems to be neither awareness of the inherent incompatibilities of these types of institutions, nor a systemic or systematic effort to bridge them.

Administrative attitudes and decisions do not appear to reflect an understanding of the inherent incompatibilities of these types of institutions. Complicating matters, much of the decision making occurs off-stage and out of sight, so that throughout this book, I use the term "administration" to describe both the administrators at the college level and the bureaucrats higher up in the Bureau of Indian Affairs. As all major administrative decisions face some amount of Bureau-level oversight, the decision making and the general administration of the school happen at all levels of the federal chain of command. I do not reference the actions of any specific administrators, as I do not know the role of each individual actor in designing, approving, and implementing policy and institutional philosophy—rather, decisions were made and handed down from the school's administrative tier with no names attached. Whether decisions were generated at the individual or the group level (another unknown to the rank-and-file employees and students), decisions routinely betrayed a lack of awareness of how they reflected SIPI's fractured institutional culture.

Student Voices

To truly understand the Southwestern Indian Polytechnic Institute, one must let the students speak. Students at SIPI are astute observers of the daily dynamics and organizational culture of the place. Unfortunately, SIPI students, like students at other TCUs, are oftentimes kept out of the discourse. Students' own perceptions of their schooling are virtually ignored by the literature on tribal colleges, which typically focuses on one of three issues: college administration, culturally appropriate curricula, or school origins and history (W. Belgarde 1993; Oppelt 1990; Pavel et al. 2001; Stein 1988). It is rare to hear the voice of a tribal college student in the literature. Tierney 1992 is an exception, but he includes only a few pages dedicated to tribal colleges. SIPI itself is mostly ignored within tribal college literature, except in the few cases when it warrants only a very brief mention or the information is hopelessly outdated (Carney 1999; Szasz 1999; Stein 1992; Oppelt 1990). The words of SIPI students specifically? Nowhere to be found in the published literature. SIPI is featured in four unpublished dissertations, but not all utilize students' words: Khachadoorian 2005 quotes extensively from student interviews, surveys, and conversations; McReynolds 1997 includes interviews with SIPI students; Machamer 2000 is entirely statistical in nature, it does not involve any interviewing of students, and SIPI is not specifically named or differentiated from HINU; and Davis 1998 is a history of Indian education.

Perhaps worse than being ignored by research, Native American students are often reduced in educational literature to generic assumptions about learning styles. Some of these assumptions effectively silence students or imply they cannot succeed in their classes. In my experience, many of these postulates do not hold up in the classroom. Early in my time at SIPI, I decided to revive a long-dormant class on contemporary American Indian issues and structure it as a series of lectures and group discussions. I expected students to participate actively and mentioned my plan to several individuals I knew had taught Native American students. I was warned away from the interactive format I wanted, as "experienced" college instructors repeated the same old cant that surfaces in so much of the literature on Native American education—"Indian kids won't talk in class." Their model of Native American students and my experiences in the classroom did not jibe. The students talked. They had a lot to say. They discussed, debated, opined, and even ranted. They brought their own ideas, experiences, and suggestions, and offered them to their peers. Silencing Native American college students by insisting that they actually do not wish to speak is an effective, and marginalizing, technique not just for stifling active debate, but for discouraging any kind of student input.

It would be impossible to teach at SIPI and hold the generic and two-dimensional view of Native American young people that appears in much of the educational literature. To teach at SIPI is to be surrounded by all the personality types that one expects from college students: the studious, the poetic, the earnest, the jokers, the jocks and student government activists, the go-getters, and the chronic "I forgot my pencil" excuse makers. There are the students who make me grin when I think of them, as well as the ones who still cause me to shake my head in dismay. All of them shaped my experience at the school and the experiences of their peers, and defined much of what is positive about the Southwestern Indian Polytechnic Institute. To leave out their voices would be to leave out much of the joy of the place.

I think back over so many students: The unfazed Alaskans who wore sandals when it snowed and were baffled by our collective shock and concern for them. They in turn expressed frustration because their peers kept asking them if they lived in igloos. I think of the student who hid her face behind a waterfall of long hair throughout her time in my class, smart but too shy to speak; a few years later, I was stunned as she cheerfully bellowed my name across the quad at the local university, turning onlookers' heads and making us both laugh. I still visualize the snake wrangler who caught one of the many bull snakes on campus (I was once told reassuringly that the campus ratio is nineteen bull snakes to each rattler found) and casually carried it into my classroom, setting off panic among the phobic and unwittingly offending members of the Navajo tribe, who believe snakes must remain unmolested and allowed to continue on their intended path. How often does a professor in an Ivy League school get to demand, "Put that snake back outside!"? Or for that matter, have to say, "Keep the door closed so the coyotes don't come in!"? I delight in the memory of students cheerfully funneling out the back door of our classroom to stand on a scrubby patch of grass under a towering line of cottonwood trees. I directed them to look at the looming Sandia Mountains, and talked about early agriculture in the Southwest, while we joked about having taken a low-cost, Bureau of Indian Affairs–sponsored "field trip."

During my decade at SIPI, I met many smart, motivated, engaging, articulate students who were more than capable of clearly and effectively elucidating and analyzing their experiences at the school. To ignore students' own words overlooks the wealth of their widely diverging worldviews—the richness in diversity of personality and persons. More important, students are the ones who see the college from the inside and experience its mechanisms daily. I assume some insider status—as all SIPI employees could—but students are the ones whose daily, personal lives are expected to bend to the rules, values, and standards of the place. They might not label the conflicts they experience at the school as growing out of institutional contradictions, but they know that sometimes they feel like they are in college and other times they are experiencing the BIA in all its bureaucracy. They see, and see through, the vagaries of the system because, as students and residents, they are far more affected by the inconsistent nature of the school than employees. I hope the reader can hear the students in this text, and make the leap from Native American students as they are represented by simple demographics to seeing SIPI students as thinkers, speakers, and three-dimensional people with self-will and valuable insights. They learn how to take the institution, with its clashing quilt of values, and make it their own. Regardless of the institutional flaws and disconnects, as one student told me, it's the students who make it a school.

Who Attends SIPI: Student Demographic Characteristics

The Southwestern Indian Polytechnic Institute attracts students from across the country, some of whom travel from as far away as New York and Alaska to attend. The majority of SIPI students, though, come from New Mexico and Arizona. There is awareness at the institutional level of the educational role the school plays for local tribes. The SIPI course catalog lists the population figures of tribes in its self-described "immediate recruiting area" (SIPI 2003:3), which includes the states in near proximity to New Mexico. The recruiting area is composed of New Mexico, Arizona, Utah, California, Colorado, Oklahoma, and Texas. In practice, though, the school attracts more students from South Dakota and Kansas than Texas.

The demographic data on SIPI students makes it clear that not all tribes are equally represented in the student body. Navajo students regularly far outnumber their peers from other tribes. There have been some small demographic shifts since 2004 when I collected demographic data for this book. In 2008, Navajo students made up 47 percent of the student body (SIPI 2008:7), a slight increase from enrollment numbers provided by the school's Registrar for 2004, in which Navajo students were 42 percent of the total students. The Navajo Nation is the largest tribe in the Southwestern United States and its reservations are located near the school, explaining the high representation of Navajo students. Pueblo students made up 17 percent of the student population in 2008 (SIPI 2008:7), a slight decrease from 2004, when Pueblo students numbered 19 percent of the student body. There are nineteen pueblos in SIPI's immediate recruiting area (Arizona and New Mexico). Although each individual Pueblo tribe is a legally and politically independent entity, for demographic purposes, they are often categorized together. Therefore, I use this general term to refer to all students from Pueblo tribes including Hopi and Zuni. The Cherokee Nation of Oklahoma is usually heavily represented in student enrollment numbers as the school has an agreement with the tribe's headquarters in Tahlequah, Oklahoma, to provide classes via distance education technology. Their enrollment numbers rise and fall depending on their participation in distance education class offerings.

According to the American Indian Higher Education Consortium (AIHEC), the typical tribal college student a decade ago was a woman around the age of thirty-one (AIHEC 1999a:D-1). More current data shows a shift to a younger overall student population, with a majority (63 percent) of TCU students falling in the eighteen- to twenty-four-year-old range (AIHEC 2005:3). Of thirty-two reporting TCUs, 66 percent of the students are female and 35 percent are male—unfortunately, the numbers AIHEC published add up to 101 percent (AIHEC 2005:1). SIPI's demographic data shows the average age of a SIPI student is twenty-six years old (SIPI 2008:7). Based on data from 2004, female students were, on average, three years older (28.1 years) than their male counterparts (25.2 years). The 2004 data, though, reflects all of the students who were enrolled in classes, including students who were rarely, if ever, physically on campus as part of the distance education cohort. As a group, distance education students tend to be in their forties and older, skewing the data for students' average ages. Unsurprisingly, the age data collected through the survey questionnaire in 2004, which was only distributed to students who attended classes on campus, diverged from that of SIPI's Registrar for the same year. Female students who attended classes on campus and answered the survey were more than five years younger than was reflected in SIPI's data. My results were more representative of the student body *on campus* (and, therefore, reflects active participants in the campus community) whereas the data provided by SIPI gave an accurate picture of ages for all students enrolled at the school.

Current data on gender ratios at SIPI indicate that female students slightly outnumber males, with women making up 54 percent of the student body (SIPI 2008:7). In the fall of 2003, which had the highest student enrollment rate in the school's history, its 914-person student body was composed of 528 women (58.8 percent) and 386 men (41.2 percent). Of the female students 61 percent were commuters, whereas only 40 percent of the males commuted (SIPI 2004). The women and men who come to SIPI, then, represent a range of ages, tribes, and prior academic experience.

SIPI's Organizational Structure and Academic Departments

There are three basic classes of permanent employee at the Southwestern Indian Polytechnic Institute. These are "administration," who have management and decision-making responsibilities; "faculty/instructional staff," who teach the college's classes (and who might act as an assistant department chair with virtually no decision-making rights); and "staff," who are nonmanagerial, nonteaching employees. All permanent employees who are not administrators are covered by the union agreement.

The chain of command at the Southwestern Indian Polytechnic Institute is led by the school's president and a fairly small group of administrators, as befitting the overall size of the school. Individual presidents have chosen the degree to which they delegate to the next lower layer of administration. The school's erratic financial status has not been helped by (or is perhaps reflected in) the fact that there have been seven different presidents at the school between 2002 and the writing of this book. Four presidents have been interim or acting. One individual, a long-time SIPI employee, served in this capacity twice, after the departure of two different presidents.

The two administrators in the level below the college president are currently labeled the vice president of academic programs and the vice president of college operations. These positions were long labeled "deans" rather than "vice presidents," but a title change was adopted during the massive institutional reorganization in spring of 2005 (detailed later in this chapter). The organizational chart for SIPI, while clear on paper, has domain overlaps that lead to confusion. For example, the vice president of instruction is tasked with managing all aspects of education at the institution. The vice president of administration handles all administrative and management functions, including acting as the director of the Personnel Department, and signing off on all hiring. Complications arise when there is a personnel issue with instructional staff. Conflicts between instructional staff, for example, could be addressed by either the head of hiring and personnel (the vice president of administration) or the director of all things teaching related (the vice president of instruction), or both. But who actually has final decision-making authority? In addition to the three top administrators, SIPI has the standard college administrative offices of Financial Aid, Personnel, Records, and Registration.

Working with, and ostensibly overseeing, the work of SIPI's president is its Board of Regents (BOR), composed of representatives from multiple tribes. The course catalog states that the school is "governed" by its Board of Regents (SIPI 1999:4), yet the standard refrain from the school administration is that the BOR serves an "advisory," rather than an administrative or managerial, function. It is unclear how much actual power the Board of Regents really wields.

Several tribes have permanent slots on the BOR for their representatives. Board of Regents positions are held for the Jicarilla Apache tribe, the Mescalero Apache tribe (both tribes are located within New Mexico), the Western Navajo tribe (this tribe has the largest, and most visually recognizable, reservation in the country), the Eastern Navajo tribe (located within the borders of New Mexico), the Eight Northern Pueblo Council, the Ten Southern Pueblos, the Southern Ute tribe of Colorado, the Oglala Sioux tribe, the Inter-Tribal Council of Arizona, and the Joint Oklahoma Tribes (SIPI 1999:4; SIPI 2000:10). SIPI's President of the Student Body is always a voting member of the Board of Regents. Not all positions on the BOR are consistently filled. For example, the Oglala Sioux tribe has its own tribal college (Oglala Lakota College in Kyle, South Dakota) and has not placed a representative on SIPI's BOR in many years.

The Board of Regents was declared a nonprofit organization in 1975 (SIPI 1999:4), which provides an avenue for individuals and organizations to donate directly to the school, as otherwise, donations are complicated by SIPI's status as a federal agency. In 1991, SIPI's Board of Regents developed a twenty-year plan that included making the shift from vocational-technical status to becoming a community college (SIPI 1999:4). The school gained accreditation in 1993 as a community college, leading to a shift away from a purely vocational-technical focus with its emphasis on job skills. Since 1993, SIPI has offered community college courses intended to prepare students for matriculation to four-year schools, especially in the fields of science, technology, and computers. As SIPI did not initially have the credentialed staff to teach college-level classes, the school hired most of their college faculty as adjuncts through the University of New Mexico's Continuing Education Department. It is through this hiring program that I came to teach at SIPI in early 1998, and I was eventually hired as a permanent faculty member.

Faculty play multiple official and unofficial roles on campus, as is typical of a small college. All faculty members typically have a teaching load of five classes per trimester, although some take on more duties as necessary. In addition, all permanent faculty members have a roster of student advisees. Students are made unusually dependent on their faculty advisors because only faculty can register students for their classes. (I present student responses to this situation later in the book.) Not only can students not register themselves for their classes, but they need their advisor's permission to change their schedule, add and drop classes, and check their grades. The learned helplessness students are encouraged to adopt creates tension between students and the institution, yet also builds strong ties between students and their faculty advisors, who repeatedly intercede on students' behalf.

For the majority of SIPI's history as a community college, there were three academic departments, each with its own department chairs and assistant chairs. Department chairs do not have teaching responsibilities; assistant chairs do. The academic departments have academic counselors who meet with students who are having difficulty, organize and operate the placement testing, apprise faculty of student absences, and act as mediators to the administration. The departments as they were organized for the majority of my time at the school were Occupational Technologies, Business Technologies, and General Education. Students must have a high school diploma or its equivalent to enroll in a degree-granting program at SIPI. The academic programs offer one-year certificates and two-year Associate of Arts, Associate of Science, and Associate of Applied Science degrees.

Until 2005, General Education was made up of two fused programs: Liberal Arts and the remediation program, Adult Developmental Education (ADE). These two programs were housed in the same building and under the same administrator for most of my time there. When I refer to General Education in the text, I am making reference to a policy or issue that affected the merged department. When I refer to Liberal Arts and ADE individually, it is because there are differences in the characteristics of the student populations and the educational goals.

The Liberal Arts Department has a two-year degree program designed to fulfill all the standard college general education requirements. The degree prepares students to matriculate to a four-year college by fulfilling the general education and freshman- and sophomore-level courses. Students can then matriculate directly into their major programs at four-year schools, with the majority of matriculating students choosing to attend the University of New Mexico.

ADE classes provide remediation for students needing to work on basic academic skills, such as math, English, and reading. Students entering SIPI for the first time undergo placement testing to determine their academic preparedness. The majority of incoming students need at least one college preparatory class when they enter SIPI. The need for remediation is typical of tribal college students, with an average of 65 percent of incoming TCU students needing remediation in mathematics, 55 percent needing it in writing, and 39 percent needing it in reading (AIHEC 2005:3).

Like most community colleges, SIPI also has a small program to prepare students to take the General Equivalency Degree (GED) exams. Free GED classes are offered throughout New Mexico, including on the reservations. The main attractions of SIPI's GED program are that, unlike other programs, students receive free housing, meals, and preparation materials, and they do not have to pay administrative fees to take the GED exams. Throughout the school's history, the GED program has dramatically expanded and contracted.

Occupational Technologies, like General Education, is a fused department. In the Applied Vocational Technologies Programs, students can major in the job-training programs that are still extant, such as Culinary Arts, Desktop Publishing, and Optical Laboratory Technology. Majors in the Advanced Technical Systems Programs include natural resources management, civil engineering, and electronics technology. In recent years, the vocational-technical programs have been severely curtailed, and are mostly limited to environmental and earth science fields. The Graphics Arts Program, which had been one of the most popular vocational-technical majors at SIPI, began to contract in size with the retirement of its longtime lead instructor. In alignment with the contemporary processes for graphic design and printing, the program became entirely digital at the beginning of 2004. The enrollment dropped after that, and the entire program was put on hold less than a year later. As more and more technical fields become computerized, SIPI is finding that the vocational-technical programs require math and language skills comparable to those necessary in the academic programs, which in turn leads to competition between majors for students.

The Business Technologies Department offers majors in business administration, accounting, and other business-related fields. This department has developed a Tribal Management Program in conjunction with New Mexico State University (NMSU). Students completing SIPI's portion of the Tribal Management Program can then transfer to NMSU to complete their degree. The major programs in this department have also become largely computerized and some classes are being taught entirely online, a large step forward for the school.

SIPI also offers distance education classes. The Distance Education Program stands apart from the other programs and comprises its own department. Distance Education offers many of the same classes as taught by other departments on campus, but it hires its own faculty, it designs its own curricula, and its students are rarely on campus. The Distance Education Program has mostly served to provide early childhood education training for students who live and work in their home communities, usually as Head Start instructors. The Distance Education Department offers classes via a range of technologies, including a balky one-way satellite feed system and teleconferencing. Distance Education offerings, like those in the GED Program, have expanded and contracted significantly over the past decade.

SIPI is taught in three 14-week trimesters, with breaks between them. When SIPI started in 1971, it had an open-entry/open-exit academic system, which meant that students worked at their own pace and received certification whenever they had completed necessary programmatic tasks and goals. An early graduate of SIPI who attended when programs were self-paced explained how the process worked:

The school didn't have a lot of restrictions back then . . . We didn't have grades. We just finished our course . . . It's kind of like, "Okay, you're going to read these books for the class that you're taking. And then, we're gonna test you." And that was it. I don't know if they gave us grades, but we didn't follow any—we didn't get any report cards or nothing. So, when we finished the section of classes we took, and at the whole end of two years—if it takes you two years to learn the skills—then you get a certificate. That was it. Saying you have finished this [program] successfully . . .

The main class that I was in had, I think, thirty to forty-five minutes of lecture, and that was not really much. It was really just to organize us, and to introduce us to what was expected in those areas and what was expected of us. What they expected us to accomplish, and that was it. You just went in there, and were shown how to do it, you know, hands on. You tried to do it also. But if the teacher decided you needed more math courses or English, and then you went and signed up for those.

The self-paced academic system was financially inefficient, with students progressing through the curriculum in their own time frame. After SIPI was threatened with closure in 1982 because of government cost-cutting measures, a trimester system was implemented, to make the classes more cost-effective (SIPI 1999:4). Another significant change from the school's early days was the shift in curriculum. The school once featured a wide range of vocational classes and programs that are now defunct, such as the dental assistant training program, telephone lineman and repairman training, jewelry making, and switchboard operator training. SIPI's campus and closets are strewn with markers of its vocational-technical past. Every workday for years, I drove past the practice telephone poles used for training students in the telephone lineman program. The poles stood for decades quietly moldering on the far eastern edge of campus. Never electrified, their wires dangled toward the ground, offering a perch for hunting falcons and representing a quaint piece of near-forgotten SIPI history. Other outdated equipment was tucked around campus where room could be found, including the massive, fascinatingly elaborate switchboard for the long-defunct telephone switchboard operator program. That device spent years pushed against the wall of an occupational technologies classroom.

In 2006, the Bureau of Indian Affairs reorganized the American Indian education section at the bureau level. This meant that the former Office of Indian Educational Programs, which was under the Bureau of Indian Affairs, became the Bureau of Indian Education. OIEP had had oversight of all federal schools for American Indians, including more than one hundred children's schools and the two federal postsecondary institutions. OIEP lumped all types of schools together, leading to odd policies for the colleges, including a requirement that a hiring authority rate college instructors on their ability to relate well to children, including their own. (Obviously, rapport with children is not usually a relevant concern when colleges seek out someone to teach calculus or political science). With the formation of the BIE, SIPI and HINU were finally placed in a category of their own within the federal Indian education bureaucracy. Philosophical changes do not appear to have followed. (The third postsecondary institution in the federal constellation, the Institute of American Indian Arts, had already declared its autonomy from OIEP.)

Chain of Command, Power, and Campus Policy

One of the most significant characteristics of the Southwestern Indian Polytechnic Institute that shapes student experiences and precludes the school from fitting the definition of a true TCU is its entirely "top-down" management structure. The chain of command model of management, typical for federal installations, provides no avenue for the nonmanagerial employees to participate in or affect administrative decisions. To have a voice in school operations, employees must step outside the chain of command or access the union. Unlike most colleges, faculty are not provided official and consistent avenues for shaping the school as they have virtually no say in the design or implementation of policy, or hiring in their departments. Many of these limitations are a function of SIPI's nature as a federal installation. Employees in federal offices are not given a vote in the hiring of their peers, while college faculty usually are. Because personnel matters in federal hiring are restricted to the upper layers of the chain of command, there is no such thing as a faculty-led, departmental-level hiring committee. In fact, faculty members are not allowed to interview, meet with, or review the curricula vitae of potential hires. During the hiring process for two of the school's recent presidents, faculty members were not allowed to know the names of the candidates, which meant that faculty members were not given the opportunity to meet the candidates, read their CVs, ask questions, or participate in the process. Faculty did not have an official vote in the adoption of the personnel system that was disputed at its implementation and later overthrown by the courts. Other examples of how SIPI's nature as a federal installation overrides its nature as a college include that faculty are paid hourly, they must fulfill a standard federal workday, and they cannot vote on matters that affect them in the classroom.

Indicative of the top-down nature of campus leadership is the fate, or rather existence, of the SIPI "Faculty Senate." As late as 2000, institutionally produced text claimed there was an active Faculty Senate on campus, and that this organization had been established in 1992 (SIPI 2000:11). Yet as I sought to attend and participate in this group, my peers were unsure if it had, in fact, been disbanded. Those who thought it might still be extant could not answer questions about how members were selected, who was a member, when and where the Faculty Senate met, and what matters it had a say in. As no administrative decisions were ever labeled as having been vetted by faculty input, the "Faculty Senate" appears to have been a rhetorical flourish rather than an actual democratically chosen, autonomous voice of instructor participation in the institution. Particularly striking was the fear that faculty had about asserting a need for an active Faculty Senate and their belief that doing so could lead to administrative censure. After a departmental meeting and prior to the start of a new president's term, a fellow faculty member waited for most of our peers to leave the room. This individual, fearful that even asking the question could lead to reprisals, nervously leaned toward me and a colleague to whisper a question: Did we think the incoming president would reinstitute the Faculty Senate? The staff has even fewer means of input as they do not have any listed campus organizations through which they can participate. The union—the Indian Educators Federation—becomes the de facto voice of all nonmanagement employees. This results in nonmanagerial employees stepping outside the institution if they want to be heard.

An intriguing coda: While the faculty and staff have no means for participating on the Board of Regents—as all their concerns are supposed to be filtered through upper-level management—the Student Senate does. The president of the SIPI student body has a seat, and a vote, on the Board of Regents. Imagine the intriguing quirk of institutional power dynamics inherent in this situation: When faculty and staff cannot directly inform the BOR of their concerns and issues, but students can, should faculty use the SIPI student body president as their conduit? Does this mean that students have more voice in the operation of the school than faculty and staff? Is it appropriate that nonmanagerial employees might have to resort to personal connections with BOR members to be heard by that group?

The heavily top-down structure means SIPI does not resemble a typical college, but it does not resemble the ideal of a tribal institution either. In order for SIPI to function more closely along the model of a tribal institution, its hierarchical administrative structure needs to be flattened from the current top-down system to one in which all employees are deemed participants—the chain of command should no longer hang heavily overhead but be wrapped into a circle. Adopting culturally traditional Native leadership and decision-making processes would benefit university leaders nationwide (Blanchard 2001), yet SIPI does not practice them, even in light of its status as a Native-serving institution. These processes (again, not in evidence at SIPI) include "playfulness"—a nonlinear, dialogic, administrator-as-facilitator approach to leadership; leadership by example, where college administrators remain active in teaching and research; consensus building; and nonhierarchical management models in which members of the organization participate in the school's decision making (Blanchard 2001:208, 210, 211). This model simply does not fit the core organizational values exhibited by SIPI, and the school's current model alienates all nonadministrative employees from contributing to the shape of the school.

The profoundly hierarchical leadership structure of the school has led to the subsequent control mechanisms imposed on students. Students are the least incorporated into the campus power structures and, therefore, the least volitional. If faculty, for example, are virtually powerless in shaping organizational culture and policy as it affects them, and department-level administrators must seek upper management's approval for all but the most minor decisions, it follows that students—the least powerful participants in the campus community—will bear the brunt of institutional authority.

The organizational structure that puts all institutional power firmly in the hands of the school leadership was additionally buttressed by Congressional approval in 1997 to implement a new personnel system that diverged sharply from the traditional civil service employment system. The bill (105-HR1337) was approved by the House of Representatives on April 15, 1997. The official title of the act is Haskell Indian Nations University and Southwestern Indian Polytechnic Institute Administrative Systems Act of 1997. The main stated goal of the act was "[t]o enhance the administrative authority of the respective presidents of Haskell Indian Nations University and the Southwestern Indian Polytechnic Institute, and for other purposes" by implementing what is known in the federal government's personnel system as an Alternative Personnel Management System. These systems can be quite effective in attracting faculty by offering comparable benefits typical of non-federal colleges to individuals who would otherwise not accept federal employment. The act allowed for the abridgement of Civil Service Laws and made the school president the final authority on personnel issues—with input from the school's governing body, although it is unclear if that is meant to refer to the Board of Regents or the Office of Indian Education (U.S. House of Representatives 1997).

Funding, Finances, and the Threat of Collapse

The Southwestern Indian Polytechnic Institute's budget and funding are designated by Congress. The amount of funding Congress allocates does not factor in student enrollment numbers. The funds allocated to SIPI have been stagnant or shrinking for many years while enrollment has grown. In the three-year period from 2002 to 2005, the years preceding and including one of the school's direst financial crises, SIPI's federal funding allocation was reduced from $5.64 million for the 2002–2003 school year, to $5.6 million for 2003–2004, and eventually down to $5.48 million for the 2004–2005 school year (Armijo 2005c:1). SIPI's budget woes are particularly vexing in light of the fact that it has virtually the same enrollment figures as HINU, yet HINU receives roughly double the funding SIPI does. For example, for the 2004–2005 school year, SIPI's budget was $5.48 million to HINU's budget of about $10 million (Armijo 2005b:2).

Many of SIPI's students, like many community college students in general, would not be easily able to attend a four-year school, owing to the prohibitive cost of schooling, the need for academic remediation, or both. The school's liberal enrollment criteria, coupled with the fact that SIPI was, for most of its history, completely free of cost, had serious budget implications and was thought to create high failure rates. SIPI's mandate for free education is based on the federal government's obligation to provide Native American youth with subsidized schooling per several treaty agreements. For example, "[e]ach of the treaties and agreements signed in Montana Territory between the U.S. government and Indian tribes—1851, 1855, 1896, others [sic]—contained a provision that education would be provided to tribal members" (Juneau 2001:13). Other treaties that include guarantees of federal support for education are the 1868 Treaty with the Cheyenne Indians; the 1861 Treaty with Sacs, Foxes, and Iowas; and the 1868 Treaty with the Navajo Indians (Rosenfelt 1974). As legally binding agreements between two sovereign nations, these treaties are still valid. There is disagreement as to the level of support and the length of time the federal government is required to fulfill these obligations (see Rosenfelt 1974).

One of the Southwestern Indian Polytechnic Institute's most attractive features for students is the extremely low cost of attending. It was, for most of its history, almost free of charge. Forty-five percent of the students (18 of 40 students) responding to a survey questionnaire in 2002 listed "free tuition, lodging" as their most important reason for attending the school. Another 25 percent of the survey's respondents (10 of 40 students) listed this as their second most important reason for attending. The fact that 70 percent of the students surveyed chose SIPI for its lack of cost points to the school's central attraction, its accessibility to students who otherwise could not afford postsecondary schooling. Housing, meals, books (lent to students for the trimester), classes, and some recreational activities had been (until 2005) essentially free of cost. Students were required to pay only a $20 nonrefundable activities fee and a low refundable deposit at the beginning of each trimester. Federal funding to the school would provide the rest.

The student population at the Southwestern Indian Polytechnic Institute has always been fairly small but has been steadily increasing since the 1990s. Because SIPI students paid only a nominal fee to attend the school, there was a significant outlay of school funds to cover the prohibitive costs of room and board, and books. The school implemented several policies to manage the budget that directly affected students. They were able to cut the school's enrollment by more than 10 percent through simple measures such as holding firmly to deadlines. Accurate enrollment numbers collected at a reasonable time prior to the beginning of a trimester allowed administrators to more accurately project costs, such as for books and food, and determine the need to hire adjunct instructors.

Limited enrollments, though, were not enough to improve the dire financial picture. Owing to increased costs for operating the school, and concerns about student retention, fees were instituted in 2005. The question of whether or not to charge additional fees (and whether to use the politically fraught term "tuition") was often discussed but not implemented prior to then. In addition to improving the school's financial health, there was also the hope among some employees that cost would impart a sense of value, so that implementing fees would lead to lower dropout rates. The hope was that by paying even a small amount for their classes, students would be more motivated to pass each of their classes the first time they were enrolled. Concern over failure rates becomes more relevant when one notices that the average GPA of students in 2003 was 2.02—meaning that the average student at SIPI was a mere .02 grade points away from academic probation. As of 2008, residential students paid $280 per term, and commuters paid $225 (SIPI 2008:22). Although there is now more cost associated with attending SIPI, it is still quite inexpensive for students to live on campus and attend classes there. Fees alone, though, were not the entire answer.

Chronic problems with SIPI's funding and budget management reached a crisis point in September 2004. A budget review by the Office of Indian Education Programs (as the BIE was not yet formed) showed that SIPI was operating with a $1.06 million deficit (Armijo 2005b:1). Multiple measures were examined for addressing the budget crisis, including a suggestion examined by the Board of Regents to close the school for a portion of the year (Armijo 2005c:1), but that option was rejected. Rumors of a permanent closure of the school were chronic, and perhaps administrators were concerned that by closing the school temporarily, students might not return. Certainly rumors of the school closing had some students worried that they would be stuck with college credits that they could not transfer. Many faculty members, myself included, were made aware that closure was being considered as an option only after seeing an article in the newspaper. The article described a visit by SIPI administrators in which they asked leaders of the Navajo Nation for help with funding the school lest SIPI be temporarily shuttered.

For virtually as long as I was at SIPI, and probably for long before that, there were consistent rumors about the college closing permanently. For example, when the Indian Health Services (IHS) clinic on campus announced it was suspending all nondental health care services, the campus administration immediately began countering rumors that the entire school was shutting down.

Clearly, cost-cutting measures had to be put in place. Three solutions for reducing costs were implemented in April 2005. First, SIPI's academic and administrative departments were completely reorganized, a measure based, it was claimed, on financial considerations. Second, there was a massive layoff, called a Reduction in Force, and known to federal employees as a RIF. Third, the administration imposed a mandatory twenty-three-day unpaid furlough for all employees. In the effort to minimize the negative financial impact of losing almost five weeks of salary, employees could select the individual dates to be furloughed, as long as all furlough days were completed between April and the end of September 2005.

A significant proportion of SIPI's staff was laid off in the RIF. Twenty-two percent of SIPI's employees were laid off: 29 out of the 130 total non-managerial employees (Armijo 2005d:1). The RIF was highly contested, and the union, the Indian Educators Federation, immediately filed suit in protest. The layoff was said to have violated thirteen separate provisions of the union's collective bargaining agreement with SIPI (Armijo 2005d:1), and the union expressed concern that the average age of the laid-off employees was fifty-two (Armijo 2005a:2). All five of the campus union stewards were laid off (Armijo 2005a:2), a move the union found deeply suspect. Also suspect was the fact that, soon after the mass terminations took place, eighteen new positions at the school were advertised. The union argued that the cost of the salaries for the new, fewer positions consumed whatever savings were incurred by laying off the twenty-nine employees, suggesting the new hiring would prove more expensive than simply not terminating the employees in the first place (Armijo 2005a:2). The official termination date for laid-off employees was April 30, 2005 (Armijo 2005c:1). The RIF was later found by a court-appointed mediator to have been legally suspect and overturned. The results of the lawsuit were publicized in September 2006. The school rehired the terminated employees, among other penalties. The academic departments, though, did not revert to their previous shapes. Departments were merged, and the department-level administration pared down. The Adult Developmental Education Program was split off from General Education into a separate department, and combined with the tutoring programs and academic counseling services. Eventually the new personnel system that had been used to justify the RIF was scrapped and employees returned to the federal government service personnel system.

The School and Its City

The campus of the Southwestern Indian Polytechnic Institute is set slightly in from the west bank of the Rio Grande River. It is an area that had long been considered the far western edge of Albuquerque, New Mexico, but in the last decade the school has been absorbed into the city's sprawl of new development. Albuquerque was founded in 1706 by settlers from Spain. The city is the largest in New Mexico, and houses about one third of the state's population of 1.5 million. Albuquerque has been growing exponentially for the past decade, but its boundaries are so constrained—tribal land to the north, tribal and federal parkland to the east, an Air Force installation to the south—that much of the growth has been westward, pushing toward the cones of the three long-extinct volcanoes that hover over the western horizon. Almost overnight, SIPI has found itself practically in the center of town. This new, more centralized orientation in relation to Albuquerque proper stands in direct contrast to the school's early days. A Navajo woman who attended SIPI in the 1970s said:

> It was dirt. All the way. And in the springtime, it was dusty! ... It was awful. The road also has really changed. It was only one lane, either way. And no lights. Hardly any lights. Once you turned off Central [Avenue, a main east–west artery through Albuquerque], off of the freeway or Central, it was dark all the way, dark. And we even had a neighbor one time who came back from there, her battery died halfway. She couldn't see. She tried to drive in the dark and ran off the road and rolled her car. "What are you doing driving in the dark?" "I have to get home. The kids. No one was watching the kids, and I couldn't stay out there. In the middle of the road. And my husband's in the hospital and I was just coming back from the hospital."
>
> Oh, dear. It was crazy, that's how dark it was. You couldn't see unless you had your headlights on all the way ... It was just dirt.

As recently as six or seven years ago, the road to SIPI was flanked by expansive fields of blue and yellow wildflowers in springtime and a clear view of the cottonwoods lining the Rio Grande. Many of those fields have been consumed by development, sprouting row upon row of nearly identical faux-adobe housing.

For its size and its centrality to the state, Albuquerque has few college options. There is the University of New Mexico (UNM), which is the flagship of education in the state, and the Community College of Central New Mexico (CCCNM), which recently changed its name from Albuquerque Technical-Vocational Institute (TVI). These two colleges are within walking distance of each other, and in addition to its own degrees, CCCNM offers the remediation programs for UNM students. Albuquerque has a longstanding history with the Bureau of Indian Affairs educational branch, as it was the home of the Albuquerque Indian School, one of the largest and most-storied of the historical BIA schools for American Indian children. The Albuquerque Indian School was founded in 1888 by the Presbyterian Church for Pueblo students. Albuquerque Indian School merged with the Santa Fe Indian School in the 1980s (Logan 2005:76).

The campus of the Southwestern Indian Polytechnic Institute stands in stark visual contrast to the upscale housing developments that bound its northern and southern ends, with its vast open acreage and dated architecture. SIPI's buildings are centered in a campus that consists of 165 acres (Harbert 1996:B2). The west side of the campus faces a large *acequia* (a traditional New Mexican irrigation canal) and the main traffic artery of Albuquerque's West Side. The east side of the campus has a small pedestrian gate for accessing the Rio Grande, and the Bosque, or riparian forest that lines the river. The gate provides a ready escape for students who want to walk, or run, along river trails, and there are myriad hidden areas where students can disappear with friends. The Bosque, prone to wildfires, is occasionally closed to the public, such as during a period in 2004 when it had been damaged by a series of devastating fires. The Bosque has seen the rise and eventual fall of several student hangout areas and party spots, as formerly undeveloped natural areas are consumed by the suburbs.

Most of SIPI's campus lacks landscaping, and maintains a sense of what the West Side of Albuquerque must have looked like before the construction boom of recent years: massive, twisted cottonwoods and elms scattered near campus buildings; tufts of sage and rabbitbrush gripping the sandy soil dotted with river cobbles; black and gray lumps of obsidian peeking through patches of desert grasses; and birds and beasts representing a broad range of Southwestern wildlife. Birds rest in the area on their annual migration, and in fall and spring the campus hosts huge flocks of geese. The edges of campus are home to ravens, hawks, and falcons. Occasionally, a pheasant explodes out from the dry grasses under the cottonwood trees nearest to the Rio Grande, startling the humans who come too close. In springtime, great croaking flocks of sandhill cranes swirl so high over the campus that, while their calls are clear, they are difficult to see against the washed-out blue sky. The campus also provides a home to pocket gophers, their noses peeping out from their burrows close by the classroom buildings; jackrabbits and cottontail rabbits guarding their young from hungry roadrunners; alien-looking large red and yellow striped centipedes; muskrats; bull snakes and rattlesnakes; and a resident family of coyotes. All in all, SIPI campus retains a flavor of Albuquerque's original, pre-irrigation ecology, while nestled within the larger reality of the city that has absorbed it.

The bucolic physical environment of the school was emotionally meaningful for some students. An Alaskan woman told me, "The campus kind of reminds me of a park."

Another student from a Midwestern tribe said of the campus, "It's like a little oasis when I drive onto campus ... [Albuquerque is] hot, it's dry, it's flat, covered in blacktop. There's no trees ... I drive onto SIPI, it's a complete escape. It's a ring of big beautiful cottonwood trees, and they smell so good when it rains here in the summertime . . . I always associate [SIPI] with the cottonwoods."

The buildings sit in the very middle of the campus, ringed by undeveloped acreage and a road laid out in the shape of an eagle's head. Because the eagle's head motif is visible only in an aerial photograph, many students and faculty were unaware of it until the campus GIS program created a poster with the aerial photograph. Even then, it is difficult to discern, as the top of the head is not aligned with north, but rather with southeast. Most buildings fall within the eagle head outline (i.e. within the campus road) except for the on-campus Indian Health Services dental clinic. The clinic is so poorly placed in relation to the overall design that it appears to be a recent addition to the campus, although it is not. In the aerial photos, the clinic sits like a tumor growing out of the eagle's beak. The centering of the buildings leads to a sense of isolation from the West Side of Albuquerque.

The main part of the campus is dominated by four buildings that bound an area that is roughly rectangular. There is not one commonly used name for the area, as I have heard it referred to as "the quad," "the plaza," and "the picnic benches." Lying low on the eastern edge of the quad is the building officially known as the IMC or Instructional Media Center. Virtually no students know it by this name; rather, the entire building is universally known simply as the Library as this is the location they are most likely to frequent in the building. To the south of the quadrangle is the cafeteria, a large, U-shaped building with dark-tinted floor-to-ceiling windows. The cafeteria has had several cosmetic changes in recent years, including, unfortunately, the painting over of a mural of traditional Pueblo dancers that had been on the wall since the 1970s.

Sunken into an artificial hill on the western side of the quad is the gymnasium. It is a significant campus location for many students, as it is a center of on-campus activities and a four-decade-long series of pickup basketball games. Many students who do not have cars are dependent on activities in the gym for social connections and stress release. The upper level of the gymnasium houses an area known as the Snack Bar and has pool tables and soda machines. The bottom floor has workout rooms boasting new, high-tech fitness equipment, staff offices, and locker rooms. The north end of the building is the gym proper, with a basketball court and bleachers.

In recent years, the gymnasium building has been targeted for a badly needed overhaul, which has led to its increased significance for students. Prior to the upgrades, the building was dark, musty, poorly ventilated, and generally unpleasant. The building's interior lighting was upgraded, the locker rooms having been so dark that it was difficult to see the numbers on one's combination lock. The workout rooms were reconfigured, windows were punched into cinderblock walls, floors were padded with rubber matting, and new equipment was purchased using grant funds. The gym is no longer dark, musty, or unpleasant. The upgrades were partially intended to prepare the gym building to take on several functions previously fulfilled by the Student Union Building, which sits at the north end of the quad. This building is commonly known as the SUB, like its counterpart at the nearby University of New Mexico. The Student Union Building originally held game rooms, a snack bar, a TV viewing room, Student Recreation Services, and the Dean of Students' Office. Commencing in 2004, many of these student services were moved to the gymnasium, so the SUB could be reconfigured as a one-stop-shop student tutoring and services center. It is now officially labeled on the campus map as the Student Support Building.

The SUB, though, was central to student social life for most of the school's history. Its centrality was reinforced by the choice to bury the school's two time capsules in a grassy area in front of it in 2001. A ceremony was held on September 20, 2001, during SIPI's thirtieth anniversary celebration, to bury both the capsule reflecting SIPI's thirty years, and the capsule that had been assembled, but never buried, for the twenty-fifth anniversary. Students and staff were encouraged to add items to the capsule during the period leading up to the burial. The thirtieth anniversary capsule was the larger of the two and looked like a sealed white plastic oil drum. It took considerable effort for the facilities crew to wrestle it into the hole. As almost an afterthought, the smaller twenty-fifth anniversary capsule was added on top, after having spent five years languishing in an office, waiting to be buried. Students seemed puzzled as to both the tone of the event and their expected role in it. The ceremony was incongruous and awkward as, in effect, participants were celebrating SIPI's anniversary by holding what felt like a funeral. The date of the event simply emphasized the strangeness in tone, as the burial ceremony was conducted days after the attacks on the World Trade Center. The priest, recruited from Santa Fe to preside over the event, was either tired, ill, or nervous as his legs shook uncontrollably throughout his benediction. Students were exhorted to toss handfuls of dirt into the hole, further highlighting the funereal feel.

An individual who was nominally affiliated with the school pushed past the facilities crew, who were still working, and upon reaching the edge of the hole, began kicking dirt into it. Eventually, this person was pulled away, and the time capsules were covered. The torn-up sod that marked where they were buried eventually grew over, hiding any evidence that they were there. The time capsules are supposed to be retrieved from the ground on September 21, 2021. Between staff turnover and retirements, I cannot help wondering if anyone will remember to do so (or remember exactly where the time capsules are located).

The quad in the center of campus is grassy, low-lying, and shaded by huge, gnarled old cottonwood trees. For a significant portion of the school's history, there was a low soil ridge along the quad's eastern side. When the school was threatened with closure in 1982, students organized two runs, one that took students to each of the pueblos north of the school, the other to the southern pueblos, to ask for their assistance in saving the school. A medicine man buried a medicine bundle in the berm. Students and staff who were aware of the medicine bundle elected to walk respectfully around, rather than over the ridge. During construction, the ridge was razed, and the medicine bundle presumably lost.

The quad space is used almost exclusively by students. The picnic tables in the quad, scattered under the trees, act as hubs for social interaction. The tables' physical centrality, as well as their position in a student-claimed space, ensures that they are equally important to all students on campus. Students recognize the significance of the quad as it is the crossroads where every student at SIPI passes at some point during the day. Because of its centrality, no one group lays a claim to a portion of the space. A former student described the picnic tables in the quad: "It's like the mailbox or the little store back home . . . It's kind of like the social center of the campus . . . There are only four out there, and we're so small [a school] that no one person, no one group or clique of people, claims a table. Not like, 'That's the jock table or the stoner table' . . . The picnic tables [are] kind of the place where people can meet and see and pass each other."

Terms such as "jock" (student athlete) and "stoner" (marijuana user) are not commonly used by SIPI students to describe their peers, although "partier" (one who drinks excessively in the search for a good time) is commonly used.

The impact of the Southwestern Indian Polytechnic Institute's restricted budget is felt across campus, with a physical plant that requires the constant and dedicated tending of the facilities staff, and embargoes on the most basic purchases, including textbooks, copier paper, and at times, janitorial services.

The appearance of the campus is dated as there have been only three buildings added since it opened in 1971. The building interiors resemble an aging urban high school with high-tech retrofits. The classrooms are cramped, holding no more than twenty-five students. The unintended benefit to students is small classes with a low teacher-to-student ratio. A detrimental aspect of the buildings is that some of the classrooms are designed without doors, and the walls of all the rooms are made of fiberboard and do not reach the interior of the roof. Noise travels freely from room to room. (I came to a long-standing agreement with another faculty member, who is as adept at projecting his voice as I am, that we would actively lobby not to have adjoining classrooms.) Positive changes to the campus has been implemented more recently as both cosmetic and structural work was initiated all across the campus. Warped plastic windows were replaced with energy-efficient ones, small patches of xeriscaping were planted, and streetlights and a sidewalk now lead from the street to the dormitories so students no longer have to walk in the gutter on their way into campus.

The most significant change to the campus is the addition of three new buildings. In 2001, the Southwestern Indian Polytechnic Institute Museum and Cultural Learning Center was erected adjacent to the administration building. The log cabin building was donated as a kit with numbered logs by the Kellogg Foundation. All tribal colleges received these kits, allowing each school to choose the building design they felt was most appropriate to their school. SIPI's building resembles a traditional eight-sided Navajo dwelling, called a *hogan*, so it is universally known as the Hogan. The choice of the building structure is far more laden with meaning for students than campus employees must have expected when they designed it.

The Science and Technology Building was completed in 2003 with more than 72,000 square feet of laboratory, office, and classroom space. Its groundbreaking ceremony took place two years prior and was attended by a variety of New Mexico's political figures. The Science and Technology Building has laboratory space for classes in chemistry, biology, robotics, electronics, and lasers. The view from the building is a spectacular vista that encompasses a grassy field and the Bosque. Beyond the river, and filling the windows although they are more than ten miles away, are the Sandia Mountains. Every hour that the building is open, students are in the study lounge reading or sprawled in chairs. The view from the building also takes in the backyard llama corral of a house directly beyond the parking lot. Students expressed affection for the llamas (even alerting me when one of them died), but gave

2. A view of the Science and Technology Building. Photo courtesy of the author.

them a wide berth, having learned the hard way that angry llamas will spit. Most recently, a new child care facility was built on campus in 2007 but, as of this writing, is not yet in operation.

The Conflict Between Institutional Models

As briefly described earlier in this chapter, SIPI has an unusual organizational model, and seems to have more conflicts about its nature than its sister school, Haskell Indian Nations University in Lawrence, Kansas. The members of the Southwestern Indian Polytechnic Institute community do not operate under a shared set of institutional values because of the school's incomplete meshing of organizational models and incompatible institutional rules and goals. Colleges are a type of community, which, like all communities, by their very nature, share a mission and a purpose. This means that, at most colleges, conflict in the system is an aberration (Tierney 1992:28–29). For SIPI, institutional conflict is not an aberration, but a constant state of being. Because the institution has not harmonized its opposing parts, and is subsequently in perpetual conflict with itself, students cannot integrate themselves easily into the institution. Failure to integrate into a college socially and intellectually leads to a failure to persist (Tierney 1992:23). To succeed, students must find a way to make the Southwestern Indian Polytechnic Institute work for them and bridge the institutional conflicts.

SIPI struggles to mesh four institutional models: community college, federal installation, BIA educational institution, and tribal college. SIPI is a community college, and strives to incorporate a community college's attendant values and structures into its design. At the same time, the school shares many of the policies, procedures, and values typical of federal installations. SIPI, though, is not just a generic federal office complex melded to a college, but derives from, and operates under, the culture and value system of the Bureau of Indian Affairs. The BIA's history of repressive and assimilative schools and their current mission of administering children's schools often diverge from the values of a college. Lastly, SIPI is classed in many official contexts as being analogous to a tribally controlled college and university, albeit a federal one.

A true TCU differs noticeably from schools like SIPI, in that TCUs are expressions of the tribal culture and sovereignty of the tribe(s) that created them. TCUs are based on tribal land. The curricular goals of TCUs are often explicitly designed in opposition to federally defined educational values, which were long considered coterminous with assimilation. Other than enrolling only Native Americans and being small in size, SIPI does not fit the model of a TCU in its core values, philosophies, and nature. This divergence from a true TCU underlies several of the school's most basic conflicts. Ultimately, while there are efforts to create a balance of these four conflicting models—although it appears at times that there is an unwillingness to acknowledge them in the first place—the school remains confusing and conflicting, with central philosophies that stand in direct contrast to each other.

How does the conflict play out? Think of the school's employees wearing multiple, ill-fitting hats, swapping them out quickly depending on the context—or even attempting to wear more than one hat at once. As a community college, SIPI struggles with standard concerns such as student retention and graduation, fulfillment of accreditation requirements, and funding. It builds ties to universities in and outside New Mexico, and creates shared programs and aligns educational goals with these other schools. Additionally, SIPI must attract students, decide which classes to offer, and move students toward graduation and matriculation to a four-year institution—all typical concerns of a community college.

The academic philosophies and functional requirements of SIPI's college side collide with its reality as a federal installation. Federal workplaces—including SIPI—maintain an adherence to military terminology: decisions must pass approval up the "chain of command" and strictly scheduled employee hours, labeled their "tour of duty," must be spent at their "duty station" (their desk). This rigidly hierarchal, inflexible model of supervision is in contrast to normal expectations for college faculty, which include the valuing of intellectual skills and knowledge over that of fulfilling hourly quotas, flexible work hours, and low levels of supervision. While community colleges expect more hours on campus than universities do, those hours are fewer and more flexible than a typical federal workplace. The requirement that SIPI follow work hours typical of federal office buildings means that faculty members are discouraged from staying late (including being locked out of their offices) and the campus library is open only on weekday banker's hours.

Worse than just mandating limited hours of operation, the federal perspective imposes infringements on students' rights. SIPI has a strong theme of *in loco parentis* attitudes underlying administrative decisions and interactions with students. This parental responsibility is still extant in K–12 schools, but for most colleges, the philosophy of protecting students from themselves has been replaced with an attitude of educating students to make good decisions rather than actively preventing them from making bad ones. SIPI's oversight responsibilities and, therefore, its opportunities to enact the *in loco parentis* attitude are somewhat larger than is usual at a community college because SIPI is both a residential school, with typically more than half of its students living on campus, and a federal facility.

Which model—college or federal installation—should take legal, cultural, and philosophical precedence at SIPI? This question leads to other philosophical and operational dilemmas: Are students wards of the government or are they independent adults? Scholars or inmates? Struggles occur regularly between students and staff as they each negotiate this minefield. Security staff at a college cannot arbitrarily search a student's backpack as that student is walking across campus. Security services at a federal installation claim that right. Can SIPI students refuse to have their bags searched? Can a campus security guard, citing a concern for public safety on federal property, search a bag without consent or probable cause? What constitutes probable cause for searching a dormitory room, a car, or a person when that individual is at a federal college? Is the student's mere presence on campus equivalent to probable cause? Dilemmas of this sort arise regularly in the daily interactions between students and staff at SIPI. They inform student perspectives of the school, and they oftentimes do not get resolved satisfactorily.

Student housing policies also raise concerns about SIPI's hybrid nature. College housing policies typically balance the students' rights and their efforts at making adult choices with the needs of the institution. Students at most schools have the expectation of privacy as long as they are not blatantly violating dormitory rules, such as playing loud music during quiet hours. Contrast that with an experience of one man from a local pueblo who described how his dormitory room was searched by a staff member because he and his friends were laughing too loudly at a comedy video. Perhaps we should assume that, to the dormitory staff, laughter is somehow suspect.

What should federally provided college room and board look like? The federal government houses a range of types of people. Typically, though, the individuals the government houses are, in some form, legal wards with legally limited individual rights because of their relationship to the government. Individuals utilizing military base housing, such as active duty military, their dependents, and cadets at service academies are bound by the Uniform Code of Military Justice. Children at contemporary Bureau of Indian Affairs boarding schools are legal wards because they are under eighteen years of age. Federal prisoners' rights are profoundly restricted during their residence in federal housing. What form should government-provided housing take when the population is adult, not incarcerated, and not in uniform? Does the school need to satisfy federal safety and security standards in the same fashion as occurs with other federal housing? Is it appropriate to abridge the rights of residents because they voluntarily entered into residency? Perhaps a more appropriate model might be derived from rules surrounding residential internships with federal agencies, such as students working for the National Park Service? SIPI has not answered these questions adequately, for students continue to complain mightily about living on campus. The school is unlikely to answer these questions successfully, as the questions themselves illuminate the inherent limitations of meshing the college and the federal installation models.

And SIPI has resisted or rejected the fundamental shift seen at most colleges in the past forty years, the rejection of the *in loco parentis* role of campus administration. Nowadays, most colleges define their role, even in the context of housing, as one of education and support for students. College administrations do not take on the responsibility of policing student behaviors and morality. SIPI's dormitories are rigidly single-sex. Members of the opposite sex cannot visit beyond the dormitory lobbies, and students engaging in consenting sexual activity on campus face severe penalties. As an institution, the leadership of SIPI is loath to transcend the *in loco parentis* role. Perhaps this derives from SIPI's identity as a federal installation; perhaps it is a direct descendent of the philosophy of schooling of SIPI's parent agency, the BIA. Either way, it represents a significant cultural lag from the vast majority of colleges in the United States, a lag that students are conscious of.

Within this mix is an injection of attitudes and rules unique to the Bureau of Indian Affairs; some of these are clear holdovers from the agency's earliest days of forcibly educating American Indian children at isolated boarding schools. The BIA has a long history of implementing policies and curricula intended to diminish Indian children's ties to and understanding of their traditional tribal communities and cultures. A perhaps apocryphal quote from Richard Henry Pratt, the man who designed the prototypical Bureau of Indian Affairs boarding school, defined his educational goal as "killing the Indian to save the man." Has this agency truly evolved past his outlook, and the BIA's own ignoble history? Can it provide culturally sensitive adult education? Has the BIA found a way to manage colleges differently from kindergartens? When the agency overseeing a college lumps it together with children's schools, both in policies and philosophies, is it a surprise that SIPI students complain of being treated like children?

Lastly, somewhere in the midst of all the conflicting organizational models, SIPI boosters chose to define the school as a sibling to the tribally controlled colleges and universities. Tribally controlled colleges and universities are founded by individual tribes for the benefit of the tribal community. They are intentionally designed by tribal governing bodies to reflect and support tribal identity. Although SIPI does have an intertribal board of regents, they play a narrowly defined role in the operation of the school. TCU mission statements, curricula and course design, campus locations, architecture, and core value systems are drawn from the specific tribal cultures of their founders. SIPI, as it serves members of all tribes, and as it is an offshoot of the United States federal government (rather than a tribal government), cannot favor any one tribal culture. Hence, it reflects none at all. It is a tribal college for no particular tribe.

It is in this maelstrom of competing systems, values, histories, and rules that SIPI students find themselves. Some are fundamentally unprepared for what they find once they arrive, while others are following in family footsteps, and were given some sense of the school's contradictory nature in advance. Ready or not, many SIPI students can, and do, find ways to adapt to the school's internal contradictions. They tell a story of SIPI that is equal parts success and frustration, peppered with metaphors and spiced with humor. It is in students' words, stories, and metaphors that the school's nature takes shape, and we begin to understand how they understand it, how they negotiate it, and how they conquer it. Discourse provides a window that, I suggest, demographics do not.

Discourse of any sort, and especially metaphorical discourse, serves an important function for students at SIPI. The next chapter shows how the literature on Native American college students in general addresses, or ignores, their discourses, and the ways that understanding metaphor helps us to understand SIPI students' narratives.

2
Thinking and Talking About SIPI
Narratives and Metaphors

It is rare to read the words of Native American college students talking about their experiences—notable exceptions are Garrod and Larimore 1997 and Huffman 2008. Tribal college students are represented even less than their peers attending mainstream institutions. Native American students are typically defined in the postsecondary education literature not by their personal stories but in terms of their retention in or alienation from mainstream institutions. Significant amounts of research have been conducted on the retention of minority students in general (Hurd 2000; Makuakane-Dreschel and Serra Hagedorn 2000). The majority of literature on Native American college students focuses on low rates of college enrollment and high dropout rates in high school and college (AIHEC 2000; Dehyle 1992; Gilbert 2000; Manifold and Rambur 2001; Pavel 1992; Swisher and Hoisch 1992), student preparedness for college and their academic engagement once they arrive (Cole and Denzine 2002; Jackson and Smith 2001), and institutional fit (Garrod and Larimore 1997; Tierney 1992). Native American student autobiographies have been only slightly featured in the literature (M. Belgarde 1992; Garrod and Larimore 1997; Tierney 1992). Even then, the focus has been mostly on students attending mainstream institutions.

Educational research with minority students has sought to explain the factors for student success or failure. Historically black colleges and universities (HBCUs) face many of the same retention issues that SIPI and tribal colleges do, yet I have found virtually no indication that there is an ongoing dialogue among these institutions. Murray and Rosalie Wax (1964) studied children's education on the Pine Ridge reservation. They described the fundamental failures of the reservation's federal schools both in regards to curricular design and teaching. Vincent Tinto's research suggests that students undergo a series of three steps—usually defined in anthropological literature as the phases in a ceremonial rite of passage—of separation, transition, and incorporation (Huffman 2008:34). The steps in a rite of passage require that an individual (within a cohort of age-mates) leaves normal life (separation), undergoes trials and challenges while being between statuses (transition), and after completing the challenges, is reabsorbed into the community in a new social position (reincorporation). Tinto argues that minority students must commit a form of cultural suicide (a process, it appears, that mimics the ritual changes of a rite of passage) in order to fit into their new, European American majority institutions, an idea disputed by others (Tierney 1999:82).

SIPI does not fit Tinto's cultural suicide model as all the students are Native American. By attending SIPI, are students entering a European American place, a Native one, or something in between? Nor does assimilation into European American culture have the same meanings or confer the same level of benefit as it might at a mainstream school. Do students who would be considered assimilated fit better or worse in SIPI? Are they more or less likely to succeed? In fact, students labeled "too white" by their peers at SIPI face social alienation, regardless of their academic success or failure. Identity takes different forms at SIPI—rather than dividing the student population along Indian/non-Indian lines, group membership can break down along tribal lines. An individual from a small tribe or one that is barely represented at SIPI could come to feel like an outsider or a minority. Then there is the always present reservation/urban continuum—represented by students who were mostly raised on the reservation to those who alternated back and forth to still others who were raised entirely away from their reservation. Nor does Tinto's model appear to address the variations caused by cultural differences among tribes.

Tinto's model has no explanation for how a rite of passage would work for an individual who is shifting from one culture to another, rather than changing their status within their own community (Huffman 2008:34–35). Tierney argues against the assimilate-or-die perspective, asserting that minority student success is more likely if "an individual's identity is affirmed, honored, and incorporated into the organization's culture" (1998:24). How likely is it that a large, mainstream state-funded college would make fundamental changes for a population of students that probably makes up less than a percent of the total student body? Few mainstream schools would be willing or able to effectively "honor" all the different tribal cultures possible at the school. Whereas previous models of student success were based on the need for students to adapt to the institution rather than vice versa (Tierney 1998:24), student success can hinge on how committed students feel to a school "as they become integrated in the academic and social culture of the institution" (Tierney 1992:23). A tribally controlled college would be the best model for fulfilling this mandate, but SIPI is not a true TCU. Could SIPI ever affirm and incorporate tribal cultures in its organizational culture? Can SIPI, with its mix of organizational philosophies, create a coherent academic and social culture?

Tinto's assumption suggests that students are most successful when they are the least attached to their culture. But this assumption has been proven incorrect or, more accurately, has complicated the discussion of student success (Huffman 2003; Huffman et al. 1986; Willeto 1999). Huffman's research (2003) with American Indian students attending a mainstream Midwestern college examined whether American Indians who participated actively in their tribe's community life and culture were more likely to be academically successful. The research showed that students who were raised on their reservation and were active in their tribal community ultimately did better in school than those who were not. The initial transition to college was more difficult for traditional students, perhaps owing to culture shock, but once it was overcome, students who maintained their tribal identity were more successful than their peers. What, then, is the solution for Native Americans to achieve academic success? Should they be encouraged to assimilate? Or should they instead be encouraged to participate more actively in their tribal culture prior to attending college? Should they wait for their school to honor their culture?

More important for our examination of SIPI is the question of how well these theories apply to a context such as SIPI. SIPI is not a mainstream institution. Native Americans at SIPI are not a minority nor are they a majority; rather, Native American students are the *entirety* of the student body. This is not to say that there are no mixed-blood students at SIPI, rather that their identity as Native is the most defining criterion for their attendance at the school. The dilemmas of ethnicity that SIPI's students would face at a mainstream university as Native Americans are avoided, but the demographic makeup of the student body creates entirely different issues of group membership and identity markers. Instead, the identity markers that students utilize to categorize their peers at SIPI are more nuanced and subtle than a simple division between Native/non-Native. We, therefore, cannot look at the experiences and views of SIPI students through the standard lens of "minority students" experiencing a majority institution.

Tribal colleges, it seems to follow, are bound to be a different experience for Natives than a mainstream school. Or rather, at a TCU concern over student-institutional fit might hinge on whether a student is culturally competent (and therefore fits) or not in his or her tribal culture. But then, what about SIPI? Native students are not a minority at SIPI, as they are at a mainstream school, nor is the school designed around and attuned to their specific tribal identity, like a TCU. Can we apply any of the current theories of Native student success in postsecondary education to explaining or understanding SIPI?

It is too simplistic to posit dichotomies of "assimilated = academic success" (the old paradigm) or "traditional = success (given a little time)" because nuances get lost in the examination. SIPI students come from a range of backgrounds, and regardless of background, many are able to succeed at the school. Some successful students were raised on their reservation, speaking their tribe's language and participating in their tribal religion, prior to attending. Others were raised in large urban settings, such as Albuquerque or Phoenix, attended European American majority schools, and spoke English as their first language. Additionally, there are students whose experiences along the traditional/assimilated continuum fall somewhere in the middle. Imagine a student born on the reservation, who returned to live there on and off throughout childhood, yet graduated from an urban high school. To researchers who seek to place students into easily managed categories, in what category would this student fit? And where would students attending a school composed entirely of Native Americans from diverse backgrounds, tribes, ages, religions, and regions fit into the various models proposed by educational researchers? It is too easy to seek a simple formula to answer questions about a reality as complex as a life history. We need a more flexible and individualistic model—that of students' own perceptions and their representation of those perceptions through discourse. Personal narratives and the conceptual metaphors that occur in many of these narratives provide a glimpse into the way that students perceive, classify, and digest their relationship to the institution and their experiences there.

I am suggesting that the majority of research on Native American college students does not directly correlate to the experiences of the students at the Southwestern Indian Polytechnic Institute. My goal is not to explain why SIPI students drop out or are retained. The stories SIPI students tell are too complex, too interesting, and too individual to provide answers to questions affecting all Native American students at all colleges or universities. I do, though, believe that students who conceptualize the school positively, and use positive metaphors, such as "SIPI is a family," are probably more likely to stay in school and complete their education. But as I did not interview any academically unsuccessful students, based on my data I cannot prove whether this is the case. SIPI has a culture—and a unique one at that—and I want their words to describe the educational, social, and cultural context they are functioning within when they are at SIPI.

The Role of Metaphors in Student Narratives

In the process of collecting student's narratives and explanations about the Southwestern Indian Polytechnic Institute, a trend began to emerge. Students at SIPI routinely use metaphorical descriptions of the school. These metaphors provide the listener with an interpretive device for understanding students' perceptions of the school and their place within it. Not all student narratives use metaphors, but the meanings of the nonmetaphorical narratives are fairly self-evident. Student narratives of life at SIPI represent many of the typical experiences of college students—moving in and living with a dormitory roommate, making friends and growing intellectually. Narratives of typical college life are imperative to painting a picture of daily student life at the Southwestern Indian Polytechnic Institute. Metaphors, I believe, serve a slightly different purpose, and therefore must also be attended to—they help to explain the qualities of the school that are confusing or illogical or outdated by the standards of a typical college.

Metaphors, at their simplest, are a verbal equation of "A is (similar to/identical to) B." I collapse the term "metaphor" (A is B) with "simile" (A is like B) as a simile is a type of metaphor, and they operate almost identically in student narratives. Early anthropologist Claude Levi-Strauss saw the importance of metaphors and analogies as useful tools that enabled members of a culture to "think" about larger, abstract concepts. A speaker uses a metaphor to make something that is unknown or abstract (Fernandez 1974:123; Kovecses 2005:5) comprehensible by comparing it to another thing—the B in the equation—(Lakoff and Johnson 1980:5) that is "more concrete, ostensive, and easily graspable in the metaphoric predicate" (Fernandez 1974:123). A metaphor that is held mentally, and that gets expressed, directly or indirectly, through speech, is a conceptual metaphor. Understanding conceptual metaphors helps us to see how an individual organizes or defines his or her world.

Constructing a metaphor does not imply that a speaker or thinker defines "A" as perfectly equivalent to "B" but rather that "A" is being understood through "B" as much as their mutual compatibility allows the comparison (Eubanks 1999:421). While it seems obvious to state, the metaphors people use represent the way they think about something. People are not ordinarily aware of their metaphorical conceptual system, yet it is there, shaping how they see and make sense of their world (Lakoff and Johnson 1980:3). Conceptual metaphors need not be conscious, nor expressed verbally. When a speaker draws conceptual links between two things through their shared characteristics, the similarities are said to be "mapped" (Eubanks 1999; Eubanks 2000:23; Kovecses 2005:6). Mapping two things metaphorically is contingent on the speaker's assumption that there are features in common between the items being compared (Eubanks 2000:92).

A metaphor choice is like a word choice—intended by the speaker to be specific and accurate, yet also subjectively representing the way she perceives what she is describing. The students at SIPI choose specific metaphors to satisfactorily explain their conceptualization, and by extension their *experience*, of the school (Lakoff and Johnson 1980:1). Building a metaphor means emphasizing some characteristics and occluding or ignoring other, seemingly just as valid, characteristics to maintain the legitimacy of the metaphor (Eubanks 1999; Lakoff and Johnson 1980:10; Merten and Schwartz 1982). If listeners judge the metaphor to be well constructed, what gets left out is obscured by the effectiveness of what was left in (Lakoff and Johnson 1980:10). For example, the fact that SIPI students attend the school voluntarily is virtually ignored in the metaphor of "SIPI is a boarding school." Speakers and listeners are aware that students attend the college voluntarily, but that fact is less relevant in making sense of the school than other highlighted characteristics, such as restrictive rules in the dormitories.

Metaphors are culturally specific so that shared metaphors indicate shared culture. Many of the metaphors used by SIPI students are so commonplace, so prevalent in conversation all across campus, they imply the possibility that individual students are not themselves generating the metaphors, but in fact tapping into an existing pool of shared and agreed-upon metaphorical constructions. The expectation SIPI students have that their listeners will understand their references indicates they recognize that shared culture. Deeply shared meanings that are no longer subject to disagreement or debate become a form of social reality in which speaker and listener interpret the world the same way (Koch and Deetz 1981:2).

I am not suggesting that SIPI students are unique in their use of metaphor to describe their school. It is quite likely that students at other colleges might see their school through a lens of metaphor. What stands out is the nature of the specific metaphors SIPI students use regularly. The most interesting metaphors are closely linked to the unusual nature of the institution itself. For example, students at the tribal college dubbed "Home College" described their school using metaphors of home and family (Tierney 1992:124), as do some of their peers at SIPI. But it is nearly impossible to imagine a TCU student describing their tribally designed and culturally attuned college as a prison, a boarding school, or a reservation (the last because a TCU is not a reservation within a reservation; rather a TCU is already *on* and therefore *of* its reservation). Even though students at other schools might experience high levels of management and oversight (such as at a federal military academy), they are not likely to describe their college as being a prison, and most certainly they are not describing their school as being akin to a historic Bureau of Indian Affairs boarding school.

It is not the fact of students' metaphor usage that is intriguing, but rather it is the wide and widely diverging range of metaphors applied to SIPI that stands out. The most common metaphors about SIPI, when juxtaposed, appear to describe two different institutions entirely. The common metaphors about SIPI are completely contradictory. SIPI is a family, except it is also a prison. It is a boarding school that is also an opportunity that in turn becomes a reservation. What an enormous descriptive project students are faced with in describing a school that is equal parts opportunity, prison, boarding school, parent (loving or restrictive), high school, haven, and reservation! Does the range of metaphors indicate confusion on the part of students? Or is this an admirable ability on their part to find sense in their experiences?

An interesting quality of one set of common metaphors used to characterize SIPI is their references to uniquely Native American experiences and cultural values. While these references might be generally understood by non-Indians, the depth of meaning intrinsic to the metaphor is going to be best understood by a Native American or an individual who has spent considerable time in tribal communities. The depth of meaning and feeling behind statements such as "SIPI is a prison" or "SIPI is a family" is fairly self-evident to a non-Indian. But the subtler meanings for "SIPI is a reservation" and "SIPI is a boarding school" are not immediately evident without shared cultural knowledge. Students know the history of federally operated Indian schools and are cognizant of SIPI's nature as an agency of the federal government. When they see the institution enforcing paternalistic rules, they interpret them as replicating the long-standing relationship between the U.S. federal government and American Indians.

A Navajo woman in her twenties used a disquieting and powerful metaphor to describe this relationship. "SIPI is this institution . . . that gives a hand up. But also puts a hand on you. It reminds you that there is a hand,

and that this hand is a government hand, and that this government hand will always be holding you up and holding you down. And that this government hand has a long... history, and that you are a major part of this federal history by coming to school here, even [if] you don't know it." Attending SIPI is not, she tells us, entirely value neutral, for by attending, students not only become part of the history of federal Indian education but also perpetuate that history, for better or worse.

Stories of federal Indian children's schools, especially off-reservation boarding schools, with their isolation of children far from their communities, are part of the oral history of many contemporary Native American families. Young people in Native American communities internalized the knowledge of this history. Debra K. S. Barker characterizes these narratives as "family stories a good number of us have heard from our parents, grandparents, and elders; especially, they recall the story of their unwilling participation in the federal government's effort to reeducate on a massive scale thousands of American Indian children" (1998:48). Comparing any institution to a BIA school, especially a boarding school, is a particularly harsh indictment of that institution, and worthy of notice.

Metaphorical Themes and Their Use for Interpretation

The metaphors that students used regularly in describing the Southwestern Indian Polytechnic Institute are clustered around one of three main themes: (1) SIPI is a system of control, (2) SIPI is network of support, and (3) SIPI is a resource for self-determination. The metaphorical clusters position students' experiences at SIPI on a continuum ranging from extreme levels of institutional control to high levels of student volition and personal power.

The metaphor cluster of "SIPI is a system of control" is the least volitional. The metaphors in this cluster include "SIPI is a prison," "SIPI is a [historic BIA] boarding school," "SIPI is a [restrictive] parent," and "SIPI is a high school." Metaphors of this type characterize students as powerless and suppressed both at the institutional level and in their face-to-face dealings with the school's representatives. They are commenting on institutional hegemony (Adams 1995) at SIPI, which mandates a range of capitulations from students and effectively minimizes, or negates, their identities as adults while they are on campus. Students using these metaphors are interpreting institutional mechanisms for managing students, such as inconsistent or outdated rules and paternalistic attitudes, as exhibiting an institutional lack of trust or respect for students. In acknowledgment of this power differential, many of the institutions that SIPI is compared to have the right, and responsibility, to modify an individual's behavior coupled with the power to punish.

The metaphors sharing the theme of "SIPI is a network of support," include "SIPI is a family," "SIPI is a reservation," and "SIPI is a haven." In these metaphors, the individual is situated in a social and pseudo-kin network on campus and the metaphors develop in response to the emotional bonds students share with other members of the school community. They are not entirely free actors, as they are responsible to their peers, but students see these bonds as affirming their individual identities. Some students spoke of feeling accepted as a person, especially as a Native American person, for the first time in their lives, and of being inspired by their peers to explore their culture and identity. Typically, the bonds are described as one-way, in that narratives about acceptance center on a student receiving acceptance from peers, not on their offering acceptance to other students. The bonds that motivated these metaphors were purely interpersonal and did not derive from a larger, institutional philosophy. SIPI simply provided a setting or context for the relationships to develop.

The third metaphor theme, "SIPI is a resource for self-determination," focuses on the ways in which students can utilize the school, leading to metaphors such as "SIPI is an opportunity," "SIPI is a stepping-stone," and most intriguingly, the meta-metaphor "SIPI is what you make it." These metaphors define the school in terms of individual choices and personal volition. These metaphors represent students acting in their own best interests and making decisions for themselves. The institution serves a functional role toward achieving their educational goals, and the emphasis is on students crafting their own future from the raw material (opportunity) offered by the school. Achieving that future requires students to make smart choices, have clear goals, and learn to manipulate the system for their own academic and professional ends. Students who see SIPI as a resource for self-determination are not waiting for guidance, and they do not bow to the institutional paternalism they encounter. Institutional control mechanisms are simply hurdles to be transcended. Ultimately, they are proud of their ability to outsmart a senseless administrative decision or use the school's bureaucracy for their own ends. This attitude is embedded in the intriguing metaphor of "SIPI is what you make it," which is asserting that SIPI is, quite literally, a metaphor, a blank slate, waiting for the imposition of a student's willpower to define it. For students who saw SIPI as whatever they made it into, the confusing and conflicting nature of the institution, and its ill-fitting intermesh of institutional structures, creates gaps into which they can insert their own will. In fact, a school with a more coherent structure would also have more consistent rules, close official loopholes, and limit the fissures successful students are so effective at maximizing at the Southwestern Indian Polytechnic Institute.

Researcher Ties to the Southwestern Indian Polytechnic Institute

I did not come to the Southwestern Indian Polytechnic Institute to do research; I came to teach. I thought I would stay for one trimester, and in the end I was there for most of a decade. I saw many changes, some of which I helped to initiate and promote. I was recruited to teach at SIPI by the University of New Mexico (UNM), where I was a graduate student pursuing a Ph.D. in cultural anthropology and looking for teaching opportunities. In 1993, when SIPI underwent the transition from being a purely technical-vocational college to a community college, the majority of SIPI's faculty at that time did not have the credentials to teach the newly offered liberal arts classes. SIPI came to an agreement with the University of New Mexico's Division of Continuing Education that UNM would locate and hire qualified adjunct faculty for SIPI.

In early February 1998, I was the least senior graduate student at the University of New Mexico in the Department of Anthropology who was teaching her own class. An administrator from the Anthropology Department had asked the more senior students if they wanted to take over an introductory cultural anthropology course at SIPI (the instructor had had to leave on short notice). Several other individuals, I was told, had already turned down the course. Opportunities to teach anthropology in Albuquerque were few and far between, and as graduate students, we were hungry to gain teaching experience and earn a little extra money. Yet teaching at SIPI had a bad reputation—it was, I had already heard, like teaching high school. Not a tempting proposition for graduate students honing their college professor personae. But I eagerly said yes and assumed SIPI would need me for only one trimester. That one trimester commitment led to my teaching as an adjunct at SIPI for more than four years and eventually being hired as the only social science instructor in May 2002. I left my position at SIPI in May 2008, after having spent a year as a visiting professor at the United States Air Force Academy.

My first day teaching at SIPI was quite different from my last, as the school and I had made some profound steps forward during that decade. I was both eager and apprehensive as I approached the General Studies Building for the first time to meet the departmental administrator tasked with preparing me for my class. The first several months I was at SIPI, there was no department chair for General Education, and employees seemed to be getting shuffled in and out of the position arbitrarily.

The air was cold but the sun was bright in my face as I waited on the exterior walkway outside her office door. I scanned what I could see of the campus while I stood there. It appeared virtually empty of people. The building I was standing next to also seemed empty. The administrator handed me the course grade book and walked me to the classroom. SIPI at that time was so profoundly underfunded and underequipped that, when I asked where I could find extension cords, I was told to bring one from home. World map? No, but there was a globe. It must have been donated, as it predated the fall of the Soviet Union. In fact, it predated the contemporary postcolonial names and borders of most African countries. I kept it in my classroom for years, along with an equally outdated National Geographic map of Africa, offering a few extra credit points to anthropology students interested in researching the current names of the countries.

Several minutes after class was supposed to start that first day at SIPI, a few students trickled in and sat down, looking at me with some confusion. Most of the students were staying away as they had been told that class was canceled for a few weeks. Confusion led to complete bafflement when I announced I was now teaching the class. Departmental disorganization was so profound that, while most of the students lived in the dormitories, no one had contacted the dormitory staff to tell the cultural anthropology students the class was being reconvened or that they would have a new instructor. The ones who attended that first day took it upon themselves to both inform their missing peers to start returning to class and to bring me coffee the first few mornings, worried that I was going to be overwhelmed by my early morning task of starting a class mid-trimester from scratch.

My enthusiasm was vast, but they were right to worry about adjuncts at the school. Permanent faculty members were bitterly frustrated with administrative decisions, basic supplies were limited, and employees felt unappreciated. There was no faculty orientation, although occasional efforts were made over the years to implement one. There was no need to design a faculty orientation because hiring permanent faculty at SIPI is rare. There is no faculty dining hall or faculty parking, and faculty offices at that time were cubicles in a bullpen layout where every person there could hear everything said by everyone else.

The students in that first class, though, were smart and motivated, and I soon looked for opportunities to teach more classes at SIPI. Students were clearly interested in the social sciences, and there were some long-neglected and untaught classes still listed in the course catalog that I redesigned and asked to teach. SIPI is a small school, and many of my students—especially those who took a class for interest rather than to fulfill a requirement—came back to take several courses with me. I came to know many of these students rather well. As a result, the students whom I interviewed had all taken classes with me at some time prior to our interview.

I started each trimester by introducing myself and my research interests to the students. One day, after informing my students of my interest in postgenocidal communities, three students stayed after class. They asked me if I had considered doing my research at SIPI. They thought it was worthy of studying and thought I was in the position to do so. It was then I realized that students themselves were interested in understanding the school more deeply and that they trusted me enough to tell me what they thought. Several years later, I interviewed for this research one of the three students who stayed behind, and we both marveled to think of the impact her words had had on me.

Another Federal Postsecondary Institution

When I first arrived at SIPI, I heard repeatedly about how a longtime faculty member was on assignment teaching as a visiting professor at the United States Air Force Academy (USAFA) in Colorado Springs, Colorado. In the spring of 2006, I applied for a similar opportunity at USAFA. I was invited to teach for the 2007–2008 school year in the Department of Behavioral Sciences and Leadership at USAFA. While SIPI and USAFA share an identity as a federally operated postsecondary institution, there are obvious differences between the two institutions and some surprising similarities.

The student populations at the two schools are dramatically different. Teaching at USAFA with a markedly different student population than I taught at SIPI shed light on the ways I had changed as an anthropology instructor in my time at SIPI. I joked to myself that I had, in fact, become quite a lazy anthropology instructor. So many concepts that are treated by European American anthropologists as exotic or somehow distant in time and place were seen by my SIPI students as commonplace and commonsensical, and over time, I came to see them that way as well. It is a rare individual at the Southwestern Indian Polytechnic Institute who has no understanding or experience with clans, totems, animism, and non-Indo-European languages. Many students are passively bilingual in their grandparents' language—meaning they understand some of what is said to them, even if they are not comfortable speaking their ancestors' language. SIPI students deeply understand the limits and losses of translation and transliteration (the movement from one alphabet to another). One of my favorite techniques for illuminating the issue is to ask a bilingual student to tell a joke in their grandparents' language and translate it into English. Their struggle to do so often led to an almost clichéd assertion, "But it's really funny in Navajo!" Apparently, the Navajo language lends itself nicely to punning, a particularly untranslatable type of humor. Truly, students did not need me to point out how words, sounds, and entire concepts are mangled in their movement from one language to another—they had already experienced these themselves. One student took the issue of transliteration to heart when I used my own last name as an example of the way in which transliteration—in this case from the Armenian alphabet to the Latin one—drops significant sounds. She asked me the "proper" way to pronounce my surname, carefully practiced it, and used that pronunciation for the rest of our acquaintance. I was quite touched.

When I started teaching anthropology to students at the United States Air Force Academy, I knew that I had changed as a teacher. They were multicultural and multiracial, coming from a wide range of backgrounds. They were bright, prepared, and eager, it seemed, to take a break from aerodynamics and astrophysics. I realized quickly, though, the terminology and concepts that I had become so used to referring to in shorthand at SIPI ("You know how you get your clan from either your mother or your father?") now required more complex explanation. The vast majority of cadets had no experience with clans and totems and translation problems. And I no longer saw these as exotic cultural artifacts done by people "out there," but rather, I had come to take those things as normal facts of daily life and taught them that way.

Teaching at the United States Air Force Academy also had a lasting impact on my understanding of SIPI as an institution. For all their intrinsic differences, the two institutions had a surprising number of similarities. The differences between the two schools (SIPI and USAFA) are so profoundly apparent that comparing the two seems unsupportable. USAFA enrolls students from the top of their classes nationwide. Cadets must have excellent test scores and the written support of their congressperson. SIPI enrolls anyone who has a legally certified relationship with an American Indian tribe or Alaskan Native village. Students' test scores and GPA prior to arrival at SIPI are practically irrelevant. USAFA is academically rigorous; SIPI is not.

Unexpected similarities between the colleges are that they both practice extensive control and management of students/cadets and their time, although for cadets, that management is an aspect of their training. At both institutions, students/cadets exhibit subtle forms of resistance to institutional expectations. There is a powerful philosophy of *in loco parentis* and a core institutional philosophy of students/cadets as dependents and as the inheritors of the older generation's traditions. Both schools have external entities overseeing them and imposing their institutional cultures (tribes and/or BIA; the United States Air Force), which in turn informs—but does not entirely define—the culture of the students or the school.

Further, both schools are federal colleges. Unlike SIPI, the administration at USAFA takes an active approach to defining, discussing, and attempting to resolve the contradictions inherent in the melding of federal, military, and college cultures (this dilemma is often framed as the Athens-Sparta debate after the work of John P. Lovell 1979). The service academies wrestle with the fundamental question: Are cadets college students with a military commission or junior officers getting a college education? A similar question arises with SIPI students—at a TCU, students are tribal members first, college students second, because their school is an offshoot of their tribe. At SIPI, students' identities vis-à-vis the institution are a bit muddled—they would not be at SIPI if they were not Indian, but other than eligibility to attend, how is SIPI an "Indian" place? Consequently, while the service academies share with SIPI (and HINU) the predicament of combining institutional models, they deal with that predicament in dramatically different ways from SIPI. USAFA favors active engagement in discussion and critical self-analysis while SIPI appears unaware that there is such a dilemma at all.

SIPI's contradictory nature grows from multiple historical precedents that shape the Southwestern Indian Polytechnic Institute. Its organizational structure and institutional culture derive from its position in the timeline of the history of Native American education in the United States and the school's provenance as an institution of the Bureau of Indian Affairs. That history shapes students' perspectives in turn. A clear picture of that history, detailed in the next chapter, informs our understanding of student perspectives.

3
"A Standing Army of School Teachers"
American Indian Education, Assimilation, and the BIA

The Southwestern Indian Polytechnic Institute is a direct descendent of the Bureau of Indian Affairs schools of the nineteenth and early twentieth century. Many of the organizational and cultural qualities that make the institution unusual in comparison to tribally controlled colleges and mainstream institutions derive from SIPI's parent agency. Yet SIPI's founders were not trying to create a modern-day BIA boarding school, but rather they drew inspiration from the first flower of the tribal college movement in the 1970s. To see SIPI clearly for what it is in the present means understanding both the history of American Indian educational projects in the United States prior to SIPI's founding, and the changes that took place in Indian education with the advent of the educational sovereignty movement.

The educational institutions founded by the United States government for American Indian children had one primary goal—assimilation. The motivation for assimilation was twofold: Assimilated Natives could participate in American life in a way that was deemed nonthreatening to European American cultural norms, and by erasing what were viewed as primitive and outdated belief systems, so-called reformists hoped to avert what they saw as the slide toward extinction of the entire Native American population. The education American Indian children received in Indian schools was intended to alienate them from their tribal culture and community, and to prepare them for absorption into the larger American body politic (Carnegie 1989:11). A note: "Indian school" designates the historic Bureau of Indian Affairs schools for Native American children. The term "BIA school" can refer to present-day schools and is therefore less specific. Federal administrators selected the curricular content of Indian schools, and parents and community leaders were given no say in what their children were learning. Curricula at the Indian schools were carefully designed to inculcate European American values. When they did teach elements of Native American cultures, those elements were carefully vetted to be "safe" from "dangerous cultural difference." The elements of Native American culture that were chosen either supported approved cultural values, were stripped of religious content, or could be used to create marketable decorative crafts (Lomawaima and McCarty 2006:44–45).

The process of assimilating children through education was part and parcel of the larger federal system of suppression of traditional Native cultural values by Indian agents and Bureau of Indian Affairs bureaucrats. Agents of the federal government had the legal right to control all aspects of Native people's lives while they were on the reservation. Native American adults were classified as legal wards of the federal government, marking them as legally little more than children themselves. As a result of "replicating an ideology of familial power relations, federal agents assumed the powers of parents over Native wards and stripped Native parents of choice in schooling their own children" (Lomawaima and McCarty 2006:44). Actual children were completely voiceless in the equation of power. The paternalistic mindset is part of the Bureau of Indian Affairs' corporate culture even today, and college students at the Southwestern Indian Polytechnic Institute are conscious of and comment on the ongoing nature of the BIA's paternalism. The BIA, and SIPI as its subagency, are simply reenacting long-standing modes of viewing Native American adults as needing guidance and excessive management.

Assimilation through education is a potent means of effecting cultural genocide, for within just one single generation, a people's language, beliefs, and daily living patterns can be erased. Colonizing governments undertake assimilationist projects as part of the process of pulling all residents under their control. Nowadays, it is considered a violation of a community's basic human rights to remove children from their parents and assimilate them through education against their parents' wishes. The United Nations Declaration on the Rights of Indigenous People states in Article 31 that indigenous communities have the right to autonomy in matters including religion and education (United Nations Economic and Social Council 2003:25). To the Bureau of Indian Affairs (and its precursor organization, the Office of Indian Affairs), education was nothing less than a tool to completely remake and redefine Native American communities. They removed children of all ages from their parents, taught a curriculum designed to indoctrinate children with government-approved cultural values, punished children for speaking their Native language, and rigidly controlled children's access to their parents and their tribe. To this end, federal Indian schools used systems of management and control that were incredibly restrictive and that, to modern viewers, seem best suited to the operation of the military and prisons. This does not mean that students universally despised their schools or that they have no fond memories of them.

The Genesis of Indian Education

Schools for Native American children developed from the educational philosophies of the early United States. Early colonists in what would become the United States viewed education as a means of promoting piety. Literacy made the Bible accessible to all members of society, thereby increasing their moral standing (Szasz 1988:28). As education led to piety, piety in turn led to civility, which then itself merged into the concept of republicanism. One result of this merger was the equating of Protestant Christian values, education, and participation in the new republic (Szasz 1988:30). Individuals, it was felt, who were educated under the American model, and inculcated with a core set of Protestant Christian values, were best able to participate in, and contribute to, the new country. This value system was applied to the schooling of American Indian children and youths in the colonial and postrevolutionary eras.

Education in the new republic for the children of former colonists was expected to serve both practical and vocational purposes, rather than the elite goals of the English educational system of the same era (Cremin 1977:13). The early American government made a conscious effort to build a truly American educational system that was "designed to create a cohesive and independent citizenry" (Cremin 1977:43). Immersing Indian children into this system would serve to pull them into the citizenry as well. Central to the early American educational agenda was the promotion of the ideology of individualism and practicality. To do so required a standardized education available to all members of society. The educational system would serve to unify the American populace through their shared learning of uniquely American culture and history (Cremin 1977). The inheritors of the early republic decided that education, which had been an effective tool for bringing immigrant Americans into the body politic, could also be used to force American Indians to do the same.

Educational institutions for American Indian youth were not limited to schools for children. Postsecondary education for American Indian youth has an extremely long history. The earliest colonists to the Americas had a mandate to create educational programs for American Indian children. The First Charter of Virginia of 1606 included the stated goal of preaching to and converting American Indians, a goal worthy enough to receive the explicit support of King James I of England (Szasz 1988:46).

Several of the oldest and most prestigious colleges in the United States were founded in part with the intention of teaching American Indian students. Schools such as Dartmouth, Harvard, Princeton, and the College of William and Mary had programs designed specifically for Native American students (Carnegie 1989:7–8; Garrod and Larimore 1997:7). The high-minded goal of these programs was to educate young Native Americans into a Western, Christian ethical and pedagogical model that they would then bring back to their peers. The graduates would provide an avenue to assimilation through the broadcast of European American values and religious beliefs, a model that in hindsight creates a disturbing mental metaphor of "contagion." Dartmouth, founded in 1769, had a charter from the king that included a responsibility to teach "all parts of learning which shall appear necessary and expedient for civilizing and christianizing children." Dartmouth's founder, Eleazar Wheelock, felt that Native American missionaries would be most effective at converting their peers, so he emphasized training seminary students. Wheelock's educational goals did not include true assimilation, as he designed the early Dartmouth campus so that American Indian students attended classes away from their English-American peers (Garrod and Larimore 1997:7). The college of William and Mary included in its charter the goal to educate American Indian youth in order for Christianity to be more easily promoted and spread (Szasz 1988:67). Education and conversion were viewed as mutually supportive processes.

The parents of the young people who attended these early programs were not particularly satisfied with the results of their education. There is a famous missive, sent by the leaders of the Six Nations of the Iroquois Confederacy, that rejected an offer from the College of William and Mary to educate their young people. This oft-quoted letter notes that "Several of our young people were formerly brought up at the Colleges of the Northern Provinces . . . when they came back to us, they were bad Runners, ignorant of every means of living in the Woods, unable to bear either Cold or Hunger . . . [and] spoke our language imperfectly . . . they were totally good for nothing" (Barker 1998:50; Carnegie 1989:9; Reyhner and Eder 1989:22). Though disappointed with European American educational standards, the authors did kindly offer to train a dozen European American young men into the proper ways of living and "make men of them" (Barker 1998:50; Carnegie 1989:10). Parental awareness of the limitations of Euro-centric education continued throughout the history of Indian education, and the implementation of TCUs represents, perhaps, the first real break from the long-standing history of Native American parental and community dissatisfaction and dismay at what their children were learning in college.

The process of assimilating Native American youth was undertaken haphazardly until the 1800s, when the first missionary schools were founded, and prior to the creation of federally operated schools (Adams 1995; Reyhner and Eder 1989:9). The early missionary schools had the explicit goals of assimilation and Christianization. Bacone University in Oklahoma, for example, was founded initially as the Indian University of Tahlequah in 1880 but renamed in 1910 for its founder after he passed away (Reyhner and Eder 2004:292–294). Bacone is a rare long-term mission school success story and is still educating American Indian young people. High-minded ideals did not completely subsume the quest for profit, as funds for mission schools were eagerly sought through donations and government grants (Reyhner and Eder 1989:7). The missionary schools of the early 1800s, though funded by the United States government, were generally unsuccessful. Their failure was partly due to the continuing conflict between tribes and the federal government, and to the swift expansion of European Americans into territories new to them (Trennert 1988:4). Federal schools soon followed and joined missionary schools in educating Indian children and youth. The door was opened for the creation of government-operated Indian schools when guarantees of government-sponsored education were built into several key treaties (Carnegie 1989:11; Reyhner and Eder 1989:39).

The goals of educating Native American youth began to shift from assimilation of non-Christians to a wholesale effort to save an entire people. There was a widespread belief that Native peoples faced an either/or situation: extinction or "civilization" (Adams 1995:15–16; Reyhner and Eder 1989:48). "Extinction" was a rhetorical device used repeatedly in the literature of the time. For a country that was effectively erasing the bison and the passenger pigeon, extinction was a familiar and distressing concept, bound to generate a response. Ironically, the question of who had been perpetrating the extinction was conveniently left unasked. Rescuing an entire people, it was felt, required separating them from their slowly failing cultural systems, or they risked disappearing with their cultures.

The educational reformists saw their goal as one of pushing Native children and youth toward Civilization with a capital C, as represented by European American culture. The reformists' agenda was based on early anthropological and humanistic thought. The reformists—uniformly European Americans from wealthy Eastern backgrounds—were well acquainted with the work of Lewis Henry Morgan and his treatise *Ancient Society* (Adams 1995:14). Morgan's rhetoric of cultural evolution suffused the reform movements (Adams 1995), fueling their efforts and shaping the educational models they adopted. Morgan's book presented a model of human progression in which entire cultures move decidedly "up" toward the pinnacle of "Civilization" by passing through a series of material and technological advances, such as the introduction of pottery. The lower levels of human existence were labeled savagery (the lowest) and barbarism. If a community lacked the material culture or technology that Morgan deemed necessary for forward or upward movement, then no matter how complex a culture's social or political structures, it was, by definition, lacking in Civilization. To move a people quickly forward on the Civilization continuum required teaching them the steps they lacked, as allowing them to reach higher levels of their own accord might move too slowly to avert extinction.

The United States government threw its support behind the project of assimilation through education quite early on by creating the "Civilization Fund" in 1819 (Trennert 1988:4), and later creating an entire system of schools. Here lies an early and interesting contradiction in federal policy toward American Indians: At the same time that U.S. military efforts were made to "pacify" and forcibly settle American Indians on reservations, the government was creating a school system intended to prevent their populations from being erased completely. The interplay between the paternalistic and the militaristic mind-sets is summed up quite nicely in a quote from Thomas J. Morgan, the Indian Commissioner in 1889, who wrote "the Indian must conform to 'the white man's ways,' peaceably if they will, forcibly if they must" (Trennert 1988:206). If tribal members did not choose to participate in Manifest Destiny or European American educational assimilation, they would be made to.

The language of Indian education embraced the language of warfare and conquest. School administrators and teachers were not seeking to gently guide their charges into a paradise of European American cultural values. Merrill Gates, writing in the early days of Indian schools, described Bureau of Indian Affairs school teachers, many of whom were unskilled and unemployable elsewhere, as an educational army, a conquering force designed to overwhelm American Indian culture through a thoroughly Westernized curriculum. Thus, he asserted, "that is the army that is going to win the victory... We are going to do it by the conquest of the individual man, woman and child... by a standing army of school-teachers" (Adams 1995:27). The ideology of conquest serves to clearly illustrate the mind-set of the early educators and the design of their schools.

Through a range of strategies of resistance and accommodation, students and their families were not simply passive recipients of the aggressive educational policies they faced, but agents in their own experience. Parents attempted to hide their children from police who, in some cases, had to "chase and capture them like so many wild rabbits" (Annual Report of the Commissioner of Indian Affairs Students 1886, quoted in Adams 1995:211). Children ran away from school, sometimes imperiling their lives. Tribes resisted government education by providing runaways with safe passage and assistance (Child 1998:90–91). Policies were enacted stating parental permission was required prior to enrolling students in out-of-state boarding schools (Reyhner and Eder 2004:149). Parents, though, were not allowed to refuse to send children to government schools entirely. Resisting federal education was a punishable offense. In 1894, nineteen Hopi men were sent to Alcatraz Island to do hard labor as punishment for hiding their children from the police who had come to round them up (Reyhner and Eder 2004:172). Other parents who attempted to keep their children out of government schools faced the punishment of having their food rations withheld (Adams 1995:211). Children who were caught after having run away from school were subject to incarceration and physical abuse. Guardhouses on boarding school campuses were pressed into duty as makeshift prisons, or children were locked into their rooms to prevent escapes (Child 1998:87).

Into this conflict-ridden mix, educators in the 1800s set specific objectives for Indian schools. They wanted to provide a basic level of schooling, enough for an individual to step into their rigidly defined gender role in an agricultural economy. They also wanted children to reject tribal and communal goals and values, and instead adopt an individualized identity. Central to this new identity would be conversion to Christianity. They also implemented citizenship training to create an emotional connection to the American nation and the national ideas encapsulated in symbols such as the United States flag (Adams 1995:21–24).

The growth of federal schooling was coeval with the reservation era, generally considered to fall within the years 1867 to 1890. This was a period of forced settlement of nomadic tribes and the restriction of the movement of Native Americans. Having entire populations under the control of Indian agents and the military led to increased interest on the part of the federal government to create and propagate a system of schools for young Native Americans. They were, in effect, a captive audience. The 1870s saw the growth of federally funded and operated schools on the reservation (residential and day schools), and then the development of an even more effective assimilation machine—the off-reservation boarding school.

On-reservation schools generally took two forms—day schools and on-reservation boarding schools (an interesting parallel perhaps to the experiences of SIPI commuters versus residents). Students who attended day schools returned to their families in the evening. Day schools made particular sense for tribes who were sedentary farmers, since the school could be placed in a centralized location in close proximity to tribal population centers. Day schools could not have complete control of children's lives, nor could they stamp out Native languages and beliefs, as the pupils still lived with their families. Instead, day schools were seen as having a "civilizing" influence that radiated out from the school into the community at large: "The influence of the Indian day school is not bounded by the educational or other needs of the pupils in attendance. It must bring all within its radius to a realizing sense of the advantages to be derived from improved methods of living. Its province includes giving advice and information on all subjects and guiding the Indian in the path of usefulness in the community in which he resides" (Office of Indian Affairs 1906:56). To contemporary eyes, envisioning the day school as a community center is laughable, owing to its inherently coercive nature and its physically marginalized location within some communities. Nor did BIA day schools share the goals and philosophies common to modern tribally controlled colleges, which actually do serve as community centers, supporting and promoting tribal culture. Bureau of Indian Affairs schools were not designed to blend into the surrounding community. They were small outposts of the federal government, meant to stand apart from the local community while architecturally promoting the values of the Bureau of Indian Affairs. The school buildings and their placement on the reservation were based on a mutual distrust among the actors—parents, administrators, teachers, children, tribal leaders—and even tribal communities as a whole. The BIA day school located at Santa Clara Pueblo was an example of mutual distrust and of the disconnect in value systems between the school and the tribe (Swentzell 1997). The school was designed in opposition to the layout of the pueblo. A pueblo's buildings are close set, and there is an obvious center to the pueblo, the plaza. A pueblo's plaza serves as both a community and a religious locus. The farther out from the plaza, the farther from the center of community life. The Bureau of Indian Affairs day school at Santa Clara was not centrally located, nor was it an inviting space, as it was surrounded by fencing. And not just wooden posts, but barbed wire, with ladders that "kept out both animals and old people" (Swentzell 1997:62), a miniature fortress of education. Swentzell argues that the design of the school was a conscious effort at control, and represented, physically and visually, a lack of trust both in the tribe and in the abilities of their children. She writes:

> The loss of trust that occurred when people moved from the pueblo to the school setting was most striking. Within the pueblo, pre-school aged children were allowed enormous freedom of activity and choice; to a great extent they were trusted as capable of being in charge of themselves. This liberal assumption created its own self-fulfilling prophecy... But within the BIA school, there was a different attitude: The overall atmosphere was one of skepticism. The fence was an expression of the lack of respect and trust in others. Although the formal reason given for the fence was that it kept out animals, everyone in the pueblo knew its purpose was also to keep people out (1997:62–63).

Ultimately, day schools proved to be ineffectual for their primary task of assimilation, simply because educators could not have the children for all hours of the day and night (Adams 1995:29). The next logical step toward assimilation through education was the introduction of on-reservation boarding schools. On-reservation boarding schools were more typically designed to serve children of nomadic tribes. Members of nomadic tribes utilize different resources, from different parts of the reservation, as those resources become available at different times of the year. For these tribes, it was easier to guarantee consistent access to the children by housing them at the school. This did not preclude parents from settling nearby, but efforts were made to make it difficult for children and parents to interact (Adams 1995:32). The children at on-reservation boarding schools, though more isolated than their day school peers, still had contact with tribal members, making total assimilation to a European American value system unlikely.

Administrators were faced with a dilemma: How best to ensure complete immersion of American Indian children into a European American cultural milieu? How to guarantee that they did not speak or hear their tribal language on a daily basis? How to control children's daily lives, shaping their activities to fit the government's preferred model? The solution came from a grand social experiment—a prisoner of war camp. And like the institution of control that inspired them, the schools that grew from it soon showed themselves to be effectively designed models of control and coercion.

A new type of boarding school was developed that was intentionally located off the reservation in order to minimize children's contact with their families, communities, and cultures. These schools were incredibly restrictive, and sought to redefine every quality of their students. It is these schools that SIPI students reference when they make the metaphorical comparison that "SIPI is a boarding school." Students at early boarding schools found themselves forced to adapt to new cultural forms and rules, many of which were intended to completely reshape their identities and relationship with their tribes. No aspect of a child was left untouched. When they entered these schools, they were often renamed (sometimes both first and last, and with little input on their part), their appearance was modified (short hair and uniforms), they were punished for speaking their traditional language (English only), they were isolated from siblings and other members of their tribes (to prevent "regression" to their tribal culture, plotting an escape, or speaking in a Native language), and their movement was proscribed (bells marking when to pray, to begin eating, to finish eating). All these mechanisms were integral to the project of negating students' cultural identities. Biographical information provided by students from the early schools provide us with a view of a Dickensian world of forced labor, harsh punishment, minimal food, endemic illness, and fear. The traumas caused by the early schools reverberate in Native American communities to this day.

The Origins of the Off-Reservation Boarding School

The first federally operated off-reservation American Indian boarding school, the Carlisle School, was founded in 1879. Its genesis is quite telling of the values the BIA held dear. What started as an earnest experiment by Lieutenant Richard Henry Pratt grew quickly, so that by 1887, there were 109 boarding schools either operated by the federal government or run by missionaries and funded by the government (Reyhner and Eder 1989:46). Pratt's design became a model for a national system of schools for American Indian youth. The educational goal was explicitly laid out in *The Rules for the Indian School Service*, which stated, "It is the purpose of the Federal plan of Indian education to prepare Indian youth for the duties, privileges, and responsibilities of American citizenship. This implies establishment of good habits, formation of character, reasonable knowledge of civic rights and duties, development of moral and intellectual faculties, and training in industrial arts" (U.S. Indian Service 1913:3).

Ironically, or perhaps logically, Pratt's perfect school derived from his assignment as a jailor. Richard Henry Pratt was an Army officer when he was made a jailor to seventy-two Native American prisoners, a group composed mostly of Chiricahua Apaches, from Fort Sill (Adams 1995:36; Trennert 1988:5–8). Pratt was to take them to Fort Marion in Saint Augustine, Florida, for incarceration and supervise them while they were imprisoned (Adams 1995:39). It is not clear what their eventual fate was intended to be. During this period Pratt devised a series of steps to rehabilitate the prisoners. He had them taught English (Reyhner and Eder 2004:133), took them on excursions, generated income-producing labor for them, introduced them to the European American community outside the gates of their jail, and converted them to Christianity (Adams 1995:39–43). One of the first steps of this assimilation and rehabilitation process was, interestingly enough, making the prisoners responsible for guarding themselves, including issuing to them U.S. Army uniforms (Adams 1995:40; Reyhner and Eder 2004:133). This self-policing policy, which implicated prisoners in their own management, set a standard that was used repeatedly in the later boarding schools.

Pratt's efforts were considered a complete, and exciting, success, and eventually his prisoners were deemed ready to be released from incarceration. While it is difficult for a contemporary reader to take a positive view of an educational model derived from a prison camp, to Pratt's superiors at the time, his prison experiment was an inspiration. Pratt was moved to expand his "civilizing" project and received permission to enroll seventeen young male prisoners in the Hampton Institute, an African American college in Virginia (Chavis 1999:1–2; Trennert 1988:5). The Native American students were successful at Hampton. Pratt, though, felt that the racism directed toward African Americans would eventually be directed toward Native Americans, undermining his educational project (Adams 1995:47–48; Reyhner and Eder 2004:134). Pratt insisted that he be allowed to start a residential school just for Native American students. He found a former Army barracks in Carlisle, Pennsylvania (Adams 1995:48; Trennert 1988:6), and the Carlisle School was born in 1879.

The Carlisle School represented the most restrictive type of federal educational institution—the off-reservation boarding school. Richard Henry Pratt's concept of the off-reservation boarding school allowed administrators to create a total institution, meaning that all aspects of a student's life became controlled, overseen, and regulated. The more physically distant the school was from a student's family and cultural institutions, the more likely it was that efforts to assimilate the children would succeed. By having to live at a school, far from family and community, it was believed that students would simply have no other choice but to conform.

Curriculum for an Uncertain Future

From the founding of the Carlisle Indian School in 1879, the number of boarding schools quickly increased. By 1902, there were twenty-five schools, all of which were built in the West and eventually enrolled almost eighteen thousand students (Adams 1995:56–58). Boarding schools were a potent force in pulling Native Americans into the ideal of landownership and assimilation promoted by the federal government. It was not the only process in place, though.

During the same era in which boarding schools became a vehicle for assimilation of children, the government was imposing legal measures to diminish tribal sovereignty and group cohesion among their families back home. The General Allotment Act of 1887 allowed lawmakers at the state level to break up reservation lands, assign ownership of eighty-acre parcels to individual tribal members, and sell off any surplus (i.e. unassigned) land. Once individuals and heads of households received their land assignments, any additional tribal land—regardless of whether it was legally protected through a treaty agreement—became surplus land for state lawmakers to sell. Ninety million acres were taken from tribes and passed on to non-Native farmers, miners, and ranchers (Stein 1998:76). The profit benefited the state, not the tribe. Parsing reservation lands into smaller pieces by state governments and selling off those pieces made it virtually impossible for tribes to recohere around land. Breaking the land into individual parcels and landownership in general were promoted because "[p]olicymakers had such abiding faith in the deeply transformative powers of America's Protestant mercantile culture that they believed the mere prospect of private property ownership would magically transform tribal Indians into ruggedly individualist, Christian, self-supporting yeoman farmers" (Wilkins and Lomawaima 2001:108). With tribal lands broken into individual parcels, including the checkerboard pattern still evident on some reservations, how best to prepare Native American youth for their new role as a "self-supporting yeoman farmer" on their own patch of land? Through school curricula.

The Commissioner of Indian Education in 1913, a man named Cato Sells, justified this agricultural bent by noting in a preface to the *Tentative Course of Study for United States Indian Schools* that American Indian schooling "emphasizes the study of home economics and agricultural subjects, because any attempt to change the Indian population of this country from a dependent to an independent people within a reasonable amount of time must give special consideration to the improvement of the Indians' homes and to the development of their lands." Sells went on to assert that students were not being shortchanged as, "The usual subjects of school instruction are not neglected, but they are subordinated to subjects which, if learned practically, lead directly to productive efficiency and self-support." Self-support was a theme that wove through the management of these schools. But it was a dependent form of self-support, one that required students to stay out of cities and close to home, not to compete with urban factory workers or professionals, and to enact government-supported changes in their own homes and communities.

To offset the costs of their schooling—voluntary or not—administrators instituted mandatory work assignments. Students were expected to spend large portions of their day out of the classroom, engaged in hard physical labor, called "details" (Adams 1995; Child 1998; Reyhner and Eder 1989:79). Superintendents for federally operated schools argued student labor was necessary, and that details were in fact a type of functional, hands-on training for life and employment outside the school. In the 1913 Office of Indian Affairs manual titled *Rules for the Indian School Service,* the fourth rule stated, "The Commissioner of Indian Affairs shall employ Indian girls as assistant matrons and Indian boys as farmers and industrial teachers in all Indian schools where it is practicable to do so" (United States Indian Service 1913:3). This implied their enforced labor was a form of employment training rather than a money-saving mechanism. Unfortunately, for some students at government schools, their labors were judged more important than their actual lessons, so that they worked far more than they were taught academic lessons (Adams 1995; Hoxie 1998:191). Many of the early boarding school students complained of the excessive amount of labor expected of them, and avoiding one's assigned duties was a common form of resistance to the institution.

In an uncomfortable parallel with boarding schools, college students at the Southwestern Indian Polytechnic Institute who live at the dormitories are also required to perform assigned chores of cleaning public spaces. These chores are called "details." Both the use of the term "detail," with its connotations of SIPI students as children and the detail duty itself as a form of modern-day forced labor are seen as offensive by students at the school. The imposition of details and calling them by their historical name practically hands SIPI students the material for one of their most negative metaphors

("SIPI is a boarding school"). SIPI students find ways to resist detail duties, much like their historical counterparts.

Only federal schools required heavy, self-supporting labor. Students at tribally controlled schools of the era, such as the Bloomfield Academy for Chickasaw Females, were not expected to do manual labor to support the school. Tribally operated educational institutions, such as the Bloomfield Academy, emphasized a well-rounded and rigorous liberal arts curriculum (Cobb 2000). Employees were hired to do the cleaning and other labor, until, that is, the United States federal government took over management of the school (Cobb 2000:100). Unlike federal facilities, tribally controlled schools like the Bloomfield Academy were not trying to train a cadre of domestic workers and farm laborers, but instead prepared their students to become leaders in their tribe (Cobb 2000:63). Even later at tribally controlled schools such as the Rough Rock Demonstration School, which was the model of tribally managed and culturally appropriate children's school, parents were asked to contribute to cultural training, but students were not expected to labor on behalf of the school (McCarty 2002).

The schools in the 1800s and early 1900s were not intended to prepare young Native Americans to enter the professional workforce or move into cities and be hired into factory jobs. Rather, they were taught agriculturally appropriate skills such as "small-scale, individual craftsmanship in harness making, blacksmithing, printing, carpentry, masonry, and other trades" directly opposite of the direction toward large-scale manufacturing that American businesses were heading (Lomawaima 1994:65). Even those students who were fully assimilated into the BIA's educational goals were poorly served by their limited and outdated education. Luther Standing Bear, a member of the first class of students at the Carlisle School, had a typical experience of being made to learn a trade and being given no choice in the trade assigned. He found after he left Carlisle that he was locked out of gainful employment.

> One day they selected a few boys and told us we were to learn trades. I was to be a tinsmith. I did not care for this, but I tried my best to learn this trade ... I made hundreds of tin cups, coffee pots, and buckets. These were sent away and issued to the Indians on various reservations.
>
> After I had left the school and returned home, this trade did not benefit me any, as the Indians had plenty of tinware that I had made at school.
>
> Mornings I went to the tin shop, and in the afternoon I attended

school. I tried several times to drop this trade and go to school the entire day, but Captain Pratt said, "No, you must go to the tin shop—that is all there is to it," so I had to go. Half school and half work took away a great deal of study time (Standing Bear et al. 2006:147).

Clearly, Standing Bear's training was useful—unfortunately, it was more useful for the BIA than it was for him. He was only supposed to stay at the school for a short time, so he sought to maximize his educational opportunities while he was there. His efforts were roundly dismissed because, most likely, his labor was too valuable to do without. When students were taught specific skills, such as shoemaking or tailoring, it was with an unfounded optimism that they would be able to find work on the reservation in those capacities. Those graduates who were unable to find work on the reservation were often no more successful in using their newly honed skills in the non-Indian world. Racist refusals to hire or house Indians with professional skills meant an end to their boarding-school-trained careers.

Dubious Successes

With all the effort and expense put into Indian schools, were they successful in the eyes of the government bureaucrats who saw the final results? Not particularly, if one reads the correspondence between Indian agency superintendents and the Board of Indian Commissioners. In 1916, the Board of Indian Commissioners, an agency independent of the federal Office of Indian Affairs, sent letters to the superintendents of all the Indian agencies in the United States. The letters, sent by the Secretary of the Board, a Malcolm McDowell, requested that the superintendents respond to questions about what were called "returning students," especially those who had completed their schooling. McDowell asked for the superintendents to write "frankly" and "informally" and forgo data-filled responses (McDowell 1916). Rather, he wanted them to speak anecdotally. Students who returned to their home communities after graduating from a BIA school had been successful in their education and represented the cream of the Indian school crop. McDowell asked that the agents supply their personal theories, based on their experiences, as to whether, or why, students who had completed their educations at BIA schools were professionally and economically unsuccessful upon their return to their home communities. Responding superintendents included commentary about all students who left the reservation and returned, no matter how long they had attended school.

Many of the superintendents responded by noting that no matter how deeply ingrained the values of the BIA day and boarding schools were, upon returning home, students were encouraged by their elders to return to their traditional ways of life. McDowell was repeatedly told in this collection of letters that returning students should be relocated to cities as soon as they graduated so as not to fall under the recidivist influence of their elders. When returning to their traditional cultural values, students rejected assimilation into European American society and reembraced traditional Native American values.

Not all superintendents agreed with McDowell's assertion that Indian students were unsuccessful. Several noted the unfairly high standards that were applied to Native American students, which if they were applied to European American students, would rate them low as well. Others noted that Native American students were taught skills that did not translate well to working on their respective reservations. For example, C. H. Asbury, the superintendent of the Albuquerque Indian School in 1916, responded by writing, "In most places the labor market is not as readily open to Indian boys and girls, as it is to white boys and girls and capital for starting in stock or form business is lacking in most cases" (Asbury 1916).

In addition to their responses regarding returning student success, many of the superintendents had their own political and social agendas, such as asserting concerns about teaching personal hygiene and cleanliness (P. R. Wadsworth, superintendent of the Jicarilla Agency) or emphasizing even stronger efforts at Christianization (August Duclos, superintendent of the Colorado River Agency of Parker, Arizona). Other superintendents described the forced loss of a way of life, such as when C. T. Coggeshall, the superintendent of the Salt River Agency in Scottsdale, Arizona, responded, "We have tried to eliminate the Indian and in his place make a white man and a white woman, and I believe in so doing we have murdered many fine and manly attributes of the Indian and given him instead things he cannot understand or place in their proper order to replace that which we have tried to stamp out." The rest of Coggeshall's letter is far less sentimental when he shifts into the familiar "assimilation or extinction" rhetoric by asserting the need for "survival of the fittest" on the reservation (Coggeshall 1916). Ultimately, by the late 1920s and into the 1930s, during the era of the Meriam report, the federal government began to rethink all of its policies in Indian Country, including the policies governing education. One example of change is that, after the Meriam report was published in 1928, curricula at these schools were overhauled and military-style marching and drilling were stopped (Lomawaima 1994:104).

As is evident from the correspondence between superintendents of Indian agencies, even in its early days the goals, values, and results of federally sponsored Indian education were in doubt. Administrators were left with a range of questions. Was the government killing the best qualities of students by erasing their cultural ties? Should students be sent home to diffuse their new culture into their old community? Was the cultural influence of their parents strong enough to override their experiences with assimilation? Was the government not doing enough toward assimilation by allowing students to return home when their schooling was complete? Who were these schools intended to serve, and ultimately, who was the student supposed to be by the time he or she had graduated?

Disciplining Bodies and Managing Minds

It is no surprise that students and their families resisted the government's educational agenda in these early schools. Children were virtually incarcerated at Indian schools. They had few rights and no real means to protest administrative decisions. Boarding schools were notoriously unhealthy places, and schools such as Carlisle had their own cemeteries for burying unfortunate children who died far from home. Even when students were ill or dying, school officials could deny them the right to visit their families. As children moved through their daily activities, there were reminders of the limits on their freedoms. Over time some students absorbed the culture of the institutions they were in, and began to regulate themselves and their peers. They were living in a Panopticon.

When Richard Henry Pratt turned his prison into a school of self-policing inmates, he unwittingly created the sort of institution espoused by Jeremy Bentham in 1791. Bentham described a new model of highly efficient public institution that both regulated and modified its inmates. He called this institution the Panopticon. The Panopticon gave its operators an incredibly high level of physical and psychological control over residents and could serve a range of functions, including operating as a prison or a school. In fact, Bentham wrote that the Panopticon would work equally well whether the purpose is "punishing the incorrigible, guarding the insane, reforming the vicious, confining the suspected, employing the idle, maintaining the helpless, curing the sick, instructing the willing in any branch of industry or *training the rising race in the path of education* [italics mine]" (1791:2).

Integral to the operation of a successful Panopticon was creating a self-policing mind-set in its inmates. The design of the Panopticon buildings supported this process. Cells are designed so that residents are visible to their jailers at all times, but the jailer is not visible to the inmate. This leads inmates to believe they are under constant scrutiny even when they are not. Bentham wrote, "the more constantly the persons to be inspected are under the eyes of the persons who should inspect them, the more perfectly will the purpose of the establishment have been attained. Ideal perfection, if that were the object, would require that each person should actually be in that predicament, during every instant of time. This being impossible, the next thing to be wished for is, that, at every instant, seeing reason to believe as much, and not being able to satisfy himself to the contrary, he should *conceive* [in original] himself to be so" (Bentham 1791:3). Residents of a Panopticon, aware of their perpetually observed state, eventually internalize the gaze of their overseers and become trained, as they are under constant view and their everyday behavior is recorded and evaluated (Foucault 1977:294). Eventually, these individuals so completely internalize the power structure that they find themselves obeying unconsciously, "caught up in a power situation of which they are themselves the bearers" (Foucault 1977:201).

Students at federal boarding schools were, like Bentham's inmates, watched, scheduled, and controlled, ostensibly for twenty-four hours of the day, from early childhood into young adulthood. They were observed during work details, in the classroom, at play. Where they were and at what time, what they looked like, what language they spoke—all were closely supervised. These control mechanisms were designed to reduce residents to "docile" bodies with school administrators imposing "uninterrupted, constant coercion, supervising the processes of the activity rather than its result" (Foucault 1977:137). We can see this focus on process over product applied to girls working in the boarding school kitchen. They learned to cook mass quantities of food for their peers, but they did not learn to cook well. It was the action (doing mandatory labor), not the result (appetizing food), that was most relevant.

Inducting new children into school became a ritualized process meant to create uniformity and ensure student docility. Upon arriving at the school, students were stripped of their individual identity and appearance by having their hair cut and their clothes seized, and often they were renamed with European American names (Adams 1995:108; Barker 1998; Standing Bear et al. 2006; Zitkala-Sa 2005). For the first class of students entering the Carlisle School, there was an odd and amusingly ethnocentric effort to allow students themselves to select their new names. Luther Standing Bear described adopting new names as the first step of the Carlisle School's intake process. His description is both comedic and disturbing. He describes his new teacher handing each boy a pointer in turn and sending him to the blackboard to "choose" a name from a list written in chalk. Neither the teacher nor the interpreter bothered to pronounce or explain the names offered. The boys were simply encouraged to walk up front and point. As a boy selected a name, the teacher wrote it on cloth tape, sewed it to the back of his shirt, and he became duly rechristened. This process was anxiety-producing for the children, not simply because students did not know the sounds or meanings of the names they were choosing, but for the fact that they were complicit in changing their own identity. Standing Bear describes the look on the first student's face as telling his peers, "Shall I—or will you help me—to take one of these names? Is it right for me to take a white man's name?" Standing Bear's own act of resistance was to visualize himself not simply tapping at a chalk mark on a blackboard but acting "as if I were about to touch an enemy" (Standing Bear et al. 2006:137)—a culturally specific act of courage.

Another preliminary step schools took to recreate students' identities was to remove the clothes that children arrived in and put them in uniforms (Barker 1998:55). Zitkala-Sa was one of the first students to attend an off-reservation boarding school. She described her shock at seeing students who had lost their sense of decorum, so effectively were they indoctrinated. They were dressed in European American clothing, "in stiff shoes and closely clinging dresses . . . who seemed not to care that they were . . . immodestly dressed . . . in their tightly fitting clothes" (Zitkala-Sa 2005:32). Her hair was also cut soon after arrival. Her friend told her, almost prophetically, "We have to submit, because they are strong." Zitkala-Sa was caught hiding and tied to a chair. Her braid was chopped off by a teacher and her hair cut into a style that her tribe used to mark cowards (Zitkala-Sa 2005:33–34). Zitkala-Sa's friend had learned helplessness in the face of the overwhelmingly pervasive power of teachers at the school.

Time at boarding schools was tightly controlled, another step toward recreating students. Students' time was strictly ordered. In some cases, children were woken with reveille and put to bed with taps (Adams 1995:117; Barker 1998:58) as would be expected in a military setting. Luther Standing Bear described his role in keeping time at the Carlisle School in its earliest days: "I was chosen to give the bugle calls. I had to get up in the morning before the others and arouse everybody by blowing the morning call. Evenings at ten minutes before nine o'clock I blew again. Then all the boys would run for their rooms. At nine o'clock the second call was given, when all lights were turned out and we were supposed to be in bed. Later on I learned the mess call, and eventually I could blow all the calls of the regular army" (Standing Bear et al. 2006:149). During her first meal at boarding school, Zitkala-Sa was surprised by the steps students were required to perform prior to eating, all dictated by the ringing of a bell (Zitkala-Sa 2005:32). Students at Chilocco Indian Agricultural School, one of the most important of the federal schools, were regimented by twenty-two different bell calls throughout their day (Lomawaima 1994:101).

Punishment was meted out liberally at federal schools, and it is argued that "violence, abuse and neglect stemmed from the boarding schools' entrenched commitment to erasing Indian identity" (Archuleta et al. 2000:42). Students from federal schools spoke of painful or humiliating punishments for infractions such as speaking their native language. One boy on record who was "caught" speaking his language suffered a broken bone after being flung by a school employee (Barker 1998:57). Chilocco students were punished with demerits that required labor such as polishing floors until they gleamed or breaking rocks in a rock pile (Lomawaima 1994). Students at some schools were whipped (Adams 1995:122–123; Child 1998:41), kicked (Reyhner and Eder 1989:89), or had their mouths washed out with soap (Barker 1998:57).

Students who did not willingly submit to their school's system of control faced harsh punishment and incarceration. Faculty and staff at off-reservation boarding schools had the absolute right to punish students. Schools had guardhouses where students, especially runaways, were locked up for sometimes days at a time. The concept of a "guardhouse" bears weighty and purely negative connotations, even into the present day. Indian school guardhouses were places of punishment, not sources of protection. Chilocco Indian Agricultural School had specialized detention rooms at each housing unit, "called the lock-up, usually on the porch, where runaways and other miscreants could be isolated and placed on a bread-and-water diet" (Lomawaima 1994:21). Other forms of control included the reading, censorship, and confiscation of student mail (Child 1998:39). Some schools had buildings that were laid out so that students could be continually observed, even when sleeping, with hospital-ward-like open dormitories—Bentham's Panopticon again. This quality of BIA boarding schools has not changed much. Intriguingly, to Grace Nez, a Navajo student in her twenties, some of those qualities carry over to SIPI as well. She described visiting her grandmother, who was a matron at a contemporary children's boarding school. "I used to go visit her there and it kind of is set up the way the dorm here is . . . The only difference is, these guys have separate rooms. Whereas in the dorm my grandmother was matron of it was just bunk beds on both sides of the wall, all the way down. It was just one big continuous room and it had bunk beds."

A military-school model was used at some schools, with student-on-student supervision to help maintain order, participation in military-style drills (sometimes with actual rifles), and student "officers" for units made up of their peers. "The imposition of military authority at Chilocco was complicated by student officers: school matrons and disciplinarians appointed older students to command the companies and theoretically, to help enforce the rules. In reality, officers' paramount loyalty was to their peers" (Lomawaima 1994:101). Ultimately, these students practiced a combination of resistance—especially in ways that could benefit their peers—and accommodation to the power structure that they were being pulled into. Students found a range of ways to resist the systems put in place to control them, even if resistance was simply to survive.

Awareness of being controlled does not negate that control. It does, though, create a context for subtle forms of resistance. Students could and did find ways to mitigate or protest student treatment and institutional control. Regardless of whether the harrowing narratives of students' experiences in BIA boarding schools were passed down through families or heard in the larger tribal community, SIPI students are all well versed in the histories of BIA schools. In addition, students know enough about these institutions to see some of their characteristics mirrored at SIPI.

Shared Themes: Then and Now

Several of the themes that appeared in SIPI students' metaphors also show up in biographies of individuals who attended Indian boarding schools. Children from the early schools spoke of the control mechanisms they faced on a daily basis. They learned how to operate in an unfair system and adapt to expectations placed on them. They described peers who were not successful at their school. They told stories of individuals who were unable or unwilling to adapt to the high level of management and control that they faced, and either rebelled, gave in, or ran away (Barker 1998:48). Much as SIPI students do, former students from boarding schools also spoke of a sense of family or kinship with their peers at the school, especially a sense of having to unite against unfair rules and harsh disciplinarians. They described close relationships forged with some faculty or staff at these early boarding schools (Lomawaima 1994), and how those connections built solid educational foundations for them, a theme that also arose in SIPI students' narratives and metaphors. Students at federal boarding schools especially spoke of the opportunities afforded them as a result of their experiences. Many of them, when telling about harsh punishment, acknowledged that it forced them to grow up, or become self-sufficient (Lomawaima 1994:107–108). Self-sufficiency became a tool for survival. Many of these themes arose in the narratives that contemporary SIPI students tell as well.

Educational Sovereignty

With such a grim and abusive educational history behind them, members of tribal communities sought to control the education of Native American children. Much of the Bureau of Indian Affairs schooling model was a failure, as many graduates were unable to find appropriate employment for their skills (Barker 1998:61). In addition, students at the earliest schools found it difficult to fit into their home communities when they returned from school. They were "alienated from home and family, culturally as well as emotionally" (Barker 1998:63) and they "experienced serious social problems ... [because] language barriers and lack of knowledge of local culture impeded the efforts of family to reintegrate these young people" (Rousey and Longie 2001:1500). Tribal leaders came to believe that only a seismic change in how Native American children were educated would help to repair the damages wrought by the old system.

Starting in the 1960s, there was a move toward tribes taking control of on-reservation schooling, removing indigenous education from the BIA's hands, and putting it into the hands of the local tribal community. More specifically, if tribes controlled their own educational systems, they could design the schools to fit their community's cultural values. Tribal leaders wanted to indigenize educational systems that had previously been designed for the purpose of indoctrination and assimilation. Changes in educational practices for American Indian youth were reflected in changes in postsecondary education. But first, there had to be a successful model for community and tribal control.

The successful model was born with the founding of the Rough Rock Demonstration School on the Navajo Nation, chartered in 1966. Prior to its opening, a few smaller efforts were made by the BIA and the Office of Economic Opportunity (OEO) to create community-controlled local schools (Lomawaima and McCarty 2006:117). Two such experiments in community education include the school in Round Rock (generally judged a success) and the school in Low Mountain, both founded by Robert Roessel, an Indian Service educator (Szasz 1999:169–171). The Low Mountain School was ultimately undermined by lack of funds and BIA bureaucratic obstruction (Szasz 1999:169–170). Roessel went on to have more success with the Rough Rock Demonstration School. An earlier experiment in community-operated schooling involved a joint effort by the BIA and the OEO to transform an existing school in Lukachukai, Arizona, on the Navajo reservation into a community-controlled one. The decision to transform an existing school failed because they had to "work with an existing staff, dual administration, and Civil Service regulations" (Reyhner and Eder 2004:259). It is from the bones of the failed experimental school in Lukachukai that the Rough Rock Demonstration School was created (Lomawaima and McCarty 2006:117).

The benchmark of tribal control of children's education, it has long been argued that the formation of the Rough Rock Demonstration School acted as the catalyst for the soon to blossom tribal college movement. In 1966, residents of the Navajo Nation decided to take educational matters into their own hands by creating the first tribally controlled children's school (McCarty 2002; Reyhner and Eder 2004:259). The new school took shape under the guidance of Robert Roessel, its first director. The Rough Rock Demonstration School offered first through sixth grade, but it was also intended to serve all generations of the community in some capacity (McCarty 2002:84). One of its stated goals was for the school to "be an economic center for the community" (Szasz 1999:262). Programs at the school were not limited to the academic needs of the children, but also included training for adults. Adult learners could receive arts and crafts training to start their own businesses and improve their economic status. Children would be taught in both Navajo and English. Parents were involved in multiple capacities such as teaching and working as dormitory aides (McCarty 2002). Rough Rock's significance was in creating a community-designed and community-supported boarding school, a type of institution that was usually viewed as "not only *not* an Indigenous institution but a historically repressive one." Rough Rock demonstration school was instead "now positioned as an agent of community empowerment" (McCarty 2002:99). Two significant factors in the success of the Rough Rock Demonstration School were the inclusion of indigenous ideas, values, and culture in the curriculum, and the idiom of family, which was both metaphoric and actual, through the presence of parents and other community members at the school.

At the same time that schooling for American Indian children was moving in a positive new direction, mainstream colleges began to implement curricular changes including the introduction of Native American studies programs. Arizona State University started the first program of Indian studies in 1954. Federal grants became available to begin American Indian studies programs (Szasz 1999:166). By the late 1960s, other schools started to create their own programs. Large, mainstream universities such as the University of Minnesota, University of California at Berkeley, and University of Michigan all created programs during this period (Szasz 1999:295n32). A college that had originally started as an institution of higher education for Indians, the Croatan Normal School for members of the Lumbee tribe in North Carolina, morphed through several iterations and names, and was eventually opened to non-Indians as Pembroke State University (Reyhner and Eder 2004:291–292). The American Indian Law Center at the University of New Mexico was started in 1967 and was quite successful in increasing American Indian enrollment in law schools (Szasz 1999:167). The last and perhaps most meaningful step had yet to be taken: the creation of tribally designed and tribally controlled postsecondary institutions—the modern tribally controlled college or university.

The Tribal College Movement

The real test of American Indian educational sovereignty, then, was not for mainstream schools to create and fund American Indian studies programs. Rather, it was for American Indians and Alaskan Natives to design and manage their own postsecondary educational institutions. Creating tribally controlled schools eventually was made easier as federal policy began to shift toward supporting tribal control, and in 1975, the American Indian Self-Determination and Educational Assistance Act (P.L. 638) was passed (AIHEC 2001:3; Reyhner and Eder 2004:159).

The era that saw the origin and growth of tribally controlled colleges was one of tremendous political change for the relationship between American Indian tribes and the U.S. federal government. Two federal policies prior to the formation of TCUs had a tremendous impact on tribal communities. Immediately after World War II, the Bureau of Indian Affairs began to promote a dual set of policies aimed at, once again, assimilating Native Americans and lessening federal responsibility toward tribes. These policies came to be known informally as Termination and Relocation. The tribal termination policy was articulated in House Concurrent Resolution 108, which Congress approved in 1953. The resolution asserted that the BIA should make every effort to quickly end all federal supervision of American Indian tribes (Wilkins 2002:114). It also meant that all programs that provided support to tribes were to be cut. Assimilation and cost cutting in one fell swoop looked like a twofold success to Congress.

Starting in 1952, the federal government also began implementing programs such as the Voluntary Relocation Program to encourage American Indians to migrate from reservations to several different urban areas, including

Albuquerque, New Mexico. The administrators of the relocation programs hoped that relocated individuals would settle permanently in cities. The Bureau of Indian Affairs did not have an obligation to provide services off the reservation. The resulting out-migration would leave fewer people on the reservation; hence, the government would need to provide fewer services. Ostensibly, participants would receive "job training, travel and moving expenses, assistance in locating jobs and housing in the cities, free medical care for one year, and a thirty-day subsistence allowance" (Olson and Wilson 1984:152). Depending on the city, the year, and the individuals operating the program, participants might have received training in an employable skill or they might have simply been transported and deposited in an urban area with no support or guidance. Poverty and unemployment were common (Olson and Wilson 1984:153). Thirty-five thousand people were relocated during the height of the program, but about one third of them returned to their reservation (Olson and Wilson 1984:152–153). Relocation efforts were intended to promote employment but were also an effort "to destroy tribal communalism" (Wilkins 2002:115).

By the 1960s, it was apparent that the U.S. government's efforts to terminate their relationship with tribes had done far more political and economic damage than good. In fact, for the tribes affected, termination seemed to be a latter-day version of the General Allotment Act of 1887. Relocation was partially successful, in that it led to the growth of urban Native American communities. It could be argued, though, that after World War II, returning veterans probably would still have made the move to cities with little prompting from the government. The policy of relocation certainly shaped the demographic face of Indian Country by creating an urban Indian population that numerically outstrips reservation populations. The attraction of urban settings was so profound that by the time of the 1980 census, urban Indians outnumbered reservation residents (Hoikkala 1998:268). Ultimately, whatever the motivation for the implementation of these programs, many of their long-term effects were socially and financially negative, both for tribes and their members.

The development of TCUs began at the end of the Termination and Relocation Era. The failure of these programs to end the federal government's responsibility for tribes and tribal members, the efforts by tribes to reclaim their children's education, and the political atmosphere in the BIA at that time led to an emphasis on tribal self-determination not just in the political arena, but in the educational one as well. Navajo Community College (now known as Diné College) jump-started the tribal college movement. In 1968, Navajo educational leaders chartered the first tribal college. Soon after, United Tribes Technical College was chartered (AIHEC 2002:43). The founding of Diné College demonstrated the feasibility of other tribes starting tribal colleges. Eventually, thirty-four tribal colleges were founded. In recent years, they have faced economic and management woes that have led to closures—or threats of the same—such as the now defunct D-Q University in Davis, California, which was one of the first TCUs. D-Q enrolled more non-Natives than Native American students and suffered from mismanagement of funds. Originally, D-Q University's name was spelled out, but school officials were informed that it is considered inappropriate to say the "D" name out loud. But in their heyday, tribal colleges grew at an exponential rate. The Southwestern Indian Polytechnic Institute, founded two years after Navajo Community College, was the sixth Native American postsecondary institution opened during this period (AIHEC 2002:43).

Major legislation of the period further supported the growth of the tribal colleges, such as the passage of the Indian Education Act of 1972 and the Tribally Controlled Community College Act of 1978 (McClellan et al 2005:7). Tribal colleges received such limited funding that legislators became concerned about their viability. They noted that the typical tribal college received less than $3,000 per student, while the typical mainstream community college received $7,000. In response to the disparity, in 1994, the Equity in Educational Land-Grant Status Act was passed (Manzo 1994:34). By designating TCUs as land grant institutions, they were declared eligible for funding appropriated for rural-community-serving institutions.

The original land grant institutions were funded by land sales legislated by the Morrill Act of 1862 (Phillips 2003:23; Szasz 1999:237). Land grant schools were built on land given by the federal government to state governments to create institutions that, among other college studies, would teach "agriculture and the mechanical arts" (Phillips 2003:23). TCUs, coming much later, could not receive the large grants of federal land that early land grant schools received. Instead, they were given an endowment of $4.6 million per year for 1996–2000 (Phillips 2003:24), access to large federal grants, and partnership opportunities with state land grant institutions (Szasz 1999:237). Previously, land grant funds were available only to state colleges that had been given land grant status in 1862, or historically black colleges and universities that had received land grant status in 1890 (Phillips 2003:25). TCUs, as federal land grant institutions, have taken on a role in teaching about resource management and environmental protection (AIHEC 2001:2).

The American Indian Higher Education Consortium (AIHEC) was founded early into the movement by the presidents of the first six tribal colleges to allow TCUs to share information, ideas, and resources (Stein

1998:82). The original tribal colleges shared the goal of supporting the community through a range of activities, including "basic education, counseling services, and economic development initiatives—that are specifically focused on communities that would otherwise be completely isolated from such resources" (AIHEC 1998:E-1). Tribally sponsored education for Native American youth focused on the role of the student within his or her family and community, rather than attempting to sever those relationships.

The participants at an early meeting of the American Indian Higher Education Consortium outlined five main characteristics that all tribal colleges shared. TCUs are: (1) located on or near isolated reservations; (2) operated by mostly Native Americans; (3) composed of small student bodies; (4) underfunded; and (5) located in areas with the lowest national income (Stein 1998:82). SIPI shares some of these characteristics. It is within a few hours' drive to the pueblos of New Mexico: the two Apache reservations, Mescalero and Jicarilla; the Navajo Nation; and the smaller, related Navajo reservations in New Mexico. SIPI's student body is quite small, and the school is certainly underfunded. Leadership at SIPI has always been primarily Native American, as SIPI has never had a non-Native president. The key difference, though, is that SIPI is a federal institution and cannot be operated in the same fashion as other TCUs.

SIPI's profound, foundational differences from TCUs have been a significant factor in its relationship with its ostensible peer institutions. When AIHEC originated, members assumed that all institutions serving a Native American majority could and should participate. Participants quickly realized that federally operated institutions, such as SIPI, Haskell Indian Nations University, and the Institute of American Indian Art (IAIA), did not fit the model of tribal colleges as derived from and culturally responsive to a tribal community, and there was an effort made to exclude them from membership (Stein 1998:82–83). These schools were funded by the federal government, and as such were not allowed to compete for other forms of federal funding. Several participants in the early meetings preferred to exclude federal schools, including SIPI, because they were concerned that including Bureau of Indian Affairs institutions into the consortium opened up the entire tribal college community to BIA interference (Stein 1998:83). Early on, SIPI was clearly not a typical member in the tribal college movement.

Why were tribal colleges necessary in the first place? Native Americans traditionally have a high secondary school dropout rate, a low rate of college attendance, and a far lower rate of college graduation. The 2000 Census listed American Indian high school graduation rates as 70.9 percent, compared to the 80.4 percent average of all Americans (Bauman and Graf 2003:5). Even reservations that have tribal colleges graduate only 65 percent of their high school students (AIHEC 2000b:8–9). Some estimates place Native American high school graduation rates in general as low as 55 percent (Carnegie 1989:59). Other research suggests that graduation rates of Native American students who attend Bureau of Indian Affairs schools are noticeably higher: 81.7 percent nationally for BIA schools, with a graduation rate of 89.9 percent specifically in the Southwestern United States (Pavel et al. 1995:21). Research on Bureau of Indian Affairs schools shows an abysmally low number of Native American students who apply to college after graduating from high school. In data provided to AIHEC by the Bureau of Indian Affairs, 11 percent of the students at BIA schools dropped out in the 1998–99 school year (AIHEC 2001:4). Only 33 percent of the students from high schools operated by the BIA applied to college, and almost as discouraging, only 45 percent of the students who had attended public schools with a high percentage of Native Americans applied to college (Pavel et al. 1995:23). The tendency to not apply to college is not particularly surprising as BIA schools and public schools with more than a 25 percent Native American student population did not offer nearly as many college preparatory classes as their non-Native-American-serving counterparts. Of the total number of Bureau of Indian Affairs high schools in 1990–91, 54 percent offered college preparatory classes (Pavel et al. 1995:23). Public schools with more than a 25 percent Native American student population offered only 0.9 percent more college preparatory classes than the BIA schools (Pavel et al. 1995:23). These numbers are low in comparison to schools with a small Native American student population—76.2 percent of these schools offered college preparatory classes (Pavel et al. 1995:23). In my time as an academic advisor, I had several experiences with students who had done well in Advanced Placement (AP) classes but had never been encouraged by their teachers or school counselors to take the AP exams, which would have given them college credit. Without proper preparation and encouragement, is it at all surprising that the number of Native American students attending college is low?

The move to create TCUs was to, in part, address the low rate of retention and graduation of Native American college students (Phillips 2003). Attendance and graduation rates for Native American students at mainstream colleges are quite low. Less than 1 percent of college students are Native American (Tierney 1992:6). Even in states with a high percentage of Native American residents, their numbers in local colleges remain below average. For example, Native Americans in South Dakota make up a little less than 8 percent of the population, but only 2 percent of the college student population (Ridgeway 1998:11). With the introduction of TCUs, students could study near home and in a comfortable cultural milieu. In addition, tribally controlled schools can act as a stepping-stone for students who wish to prepare academically and socially to enter mainstream schools. Native American students who first attend tribal college and then move on to mainstream schools have a completion rate as high as 90 percent (Community College Weekly 2000:17).

TCUs and Their Communities

TCUs are inherently community institutions. They are designed to be "fully reflective of the tribe and fully committed to the betterment of all its members" (Boyer 2002:15). It is this community-centered perspective that informs all key decisions at TCUs, including where they are located, who they are intended to serve out of the larger community, and what courses and programs they will offer. Because they are so tailored to their home community, TCUs can quickly adapt to the tribe's educational needs, virtually as soon as those needs are identified (Phillips 2003:31–32). TCUs are created by, born of, and built for their home communities. Where, then, does SIPI fit in the definition of a TCU? What community is SIPI designed for and responsive to? If SIPI is not a true TCU (and I would argue that it is not), what exactly is it?

The traditional culture of the founding tribe(s) is the foundation of all tribally controlled colleges and universities. A tribal college that does not integrate tribal cultural values and beliefs would, in effect, negate its identity as a TCU. "Culture permeates the entire tribal college campus" (Phillips 2003:27). Culture is the fundamental basis of tribal colleges—and lack of that culture is the most fundamental reason why the Southwestern Indian Polytechnic Institute cannot truly count itself a peer to TCUs. What culture—other than that of the BIA or the federal government's civil service corps—permeates SIPI? And as TCUs are designed "to provide an education that reinforced tribal culture and identity" (Tierney 1992:118), what comparable identity is SIPI reinforcing?

Based on the assumption that, by their very nature as tribal institutions, tribal culture suffuses TCUs, John L. Phillips makes culture the central tenet of his proposed heuristic for the tribal college land grant perspective (2003:26). Of his suggested four guiding principles for these schools—identity, sacredness, holism, and viability—only one (viability) can apply to SIPI. Yet viability, on its own, is most certainly not enough to validate SIPI's institutional self-perception of being a type of TCU. Phillips's heuristic works beautifully for explaining the underlying philosophies of tribal colleges, and in turn it serves to support the argument that SIPI is not a true member of the tribal college sisterhood.

A Carnegie Foundation report points out that "tribal colleges provide essential services that enrich the communities surrounding them. These colleges are, in the truest sense, *community* institutions. Located on reservations, nearly all colleges offer social and economic programs for tribal advancement" (Carnegie 1989:4). The economic need on reservations is huge. Reservations that feature one tribal college have significantly lower average personal income ($4,665 per capita) than other residents of their states ($17,281 per capita) (AIHEC 2000b:9). Tribal colleges play numerous roles within and for Native American communities in addition to providing academic opportunities. Tribal colleges are a bridge to four-year schools (AP 2000; Gilbert 2000; Monette 1997), but bridges that help to maintain and, in fact, support tribal identity and values. They are preservers and promoters of tribal culture (AIHEC 1999:A-2; AIHEC 2001:6; Monette 1997; Pavel 1992). TCUs are job-training centers designed to help fill positions critical to the individual tribal community, and they are sources of economic and political growth and change (AIHEC 2001:6; Monette 1997).

There are multiple beneficial secondary effects that come from TCUs, such as the improvement of local tribal economies in the areas where tribal colleges are located (AIHEC 2000) and community education projects tailored specifically for the needs of that tribal community (Carnegie 1989:4). Virtually all tribally controlled colleges are located within the governing tribe's reservation. Tribal colleges are intimately connected with the tribal homeland, a place that has complex and long-standing meanings already in place. Homelands are "the foundation of our identity as individuals and as members of a community, the dwelling place of being" (Relph 1976:39). Diné College has the motto that "the Navajo Nation is our campus." Their perspective exemplifies a community- and culture-centered pedagogy. In addition, the layout of Diné College in Tsaile, Arizona, is based on the traditional Navajo value system. The campus is circular, the buildings are oriented to the east, and the residence halls are shaped like *hogans* (traditional Navajo housing), further exemplifying the community basis of TCUs.

Tribal colleges are important for their role in preparing tribal members for success in mainstream postsecondary institutions. They build students' academic self-esteem and skills, allowing them to more easily transfer into non-Native-American-majority academic institutions. Community colleges in general play a significant role in the postsecondary education of Native

Americans. For example, in 1988, 54 percent of Native American college students attended community colleges (Pavel 1992:1). By 2006, 8 percent of American Indian and Alaska Native college students were attending tribal colleges (NCES 2008). Tribal colleges are often the community college of choice. As Oppelt notes, "The two-year colleges could offer flexible admissions standards, remedial services, and delivery systems tailored to the circumstances peculiar to the non-traditional students on isolated reservations" (1990:32), strengths most four-year colleges lack. Enrollment at tribal colleges grew 23 percent between 2001 and 2006 (NCES 2008), further evidence that Native American students are choosing tribal colleges for their education.

It is believed that there is a direct correlation between higher Native American college enrollment rates and the continued growth of tribal colleges. This means that Native American college students entering school are choosing tribal colleges (Woodcock and Alawiye 2001). Tribal colleges, and SIPI, were designed for students who have the lowest likelihood of persisting in college: "those with poor academic records in high school, low aspirations, poor study habits, relatively uneducated parents, and small-town backgrounds" (Tierney 1992:21). Research on tribal colleges asserts that they have a high student retention rate (AIHEC 1999:A-2; Rousey and Longie 2001), including SIPI (Uyteebrouk 2001).

There are limits to the success of TCUs, though. Fully one half of tribal college students enter without the intention of staying to earn an AA (Machamer 2000:28), either because they matriculate to a four-year institution, or they simply permanently drop or temporarily stop out. Typical factors for dropping out of tribal colleges include family obligations, which can include personal or family problems, off-campus jobs, financial problems, lack of preparation, and lack of reliable transportation (AIHEC 2005:3; Carnegie 1989:31–32). The term "stop out" refers to repeated leaving and returning to college. This trend is common among SIPI students. In fact, stopping out—taking a semester or two off for personal or financial reasons—is common at TCUs in general (AIHEC 2005:3). It is also common for SIPI students who matriculate to four-year institutions to return to SIPI soon after, saying that they did not like the four-year school. The rhetoric of not liking a four-year institution encodes multiple dilemmas, including a lack of student preparedness for the academic expectations of a university, discomfort with no longer being in a purely Native American cultural milieu (for disliked as it is, even the BIA bureaucracy is familiar), the impersonal nature of large universities, or a combination of factors. Literature on tribally controlled colleges, as well as historically black colleges and universities (HBCUs), asserts that "feel[ing a] bond to an institution causes the [dropout] rate to diminish considerably" (Hurd 2000:44), leading students to be academically successful.

Tribal colleges provide personal models of success to Native American students. As AIHEC reports, in 1996–97, 30 percent of the full-time faculty and 79 percent of school staff at TCUs were Native American, whereas less than 1 percent of the faculty at mainstream institutions were Native American (AIHEC 1998:E-2). Prior to the tribal college movement in the 1960s, few Native Americans attended college (Phillips 2003:23). It is commonly assumed that tribal college enrollment and retention are high because students are more comfortable as classes are taught in a manner that respects, and possibly incorporates, Native American cultural values (Gilbert 2000; Monette 1997; Pavel 1992). In a special report by the Carnegie Foundation, the authors acknowledged the cultural characteristics of tribal colleges by noting: "*Tribal colleges celebrate and help sustain the rich Native American traditions* [emphasis in original] . . . While non-Indian schools and colleges have long ignored Indian culture, tribal colleges view it as their curricular center" (1989:4).

Tribally controlled community colleges are not viewed solely in terms of their status as academic institutions, but as institutions intended to, first and foremost, serve the community where they are located. Because TCUs are community-based organizations, they have an obligation to satisfy the needs of the tribe. For example, Turtle Mountain Community College describes itself as having a "unifying principle" that obligates them to provide "direct community service to the Turtle Mountain Chippewa Tribe . . . The college seeks to maintain, seek out, and provide comprehensive higher education services in fields needed for true Indian self-determination" (Turtle Mountain Community College 2002:10). Diné College describes the school's goal as that of preparing Navajo youth to contribute to the world, and to the Navajo Nation (Diné College 2001:2). Many tribal college programs are crafted to fill local needs, training students for jobs such as teaching and nursing. Diné College notes in its catalog that "the distinctiveness of each campus program derives from the needs of the community it serves" (Diné College 2001:2). A tribal college is intimately tied to the tribe that founded it and takes as its mission the satisfaction of community needs.

TCUs *belong to* their tribal communities. TCU administrators are always cognizant of the fact that their students are drawn from their immediate community. Students are community members but not necessarily tribal members. On average, 79 percent of the students at TCUs are members of the founding tribe, with the rest of the student population composed of American Indians of other tribes and European Americans from surrounding communities (NCES 2008). To maintain its status as a TCU, a college must have a student body that is at least 50 percent Native American. TCUs teach from the cultural perspective of their home community and ground much of the curricula within tribal values. SIPI has no home community and, therefore, has no one culture to draw its identity from and no one community to serve.

Because tribal colleges draw their students from the school's governing tribe and from local communities, students are not faceless bodies filling a large lecture hall. Instead they are known by school staff for their individual identities. Students at TCUs are members of complex webs of interrelationship between individuals, families, clans, and communities. A TCUs organizational structure is shaped by the founding tribe's social structure, which is in turn based on extended family (Tierney 1992:122). TCUs become microcosms of the tribe's kin networks and social ties. Research on the community-based interpersonal links between students and TCU staff notes that the bonds are so strong, and TCU staff so informed, that they can actually factor student deaths into their overall enrollment statistics, a virtual impossibility at a large, impersonal mainstream school (Rousey and Longie 2001). SIPI does resemble TCUs in this fashion as we were often apprised of the deaths of our students, even after they had left the school. Sadly, on several occasions I had students or another employee inform me of the loss of a favorite student. At as small a school as SIPI, where students might have taken several of my classes over the course of a few years, the loss of a student is profoundly felt.

Neither Here nor There: SIPI's Place in the Tribal College Constellation

SIPI, which was created only three years after the first tribal college, at first appears to be a member of the TCU movement. Much of what makes SIPI such a conflicted institution is that, while it was developed during the era of the tribal college movement, the values of the movement were either rejected or impossible to institutionalize at the school. Several of the most important characteristics that set SIPI apart from TCUs are their differences in organizational philosophy and institutional values. The Southwestern Indian Polytechnic Institute is not entirely unique in the manner of having to meld several organizational models, as other tribal colleges have had to make some adjustments in order to receive federal funding. Tribal colleges have had to adopt "formal administrative structures that resemble those of the external society but have moved towards using Indian social norms for day to day interaction" (W. Belgarde 1993; Reyhner and Eder 306:2004). The difference is that true TCUs operate from a core set of values derived from the tribal culture of the community that founded it. They might make organizational concessions in order to better suit federal funding agencies, but they never lose sight of the cultural values, beliefs, and relationships that inform every other aspect of the school. SIPI, though, is not a culturally Native American place that has had to loosely apply federal management styles. SIPI is a government agency, and federal management is not an imposition, but a core value of the school.

SIPI cannot favor any one tribe or set of tribal traditions over any others. There is no one Native language that grounds the curricula, no single culture that informs the institutional value system or course content. SIPI struggles to find a culturally sensitive middle ground to provide a "Native American" atmosphere but without focusing on a specific tribal culture. The most obvious "culture" that one could assign to SIPI is that of the Bureau of Indian Affairs. Most Native American people would argue that there are specific values, attitudes, and behaviors that one can associate with the BIA, many of which are typical to the federal government in general. Intentionally and blatantly promoting BIA culture would be highly controversial, as would constructing an organizational culture for SIPI based on any one specific tribal culture. Managing the resulting ambiguity requires school administrators to make at least token gestures toward "authentic" culture of some sort. Largely, how this question is handled seems to depend on the individuals in leadership positions. With the near constant flux in institutional leadership, policy changes often.

I was witness to a range of approaches intended to (unofficially or perhaps unconsciously) create or at least imply a unifying culture. Four main solutions came in and out of vogue during my time at the school, although there was never, to my knowledge, an institutional-level discussion of the need to find a way to balance the different tribal cultures at the school. These solutions included: (1) placing public emphasis on the tribal cultures that are most highly represented in the student body, such as choosing a *hogan* design for the log building donated by the Kellogg Foundation, (2) representing the tribal cultures of the school's leadership, by having the school leaders offer prayers in their Native language at school events, (3) making abstract and generic references to rhetoric and imagery associated with Native American cultures, such as vague remarks about eagles and the cardinal directions, or (4) bypassing traditional Native American cultures altogether by promoting evangelical Protestant Christianity in public functions, including in benedictions offered at campus events.

Unlike TCU programs designed to fulfill a clear and specific professional or educational dilemma on a reservation, it is difficult to accurately gauge the impact of SIPI on local tribes because it is an urban school. While SIPI's programs have no doubt made an impact on certain sectors of local tribes' economies or community needs, it is difficult to attribute larger-scale successes to SIPI. For example, the school has clearly been instrumental in training Native American Head Start teachers throughout the state as mandated by the state government. Economic and social effects, though, are harder to see simply because the school serves multiple communities.

Whereas TCUs are located on tribal land, with all the meanings associated by the residents with that land, SIPI lacks these meanings. It is not located on a homeland, within a specific cultural setting. It is a federal school, on federal land, surrounded by the sprawl of Albuquerque, and serves students from multiple tribes. No one community can lay claim to the school, nor can the school pull cultural values and meanings from any one (or even several) tribal cultures. SIPI's own institutionally produced text presents the school as an educational hub, located so as to serve all Native American people throughout the West. SIPI's actual physical location is relevant to the role it plays and its technology focus, as the catalog notes that it is "located in the heart of Indian Country, the center of New Mexico's high-tech corridor"(SIPI 1999:3). Pevar (1992: Appendix E) defines Indian Country as all lands within a reservation, under Indian control, and/or land that Indians have title to. In common usage, this term refers to areas of predominant Indian population and/or the American Indian imagined community. SIPI's course catalog supplement states that "SIPI continues to develop . . . course offerings that respond to the economic development and workforce needs of the modern American Indian tribal economy as well as industry, local, state and federal government needs" (SIPI 2003:3). This is a very broad mandate, not specific to any one tribe, and that reaches far beyond Indian Country.

SIPI shares some significant characteristics with TCUs. TCUs have high student retention rates and prepare students for the workforce or for matriculation into a four-year institution. SIPI, like TCUs, takes retention issues seriously. Students who are withdrawing from school meet for an exit session with an academic counselor. Tremendous effort is made at keeping students enrolled in school and attending classes. SIPI, like TCUs, is open to community members with a wide range of skill levels. The school is structured so that students are tested upon arrival and immediately placed in remedial classes if necessary. SIPI's scope is to allow any interested community member the opportunity to get a college education, and to remediate any individuals who are not yet ready for college-level classes.

In one intriguing contrast to the tribally controlled colleges and universities, SIPI's student body is entirely composed of Native Americans. The only TCU with an entirely Native American student body as of fall 2002 is Sinte Gleska University in Rosebud, South Dakota (Pavel and Inglebret 2007:141). Tribal colleges, while geared to the needs of their local reservation and culture, accept non-Native students. Because SIPI and HINU are seen as fulfilling treaty obligations, all students must show they are enrolled members of recognized American Indian tribes or Alaska Native villages. When applying, students are required to submit their Certificate of Degree of Indian Blood. Student cannot attend SIPI without this document. What this means is that SIPI's student body is numerically "more" Native American than other tribal colleges, yet more ethnically diverse than other schools as it enrolls students from a wide range of tribes.

How does an institution like SIPI fit into the history of American Indian education in the United States? And how does it compare with other types of American Indian educational institutions? The history of Native American education in the United States shows a move from schools designed as tools for assimilating Native children to schools as expressions of tribal self-determination and community identity. It becomes clear when we trace this complex history that SIPI is related to both the institutions of the past and those of the future. It also becomes clear, as described in the next chapter, that SIPI has its own history, one that can shape students' decisions about whether to attend or not.

4
Taking a New Path
The Decision to Attend SIPI

The Southwestern Indian Polytechnic Institute—owing to its small size and the specialization of its mission—is not widely known outside the Native American community, even among longtime residents of Albuquerque. When it is known of, SIPI is seen as the less storied, less mythic younger sibling of the venerable Haskell Indian Nations University. For some students, SIPI is the stuff of sepia-toned and joyful childhood memories, of visits to family and playing on campus. Other students know about SIPI from older relatives' family stories of hazily remembered wild college days. A few acknowledge never having heard of the school until immediately before deciding to attend. What students expect to find at the Southwestern Indian Polytechnic Institute, and what they indeed do find there, create a fascinating set of stories. The SIPI they hear about from relatives, or see in the brochures, read about on the Internet, or remember through the lens of childhood memory, is never quite the place they expected. And in the end, they create their own SIPI stories.

SIPI Is a Family

SIPI is, in many ways, a family affair. Many SIPI students have family members who either attended while they did, attended prior to them, or worked at the campus. Forty-eight percent of my interview participants mentioned having at least one family member who had attended the school, was currently attending, or had been employed at SIPI. Many survey respondents did as well. This familial connection means that SIPI has strong emotional undercurrents for students. Family connections to the Southwestern Indian Polytechnic Institute serve to attract students to the school. Family history at the school or the presence of kin on campus lends the school a sense of familiarity and safety. The overlap of family and family history with the Southwestern Indian Polytechnic Institute leads to multiple metaphorical representations of the school as an extended family or even as a reservation community, which is, in effect, a type of extended family writ large.

For students who had a strong or long-term family connection to the school, their first impressions were developed as children. Once they became students, their views of the school were mediated by childhood memories and experiences or by the stories they heard from older relatives. For some SIPI students, such as Kira Thomas, the decision to attend the school, their first impressions of the campus, and their experiences as students are intimately linked with childhood memories and family ties.

Kira Thomas is a perceptive, articulate, and analytical individual who has spent considerable time pondering the significance of SIPI both personally and in relation to the larger Native American community. She approaches her relationship with the school playfully and with restrained frustration, as if she were talking about a beloved but exasperating relative. She is a gifted storyteller, shaping her words into visually striking pictures for her listener.

Kira's perspective on SIPI came through multiple filters and time frames: her father's experiences at the school in its earliest days, her childhood memories of visiting SIPI with family members, her own experiences as a student at SIPI, and later, her perspective when looking back at SIPI as a graduate and a professional.

Kira's parents came to SIPI in the 1970s in order for her father to attend during the school's earliest days. The education he received there had a profound impact on their subsequent life as a family. In reference to the way SIPI shaped her family's future, she says, "SIPI is, for me, specifically, what started it all. I can trace myself back to SIPI." She jokingly announced that she was a legacy SIPI student. Mock dramatically she announced that, "SIPI's always got a place in my heart" but then turned more serious when she told me, "It's impossible for myself to turn my back on SIPI. I can take a break from SIPI but I couldn't turn my back on SIPI. And if SIPI ever left, I wouldn't be able to handle it. I hope thousands of kids get to have experiences like I do."

Her experiences at the school date back so far that her first impressions of SIPI have the specificity of a child's memories.

> Before I was a student, I came onto campus when my father would play basketball. I guess there's leagues . . . He played basketball games

here, so I spent a lot of time in the bleachers. Playing in the bleachers, jumping off the bleachers. I know the smell of the SIPI gym since the early eighties. Still smells the same! I came to campus that way. Then I had [family] who went here. I have fond memories of this Pac-Man machine in the SUB [Student Union Building]. When I first got here, [it was] the first thing I went to, and it was still there when I first got here.

And then I have memories of playing pool with my aunts and various uncles who came to school here ... I remember it being a fun place. I remember hearing stories about the trailers [a trailer park to the north of campus that served as informal married student housing and that has been replaced by apartments] and [relatives] doing crazy things on campus ... That's how I knew of SIPI. And I always remember, as a kid, tennis courts, because that's not a sport that Indians play. That's what I thought when I was younger, my first impressions as a child.

Revisiting the campus locations featured in her family's stories or remembered from her childhood visits provided her with a comforting connection to family history. Several family stories centered around a particular location on campus, now serving as a conceptual locus for her memories, which seem to echo outward from that central spot. No matter how alien some aspects of the college might have been when she attended as a student, she has a positive, nostalgic model through which to interpret the school. Leaving for college was less intimidating than it would have been had she not had happy memories of and family stories about the school.

The SIPI that Kira knew from family stories and from her own childhood experiences is far less confusing and frustrating than her own experiences as an adult and a student. Filtering the school's conflicting qualities through her affectionate memories allowed her to make sense of her experiences and ground herself at the school. When Kira describes emotionally meaningful places on SIPI's campus, she is not talking about places that are meaningful to her adult self, through her own experiences in that place. Rather, these places are important for their role in her family history or they were imbued with meaning when she was a child. The stories were a reminder that her family was part of the fabric of the place, and she drew comfort from the sense of her family's presence on the campus.

Nancy White also assigns tremendous significance to the Southwestern Indian Polytechnic Institute based on her deep-rooted ties to the school. Nancy, in her mid-twenties, comes from a Midwestern tribe. She looks much younger than she is. Nancy is extremely bright, driven, and outgoing, often bursting into buoyant laughter. She is energetic and organized, able to easily juggle details and deadlines.

Like Kira, Nancy often sees SIPI through the lens of her childhood memories there. Those memories are both positive and motivating. As a child, Nancy visited the campus with an older family member when that relative was employed at the school. Attending SIPI as an adult was a link to her childhood, and when she is on campus, she is reminded of the happy memories she has of visiting the school. I asked what role blood relations and fictive kinship had at SIPI. She understood immediately, noting the common student experience of having kin at the school:

> Because their families are all here . . . SIPI serves its purpose for a small portion of Indian Country and it's kind of a perpetual cycle. If someone can be successful here, naturally you'll encourage your family members to be successful . . . because that's the one thing that all ties us here. It's literally about your blood connection to . . . your lineage . . . your tribe, and your nation. That's [the Certificate of Indian Blood] what gives us the right to be students here, so I think that that in part is a key piece . . . I'm obviously going to encourage my cousins, or my [sibling], or whomever if they're looking to get their education, [and] (a) can't afford it, or (b) [it is] common sense, it's easier for them to come to a community college and get their degree. I'm going to . . . tell them to come here. You have free room and board, you can get a job, you can work-study, and you can take classes. I think it's a good opportunity.

Nancy's response is intriguing in that it points to the assumption that students at the school typically have a preexisting tie there. SIPI, to Nancy, is not the national community center I once assumed it to be. Rather, it is a family secret, a resource available to all Native Americans but used by only a well-informed few.

SIPI also served as both the backdrop and the answer to an educational dilemma Nancy found herself in. During a visit to the school as a teenager, she and her older relative attended an event on campus. Nancy had been debating attending college and had been thinking of taking a low-paying job instead. As Nancy was served dinner, her relative leaned over and asked her whether, in ten years, she would rather be getting served the meal or serving it. That question and her visits to the school had a profound impact on her perspective of SIPI and of the value of setting educational goals. The question from her relative, and her own reaction to it, "sort of spurred me back in the direction of my education." Her existing tie to SIPI made the choice to attend a logical one.

The Choice to Attend College

Students at SIPI share many of the motivations for attending college that students all over the country express. Some state their motivation bluntly—acknowledging that without an education, their career choices are limited and they face seriously constrained finances. Professional opportunities are severely limited on most reservations, and even low-wage jobs are hard to come by. Employment on the most impoverished reservations usually involves either working for the tribal government in some capacity or working for the federal government. A college education offers more opportunities. Students come to SIPI fully aware of the financial limitations they will face without postsecondary education, like the Navajo woman from Kayenta, Arizona, who wrote, "I don't want to end up flipping burgers for a living" or the Navajo man from Greasewood, Arizona, who wrote, "I got sick of being poor and working dead-end jobs. I want to make my dream a reality." College could liberate them, several wrote, from a dreary round of physically demanding, intellectually deadening, low-paying jobs. They chose to attend college because "you learn to use your mind in college. It expands your view." A college degree did not guarantee a job on their reservation, but it did offer more life choices.

Others spoke in more abstract terms, such as self-improvement, bettering themselves, and personal growth. One student wrote that she decided to attend college simply to "become a better person in the future." Another student saw college as a means to counteract the inertia he was experiencing, so he "decided I need to move on with my life." Some voiced the want, or need, to leave home, as described by a man from Fort Defiance, Arizona, who wrote, "I decided that SIPI would be a great place to 'find myself' again. A place to 'run away' to, where I can be alone and think." Others saw the school as a way to be closer to family, like the woman from California whose family lived in a local pueblo, who both "wanted to get away from my reservation and experience something different" while also getting acquainted with the side of her family that lived locally.

Still others defined their goals in relation to their family, such as "I wanted to be the first one in my family to complete college" and, written by a woman from a Great Basin tribe, "I felt I needed to go. No one in my family had really gone to college. Why not?" Students at SIPI know the benefits of a college education for their own life path and future earnings, but also the positive impact it would have on their families. Having a college education means that students can make a more substantial contribution to their family, benefiting even those family members who did not attend college themselves. While the choice to attend college is motivated by fairly straightforward goals, the choice to attend SIPI is a bit more complicated.

Advance Warning and Introductions

Even for those students who do not describe childhood visits to SIPI, choosing to attend SIPI could still be influenced by family. Those relatives who knew or had experienced SIPI themselves shaped students' perspectives of the school and the types of experiences they would have there. Many students learned about SIPI through family members. Forty-five percent of the students who participated in the brief 2002 survey heard about the school from relatives, some of whom they listed as having attended SIPI. While describing their first impressions of the school, 11 percent of the respondents from the 2004 survey specifically mentioned having heard about SIPI from their relatives.

The contribution of family members to a student's decision to attend could involve significant commitment from an older relative, such as the man whose aunt drove out to his reservation, several states away from her home in New Mexico, to move him in with her so he could attend SIPI. Or it can be as simple as pointing the school out.

Steve Tsosie, a Navajo student from Kayenta, Arizona, arrived at SIPI as a teenager. Upon meeting him, Steve appears quite shy, but once he becomes comfortable, he shows his quirky sense of humor and his pleasure in wordplay. He speaks quickly, throwing out asides and puns so rapidly they often pass the listener by. When he thinks deeply about a new concept or theory, Steve develops a serious-looking scowl, an expression quite at odds with his playful personality. Steve told me that he had heard very little about the school until his mother raised the idea of his attending. "I heard it's a pretty good place to go for students who need to develop themselves to go to an Ivy League college. My mother told me . . . about this school and I thought it was a really good place for me to start out. 'Cuz I just got out of high school and I pretty much did not know where to go from there. Yeah, it's a good place to get [started for] a four-year college . . . Honest? I would say that SIPI is a good place to start." His mother's encouragement—and the occasional drive past the school while she pointed it out—helped shape his decision to attend SIPI. He had not, it seems, heard any of the negative stories that other students spoke of.

Knowing that they have kin on campus offers comfort to some students who wish to attend. SIPI sees a wide range of kin relationships between students. At any one time there might be spouses, parents attending with their children, cousins, and siblings, all attending, carpooling, rooming together. A man from a local pueblo described being a student at SIPI while members of three generations of his family were also in attendance. Kin not only look out for each other, but encourage each other as well. I will always remember the cousins—who were so different in personality, appearance, and demeanor that I had not realized they were related—who stopped some distance from me on the walkway between buildings one morning as I hurried across campus. As the younger man stood by, looking sheepish, the older one asked me if his rough-and-tumble cousin was fulfilling his course obligations. This type of interaction happened on more than one occasion, where older cousins or siblings sought me out to ask how their younger relative was doing in my class, only to be surprised when I let them know they were not legally allowed to ask that question.

The attraction to attend with family means that a student might not have chosen to attend SIPI if it were not for the presence, or the active coercion, of close kin. Lynae Archuleta described her amusingly coerced decision—if it was in fact her decision—to attend SIPI. Lynae was raised in her pueblo and still lives there. She is in her twenties, and she is one of the students who, years before, had suggested that I do research on SIPI. A small woman with huge dark eyes and long black hair, Lynae is jolly and soft-spoken, but she takes her education seriously and is comfortable standing up for herself and those she cares about. Her passionate, lifetime commitment to her tribal culture and community is evident when she speaks of them.

Her equally strong love for and commitment to her family had a direct but unexpected impact on her decision to attend SIPI. Lynae and her younger sister are quite close—so much so that her sister even sat in on her interview. Her younger sister defers to Lynae in many ways, but when it came time to apply to SIPI, Lynae found herself being lovingly strong-armed. Lynae's sister decided she wanted to attend SIPI and she wanted Lynae to attend with her. Lynae told me:

> To tell you the truth, I thought long and hard. I don't think I would have ever gone back to school. I was so headstrong. I said to myself, I would've just graduated high school and got a job. I wouldn't have

come to school at all. It was my sister who forced me. I never filled out my SIPI application to come to school here. Nothing! I remember it was like two weeks before SIPI started, and she was all, "C'mon, you're going" and I'm like, "Yeah, right! I don't even want to go." I was not even into school. And she was all, "I'm gonna fill your application out." So she filled my application out. She even packed all my clothes.

Forced me to go to school! And then, all I did . . . I just remember signing papers. That's all! [laughing] I was just [mimes signing papers]. Then she returned it here. We got accepted. And then, I was so not even into this! I was a little mule. A little donkey. I was like, "No! I ain't gonna go!" So she packed my clothes, got them here. Set me up in my dorm and stuff. And I was like, "Sigh." Then school started, and I was like, "Okay, I'm here." I just thought it was like another thing. Like, "Oh it's high school again." I didn't really know that until after that it's totally different. But if it wasn't for her, I don't think I would've pursued education after high school.

In the end, she was glad to have attended the Southwestern Indian Polytechnic Institute, and she described it as a safe and supportive environment where she grew confident in her academic abilities.

Lynae's experience at SIPI was defined largely by the role her sister played, yet not all students want to attend college with their family members. A woman in her twenties who claimed both a West Coast tribe and a local pueblo expressly selected SIPI for its distance from her home state and the absence of family. She said, "It's a place where I can be on my own, away from family members and other people back home." Other students spoke of attending SIPI as a way to absent themselves from the home communities, but in a manner that was approved and productive.

Not all students had known about SIPI prior to deciding to attend. Some students arrived with absolutely no prior knowledge of the school, like one young woman who claimed several Midwestern tribes. She wrote, "Before I found SIPI on the Internet, I hadn't heard anything about it. My first impression was a positive one." The lack of advertising for SIPI, and other TCUs, bothered Robin Hale. She claims two tribes, both of which she is actively learning about while at SIPI. Robin's affect is so upbeat that someone could miss that she is a hardworking, dedicated student. She often mentors other students and participates in on-campus activities.

Robin had vague memories of a family member attending SIPI, but "after that, I didn't hear anything . . . The other TCUs, I never knew of . . . I didn't know there were so many. And so it was kind of like, 'Whoa. Why aren't they marketed more?' Or at least pamphlets given to some schools about tribal colleges . . . Because a lot of students don't know about the tribal colleges. And myself, growing up off the reservation, I sure as heck didn't hear anything about it." Luckily she had a friend who knew about the school and recommended it to her. The lack of external advertising almost implies that one factor for the high levels of family attendance is simply the fact that word-of-mouth among extended families is the major form of advertising for SIPI.

First Impressions

First impressions of the school ranged from the extremely positive—such as the nineteen-year-old Navajo woman who wrote, "I heard it was a good school. My first impressions would be 'Wow!'" to the extremely negative, such as the student who had grown up hearing that it was "just a school for drunks" and then, upon arriving, asked himself, "What the [heck] am I doing here?"

The appearance of the campus shaped most survey respondents' first impressions of SIPI. The state of the architecture and amenities was distressing to them. Students commented on the dated appearance of the school's architecture, with one Pueblo woman telling me that it looked like a 1970s flashback. A Seminole man (who overall had positive things to say about the school) described it physically as a "small, kinda old school, seventies-like." Several students described it as run-down, and one affectionately described it as old, but that it "must have been a school with style back then."

An Eastern Shoshone man was profoundly disappointed by his introduction to SIPI. He had heard that "it was a great school," but once he arrived, his "first impression was terrible because the football and baseball field was trashed. The dorms was [sic] old and the campus is old." He felt that most of the faculty was rude, students were unfriendly, and he expressed his belief that school officials "get rid of you any way they can. They don't give nobody a second chance." His perception of the school is in direct contrast to that of a twenty-four-year-old Sioux man who described hearing about SIPI from an ex-girlfriend. He wrote that she was quite impressed with the school and that when he got to SIPI, "I liked it. I still enjoy attending classes at SIPI." He added, "I like the teachers, the people here are also friendly."

First impressions were quite positive for some students, like the nineteen-year-old Hopi woman who was first introduced to the Southwestern Indian Polytechnic Institute through a campus career fair. She took a tour of the campus, and that made her mind up to attend. A Sioux woman summed up the irrelevance of appearances when she wrote, "At first, SIPI looked boring until I realized I wasn't here for the looks. I am here for the education."

Comparisons between the Southwestern Indian Polytechnic Institute and a high school repeatedly cropped up in the survey responses. The traits students used for comparison include: the behavior and attitudes of their peers, how students are treated and viewed by employees, small class size, easy or unchallenging coursework, and the fact students share a similar daily schedule. One student described SIPI as both "a good school and just like high school." Another student, a young Navajo woman from Kayenta, wrote of the positive descriptions of SIPI she had heard. She wrote, "I heard that SIPI was an affordable school and that it was good with small classes and teachers that enjoyed teaching. Mostly a lot of good things. When I got to SIPI, my first impression was that I was glad to be in a class that was the same size as a high school class." Resembling a high school, then, was not a universally negative comparison.

"Am I Going to Be a Party Animal, Too?"

Unfortunately, the Southwestern Indian Polytechnic Institute has a conflicting—and in fact, deeply contradictory—reputation. SIPI has a well-known reputation as a "party school," a common college euphemism for a school where inebriation is pursued more passionately than education. According to students, that reputation is well deserved. The party school reputation arose repeatedly in conversations with students and in their survey responses. Several students who responded to the 2004 survey questionnaire made it explicitly clear that they had not heard positive things about the school, yet they chose to attend anyway. Efforts have been made to quash student drinking with the implementation of the campus zero-tolerance drug and alcohol policy, but it is unclear to what degree this has been successful. Students describe the school as less violent than it had been in the past, implying the zero-tolerance policy is effective.

For every student who was actively encouraged by relatives to attend, there were several who mentioned relatives just as actively *discouraging* them from attending SIPI. Tales of drunken "partiers" and "potheads" dominating the social fabric of the school, and stories of physical violence shaped some students' impressions of the school. Students were warned about violence on campus, or conflicts that started on campus and were followed by assaults off-campus. A Hopi woman and a Navajo woman, both in their twenties, stated that they were vigorously warned away from attending the

Southwestern Indian Polytechnic Institute by close relatives and that they actively rejected the advice. One woman stated that she entered the school knowing that it might prove difficult to fit into a party school atmosphere but that she appreciated the challenge. The other woman said she received several warnings from different family members to stay away from SIPI. Her family legacy with SIPI was not a nostalgically told tale of relatives changing the course of their lives through education. Instead, "My dad used to tell me that it was a party school, and everybody used to get drunk. My uncle used to come here, like a long time ago, back in the seventies. He said it was a party school and that he used to drink all the time. That I shouldn't go to school here because I'll only get in trouble. Stuff like that . . . Like, all they do is drink here. There is no real education, and . . . that this place is just a place to party . . . not really go to school." She explained that her choice to attend SIPI was an expression of willfulness, in part "just to show them that I could finish here," a willfulness that she has since outgrown. But she did not regret attending, because "I think it's cool here . . . You can get your education." Undoubtedly, SIPI must lose potential students who hear the descriptions of it as a party school and, unlike the women quoted here, do not consider themselves up to the challenge.

Students were also concerned about violence and physical safety at the Southwestern Indian Polytechnic Institute. A twenty-five-year-old Navajo man wrote that, prior to attending SIPI, he had "[h]eard it was a wild school. Fights, beer, drunks, drugs, gangs, etc. . . . First impression? It was mind-boggling." Another student said that her friends in high school warned her against attending SIPI, telling her that she would get beaten up if she came. Nancy White said, "I never knew what SIPI was . . . until I came here. I heard a lot of stories about SIPI, like in the seventies, how unsafe it was. Women couldn't walk across campus without being accosted and in some cases raped. People were always getting stoned in the quad and protesting. All kinds of crazy stuff was going on. But I didn't really have any frame of reference for that."

Violence on campus was perhaps no more or less than on a mainstream campus, but in as small a community as SIPI, the reverberations from a violent act quickly spread to the entire campus. In addition, assaults on or near campus have been reported in the local news media, including the story of a woman who was beaten by two other women in the dormitory in 1998 (Jones 1998:C2), a man whose face was slashed in a fight in the bathroom of the men's dormitory in 1997 (*Albuquerque Journal* 1997:1), and the brutal rape of a student by another student in 2006 mere yards from campus (*Albuquerque*

Journal 2006:2). Ironically fulfilling the axiom that there is no such thing as bad publicity, one student responding to the 2002 survey first learned about SIPI after hearing "news reports on violence." On the bright side, a man in his late twenties from an Oklahoma tribe wrote, "SIPI has really come a long way since I was here last. It is not as violent as it used to be. More classes are offered." His words echo those of an Alaskan man who described fights between SIPI students at off-campus party locales, including one assault that took place right before he started at SIPI, where one female student stabbed another in the stomach. When he entered the school, "I kind of had an idea of how rough it could be, so I just wanted to keep my nose clean and work." He added that on-campus safety had improved tremendously in the time he had been at the school. "They're cracking down pretty good . . . It's not nearly as bad as it was back then. I hear stories from . . . relatives that came down here in '90, '91, and it was even worse than when my cousin came down in '95." He described the majority of conflicts as having originated on campus and being exacerbated by alcohol.

Another student who claimed membership in both the Navajo Nation and a local pueblo summarized the "party school" dilemma succinctly: Drinking becomes more of a motivation than the pursuit of academic goals. He wrote that his first impression of the school was "that a lot of people party, and some graduate."

Nancy White entered SIPI unaware of its reputation, saying, "Once I was here, I started hearing students refer to it as, like, a party school. For a long time, I didn't know what that meant, because I didn't see that side of it. I came to class and went home. I didn't stay in the dorms, so I was always . . . I'd drive down the hill . . . go to class, come back . . . That was really the extent I was involved with SIPI, until I started hanging out with these guys [friends she met on campus]. But even then, none of them really partied hard." Nancy did not see the Southwestern Indian Polytechnic Institute as a "party school" because she did not go there to party. One cannot help wondering if the party school reputation becomes a self-fulfilling prophecy. A young Navajo woman from Alamo, New Mexico, seemed downright enthusiastic about the school's reputation when she wrote that she had heard that SIPI was "a cool school, because it was a party school." She added that her first impressions led her to ask herself if she would turn into "a party animal, too?" In light of her enthusiasm for the school's partying reputation, it is unclear whether becoming a party animal was a concern or a goal.

SIPI's party reputation also shaped students' arrival experience. Robin Hale said of her first impressions, "It was kind of a mixed thing. I guess it was just 'the new girl on the block.' Right when I got here, within the first few weeks, I could tell the white and black area [the divide between academics and partying]. You could see it. It was very predominant. And it is still predominant. That's where I was like, 'Whoa. What kind of school is this, really?' Now that time has gone on . . . I can see why some parents are very hesitant on letting their kids come here, because of the stories that they hear about SIPI."

One Pueblo woman in her twenties said she was repeatedly warned about the school prior to attending. She visited SIPI when she was in high school, and found the campus dirty and "out of the ordinary." The physical appearance of the campus was not enough to keep her from attending. The warnings she received, though, gave her pause. "Honest? Okay, that it was a party school. It's just mainly a party school. Then people back home would say, 'Oh, you're going to school there? I hope you don't come back pregnant!' That's the first thing [they say]! . . . I heard about . . . 'the SIPI thing,' that you just come here to date somebody. It might just be for a trimester. That's called 'the SIPI thing.' Or if you end up dating here, you have a 'SIPI baby.' I heard constantly, 'Your kid would be a SIPI baby.' It's weird." In the end, she found the school to be intellectually and academically satisfying, but the school's reputation was enough to initially scare her away. A Cochiti man who was commuting to the school expressed dismay at the attitude of his fellow students—rather than reject or transcend the school's reputation by immersing themselves in their education, he was sad to note negative stories were true. "I heard it was a party school and students acted like they were still in high school. My first impressions were the students don't care too much about their education. Not all the students come here to better their lives." Ultimately, though, partying is a choice. Students who attended with a clear vision of their end goal would be successful. And just as academically motivated students built friendships with like-minded peers, the students who just wanted to party found each other. They even created their own enclave of compatible individuals in the dormitory. A Sioux man explained to me that students self-select their housing area in the men's dormitory based on their shared interest of partying. "The D wing, they call it 'the war zone' because that's where most of the 'party people' are." There is perhaps a positive result of this self-segregation—the more academically motivated students are left to themselves.

As a Navajo woman in her thirties from Arizona pointed out, "It would depend on what you want in life; you can start an education here. It's a good place if you want education, but a bad place if you are just here to party." A

Sioux woman dismissed SIPI's reputation affectionately by saying, "I knew nothing of SIPI before I came. I love this school. SIPI does have its reputation, though. It is made fun of, but I think it's just insider jokes between people who have attended here." The ongoing nature of SIPI's party school reputation was seen by one student in his late twenties as anachronistic. He noted that "first thing is how ... older people think of SIPI as a party school. It's like, 'No, here [it's] really serious about school.'" To this student, warnings from older people about SIPI are a disservice to current students because they unnecessarily scare students away from attending and unfairly discount the education students are receiving. Whether SIPI's reputation is mostly true but a matter of personal choice, an outdated artifact of an earlier time, or a playful ribbing at the hands of those who know it best, that reputation does not dissuade the most motivated students from the opportunities presented at the school.

SIPI's reputation as a party school has been detrimental to it. In response, the Board of Regents instituted a zero-tolerance policy for drugs and alcohol in June 1992 (SIPI 1998:15). The SIPI Handbook describes violations of the zero-tolerance policy as: being under the influence of drugs or alcohol, possessing alcohol or controlled substances or paraphernalia, or transporting it or trafficking it on campus (SIPI 2001:45). The goal of the policy was to forcibly change student culture by instituting severe penalties for violations. The hope was that the penalties for violating the policy would make it too costly for students to risk getting caught. The zero-tolerance policy provides the administration with a codified avenue for addressing alcohol abuse on campus. Instituting and enforcing the policy have led to changes in the campus "party culture."

"I Don't Care What They Say, I'm Going Anyway"

Stories emphasizing SIPI's reputation are not enough to scare off all potential students. Students refer to individual choice in their explanations of why they choose to attend. They acknowledge that while some individuals come to the school without the unambiguous goal of getting an education, those who know why they are there benefit from attending. A twenty-year-old Navajo woman wrote, "I first heard that this was a party school, and there are a lot of ghosts in the dorms. I didn't believe them, because I had to experience it myself." A thirty-two-year-old Navajo woman from Gallup, New Mexico, wrote that she had "heard it was a party place, but I knew I had to come for myself and besides I wasn't going for parties, I was coming to SIPI to be educated."

Students who are confident in their decision to come to the school find themselves having to make rational economic choices while gently ignoring the advice of friends or family. Renee Verde, a Navajo woman in her twenties, insisted on the multitude of opportunities available at SIPI. She is an active figure on campus who volunteers for virtually every committee or activity that she can. Renee is self-motivated, confident, and a naturally gifted student. She understands her position as a role model and takes troubled students under her wing.

Even with her faith in her decision to attend SIPI, she also had to surmount parental skepticism in her decision to attend.

> My parents didn't want me to come here. My parents didn't want me to come here at all. They didn't like it. They thought it was a party school ... They didn't think I was going to be able to fit in. I thought the same thing, but I also thought it was challenging. Because I had had so many problems in the past going to a BIA-funded school, going to school on the reservation. That this was very challenging. So, I did it.
>
> Then on top of that, the whole financial aspect of it, too. It made a lot of sense. I did a lot of research with UNM and TVI [now CCCNM] and, you know, SIPI. What was in the immediate area, and what I could—what was available to me, at that time. And the degree programs are very similar, as far as TVI and SIPI. On top of that, they [SIPI] had dormitories, [whereas] you had to pay to live in their [the other schools'] area. So, a lot of it had to do with the financial aspects.
>
> [SIPI] also had a lot more—they had associate's degrees that I could start at to build that foundation, as far as where I wanted to be ... which was transitioning to a four-year college. So, I think a lot of it was weighed on the financial aspect, but other things were weighed based on the credibility of the school. So, I did a lot of research on it before I actually made the decision. My parents were actually not in favor of it, but I did it anyway, because I thought it was challenging.

Renee explained that part of the process of meeting the challenges of attending SIPI is to look into all of the different student organizations, again making rational choices, this time in terms of participation. Which campus organizations would be the most beneficial professionally and personally and the most interesting? Active participation in campus activities served, for her and others, as an antidote to the campus party culture.

What They Found: "It's a BIA School. Where Did You Think You Were Going?"

Students entering SIPI bring a host of preconceptions about the school. Some, like Clayton Griego, enter the school unconcerned with the external qualities of the school. When Clayton decided to return to college after having worked for years, he already knew about SIPI. He called an old family friend to help him figure out the process. The appearance and trappings of the school did not affect him as much as the intellectual atmosphere that he stepped into on his arrival. Clayton said his first impressions were purely positive and that he "clicked right away" with the school. He was immediately struck by the passion of his instructors, especially one instructor who pushed him to excel and helped to build Clayton's confidence by telling him, "You can do whatever you want." Clayton found student complaints about the food or other institutional qualities to be somewhat insincere since, as he noted, he had grown up eating at BIA and public schools.

The physical appearance of the campus did not impress students, who described it as alternately, "small, brown, and dry" and "real spacious"; "isolated, old buildings" and "unique"; and most tellingly, "it's a nice school if you make it." The Southwestern Indian Polytechnic Institute that appears in the school's self-produced promotional literature rarely matches what students see when they arrive. What they think they are getting are lush lawns and new facilities, and what they get when they arrive is so significantly different that some students feel they were deceived.

A woman from a Great Basin–area tribe wrote in her survey response, "It's nowhere near as nice as the pictures [in] the catalog or brochures." Her observation was accurate and was commented on by more than one of her peers. School-sponsored brochures and documents were known for reusing outdated photographs or for touching up current ones with computer-generated lawns and landscaping. Soon after the new Science and Technology Building opened, a poster was produced on campus in which the building was surrounded by green landscaping and new trees. I had a few students approach me to point out the digital landscaping in the image. One woman even thought that perhaps she had simply walked past the digitally rendered lawn by approaching the building from the wrong side.

Cody Daniels, a man in his mid-twenties from a Midwestern tribe, described his surprise and disappointment at seeing the state of SIPI's campus, especially as he had been drawn to the school in part because of the appearance of sports facilities in the promotional literature. He made a place for himself at the school, but he said, his first impressions were distressing.

> The catalog that I got had this big old green campus. The map had three softball diamonds and a big old track and football field. I was like, "Cool, cool. This place looks like a regular college." When I pulled in, it was a different story . . . I wasn't thinking a big stadium but I was thinking something. I came around the corner and there's nothing but two old—thirty-year-old—galvanized steel field goals . . . The area they mowed down. That's supposed to be a football field. There's like a dirt track, a dirt circle around it . . . At the time there was only two sets of bleachers. Old steel bleachers.
>
> And then the dorms . . . I walked in the dorms and I was like [sound of disbelief]. I was really surprised at the condition they were in . . . But then, my grandma and everybody else was, "It's a BIA school. Where did you think you were going?" [laughs]. Things have been there for how long now? Overall my general impression was [in conflict with] what they had and what my perception was . . . I was looking for this big old green campus, new buildings, and everything else. The Science Building wasn't even up. They were just putting in the foundations for that. So, it was kind of . . . "New building!" . . . I thought, "When they usually build one new building, they usually build a couple more!" . . . That was the first new building in thirty years, so I guess I was thinking way outside the box on that one.

The negative visual impression given by the campus is not exclusive to students. A guest speaker who drove around the campus was shocked by her first view of the school. She thought the campus looked like a dilapidated 1960s high school, and she worried the outdated, run-down, and decidedly noncollegiate appearance of the campus buildings would undermine students' self-perception as college students. Since it looked like a high school, she wondered, did they feel like they were really in college?

Institutional Skepticism

If students are expecting to be welcomed with open arms when they first arrive on campus, their expectations could be frustrated. For many years, there was no standardized student orientation—one has been implemented in the past five years. Students who attended the previous versions of orientation were sometimes introduced to faculty as a group, sometimes not. They were always given dire—and overlong—warnings about the many punishments they faced for violating the zero-tolerance drug and alcohol policy, which created neither a warm nor welcoming tone. Meeting one's academic advisor should signal the happy start of a student's academic career at the school. Faculty frustrations with the school's administration, though, sometimes seep into their interactions with students. Students take notice of faculty frustration.

Renee Verde is particularly frustrated by instances of lethargic bureaucracy or moments when school staff work against the best interests of students. To Renee, the first conversation a student has with her academic advisor to plan her academic career is critical. Her advisor is the first, and perhaps staunchest, supporter of a student in her academic career at SIPI, and the tone set in their first interaction, Renee thinks, shapes how a student will see the school. Renee described a student's first impression, saying, "I think a lot of it has to do with the first people they're exposed to when they start their career, which is their advisor. Some of the advisors—there're some advisors that are real in tune with where their students want to go. And they want to help them, naturally. They want to help them go, get there . . . Starting here. I think overall it's a great place to do that . . . Start in that direction, anyway."

Renee excitedly met with her own advisor soon after arriving. She anticipated her advisor would respond with his own enthusiasm and guidance. Instead, under the guise of helpfulness, this individual indulged in a negative and off-putting rant. Renee described how a student's first impression of the Southwestern Indian Polytechnic Institute could serve to negatively shape her perception of the school and her subsequent experiences:

> I think the first people that they're exposed to, that's their first impression. That was my first impression. Wasn't real great. Because a lot of things I could figure out myself, as an adult. But at the same time there wasn't a whole lot of help, and there was a whole lot of bad attitude, a lot of complaining. A lot of complaining that should not be complained to a student . . . There's just a lot of politics, which were conveyed to students. It was uncalled for. Even on my first day of [school] my advisor . . . was like, "Whoa, this place has got major problems!" Even the first day of instruction, the second people you're exposed to, there's just a lot of . . . bad-mouthing.

Renee worried that students who were unclear of their goals or who were intimidated by being in a college setting would be so unnerved by their advisor's negative comments that they might simply leave.

Culture Shock and Heightened Awareness

A particularly intriguing theme arose in conversation with students in which they described themselves as having experienced culture shock when they entered the Southwestern Indian Polytechnic Institute. For students who had been raised in primarily non-Indian environments, and who had known few Native Americans other than family members, arriving at SIPI meant instant immersion in a totally different cultural and ethnic setting. Clearly, this would come as a surprise to some people. For example, an editorial in the *Albuquerque Journal* asserted, "Culture Shock 101 Not Required at SIPI," based on the fact SIPI "has one of the better retention rates for Indian students in higher education" (*Albuquerque Journal* 2001:A10).

Autumn McWright, a funny, self-deprecating Pueblo woman in her early twenties, spoke of culture shock. When I think of Autumn, I immediately visualize her big, dark eyes twinkling behind small glasses, and dimples framing an impish smile. She admitted, "I didn't know there were so many tribes . . . I only knew like Navajo, Hopi, Apache. That there were little ones. Not in Arizona, or something. I never heard of the ones in California, Wisconsin, and other parts of the States." Ultimately, the culture shock that Autumn experienced added to her personal growth. She described herself as being more open-minded and informed, because feeling out of place pushed her to learn about other tribes and develop a connection to them. "It's really changed me, though . . . I grew up around white people. That's all I've known. Before I came here, the majority of my friends were white. They didn't know what I was talking about, stuff I would learn, they never knew it. I was kind of cut off from different tribes." In this way, SIPI does fulfill part of its mandate to create intertribal awareness.

Robin Hale described her experience: "When I first, initially got here, I went through about two trimesters of culture shock because I had not been surrounded by Native American people." By actively participating in school-sponsored social activities and making conscious efforts to learn more about her tribal culture, she was able to find her footing.

Yvonne Kee, an older Navajo woman who was raised on her reservation, sees multiple reasons for students' culture shock. She argues that some students are not suffering culture shock from being immersed in an all-Native milieu. Rather, she believes that many of them are leaving home for the first time and entering an alien culture—postsecondary education—that their parents have not prepared them for. They are family pioneers but they do not have the emotional or experiential resources to succeed. She worries that their culture shock means they lose a valuable opportunity at self-improvement.

> I see SIPI as a big advantage for a lot of students. A big stepping-stone for better things. If they take advantage of it. It can also be a bad experience for some people that are just not used to getting off the reservation. Lot of culture shock. They're not used to being on their own. Not used to being away from the family. The family network that holds them together is gone, and they can't really function. I notice a lot of students can't function alone . . . Normally, they get kicked out of school. They fall behind on their studies. They can't study because they're emotionally . . . shocked. They can't function to the smallest thing, like getting up on time, doing their own laundry. Also, just where to go for your basic needs, who to ask for what they need . . . The parents are normally not the first generation [educated] past high school. These students are pretty much first generation, venturing out to do what their parents didn't do. They have no support from the parents, [do not] know what to expect, what to do, how to go about it. And no one to turn to. So, a lot of them just quit.

Conclusion

Students who choose to attend the Southwestern Indian Polytechnic Institute come with a myriad of preconceptions about the school. Whether these are based on assumptions about college life in general, family stories, warnings, or childhood memories, what they find might not reflect what they expected. Even for students actively warned away from attending, the low cost for attending and the opportunities available at the school draw them anyway. Unfortunately, the school's reputation—especially that of its earlier, wilder days—serves to intimidate some students who might want to enroll there. They might find themselves in direct conflict with their family, who worry about their safety, or about the social environment on campus. Despite the warnings a student may have received from family and friends—and there are a surprising number of warnings about the school considering that they are warning students away from attending a college—they decide to attend anyway.

Unfortunately, some students fall prey to the social chaos or leave the school prematurely in order to escape the environment they find themselves in. It is especially unfortunate for the students who leave and those who get lost along the way that they are giving up an opportunity. The possibility of attending the first two years of college in an almost-tuition-free and all-Native-American context is a valuable opportunity, one that unfortunately, some students feel safest not accepting.

The students who find their way, follow their goals, and ignore the temptation to party will soon discover themselves immersed in SIPI's culture. As described in the next chapter, living on campus and attending SIPI mean both a wealth of interesting experiences and a web of frustrating bureaucratic rules.

5
Life Within the Eagle's Head

As with all institutions, the story of the Southwestern Indian Polytechnic Institute is told not only through the big picture and the significant events, but also through myriad mundane details, the minutiae of life on campus. The organizational structure informs that culture, but it is students—through their responses to the organization, their daily activities, and their interactions with their peers—who construct the day-to-day culture of SIPI. The accretion of students' actions, attitudes, and experiences create a student culture that responds to, but also stands apart from, that of the school's official institutional value system.

SIPI has the unusual quality of being a residential community college, and typically more than half of the students live on campus. Whether they are active participants in student life, or whether they are simply commuting to SIPI to attend classes a few hours a week, each student contributes to and reinforces the culture of the school. Residents shape it through the sharing of their daily lives, and commuter students bring their perspectives of life outside of the campus. Commuter students do not participate as deeply in the on-campus culture, as many of them have jobs, children, and other responsibilities. But whether they are residents or commuters, each student adds his or her own layer of experience, and interpretation of that experience, to the larger picture of SIPI.

Metaphors of Campus Life

Student life at the Southwestern Indian Polytechnic Institute is the subject of a multitude of metaphors, and several of the metaphors have both positive and negative variants. When students use metaphorical descriptions of the school, they typically base those metaphors on one (or more) of four facets of SIPI: how the school system defines and views them; the physical appearance of the college; their experiences at the school and their interpretation of those experiences; and their interpretation of their peers' behavior and experiences. When students describe the school as a prison, for example, they might be basing their interpretation on the appearance of the campus buildings and the fence that surrounds it. Or they might be referencing the underlying value system of the school that surfaces in the rules surrounding student behavior. Or they could simply be noting that they feel constrained and controlled.

Typically, when describing their nonacademic, nonsocial life experiences on the campus unrelated to academics or socializing, students use four main metaphors: "SIPI is a prison," "SIPI is a boarding school," "SIPI is a parent/family," and "SIPI is a high school." When "SIPI is a family" is used as a positive description, the people at SIPI (students and employees) are defined as members of a supportive and caring community much like a loving family. When students use the negative variant of "SIPI is a family," they are likening it to the most distrusting and controlling type of parent. It is a high school because students are treated like children or behave as if they were in high school. And it is a boarding school, because at odd times and in unexpected ways, the school exposes its own provenance as an inheritor of the Bureau of Indian Affairs educational system.

Negative metaphors about life at SIPI focus on four main characteristics: (1) constraint and control of students as a central institutional value (perhaps drawn directly from SIPI's parent agency, the Bureau of Indian Affairs); (2) unequal power dynamics between students and staff, with students expressing concern that they have no consistent, official avenues to participate in decision making; (3) behavioral training being as valued by the administration as education, with mandatory cleaning assignments for residential students and those facing punishment; and (4) lack of trust between students and the institution, leading to rules that seem arbitrary and patronizing and that negate the students' identities as adults.

Regardless of their metaphors or the conceptualizations of the school they eventually develop, students tend to approach move-in day with the optimism of a new start—whether it is simply the beginning of a trimester or the beginning of their entire college career.

A New Trimester Starts

College begins for many SIPI students as it does for college students across the country—at move-in day. Students typically enter the dormitories on the weekend before classes start. Claiming their dormitory room in preparation for the start of classes is a crystalline moment of change. The dormitories at SIPI encapsulate a host of meanings for students, even for many commuters. They are a center of social life at the school. The two campus dormitories are known as the Lodges. Four Winds Lodge, the women's dormitory, sits closer to the center of campus than Golden Eagle Lodge, the men's dormitory. Each lodge can hold up to 250 students. For many years, there were three to four students assigned to each room, necessitating double bunk beds and leading to tensions. The condition of the dormitories has been dramatically improved in the past five years, and there have been efforts to limit the number of students per room. Typically, slightly more than half of the student body lives on campus.

Move-in day is bittersweet, as described affectionately by a Navajo woman looking back on watching families arrive on campus, having driven long distances, bearing their new freshmen. She talked about seeing new students move into the dormitories after she had been at the school for a few trimesters, "watching the students come in, in vans, and cars, and trucks. Filled to the brim with family. Uncles, grandmas, aunties, cousins, nieces, brothers, sisters, distant cousins. All piling outside of this dual-wheel-tired truck monstrosity. That's brand new, brand spanking new. You and the family unloading your material . . . your life into this dorm . . . That's one of my favorite images . . . the family's there." Her image emphasizes two points: First, a child leaving for college is not meaningful just for parents, but for the extended family as well, and second, the optimism and excitement of college move-in day is a universal rite of passage, as meaningful for Native families as for their European American counterparts.

SIPI's residential Lodges are much bigger than they first appear from the outside. The layout of the Lodges is identical, and they are built on the same axis. Once inside, the only way to distinguish Four Winds Lodge from Golden Eagle Lodge is by their wall art and color schemes. From the outside, each lodge resembles a two-story cinderblock L. The residence wings meet at a right angle, with the entrance to the buildings located where the two wings meet. Long hallways extend from the entrance and terminate in the two-story residence wings. Even in daytime, the Lodges are dark, and the air smells slightly damp with a strong whiff of industrial cleaners. To the left of the dormitory entrances are the public spaces, with sunken sitting areas, televisions, and pool tables. The dormitory staff office is immediately inside the doors, and they can see everyone who passes through the main entrances.

3. A view of the two-story residential area of the dormitories showing the dark, narrow dormitory windows. Discoloration on the walls reflects areas where graffiti was painted over. Photo courtesy of the author.

Dormitory staff at the Southwestern Indian Polytechnic Institute are called "matrons." Matron is a gender-neutral term at SIPI and simply refers to dormitory staff with supervisory duties over students. As a result, in the women's dormitory the matrons are women, and in the men's dormitory, the matrons are men. There is significant cognitive dissonance in referring to a man in his twenties as a "matron." The term "matron" is drawn directly from BIA boarding schools (where matrons are typically female). This term operates as a linguistic cue to SIPI's provenance and cues listeners to the value system of the dormitories as well.

Both men and women frequent the common areas in the women's dormitory. Students insisted the public areas in the women's dormitory are nicer and more inviting than the men's. Deeper in the buildings, there are study lounges, cooking areas, and banks of vending machines. The study lounges have multiple doors leading deeper into the building and to the outdoors. The lounges have seating areas and a television. Students routinely complain about not having a quiet place to study, since the study areas serve as additional social space and even host romantic assignations. A female student described abandoning efforts to study in the lounge, and instead relocating to the white noise and warmth of the dormitory laundry room. A male student described finding a quiet hallway in the back of the dormitories where he would hide himself and study.

My introduction to the inner sanctum of a dormitory came when students in a summer school class were complaining mightily about life in the Lodges. They asked if I would be willing to take a tour of the Four Winds Lodge to see conditions for myself. We entered in a group. Two students, one female and one male, took deep sniffs of the air and announced, with a mix of nostalgia and disgust, that it smelled just like the Bureau of Indian Affairs boarding schools they had attended as children on their reservation. I asked what the smell of a boarding school is composed of, and they told me dampness and Lysol.

The female students took me on a tour while the male students waited in the public area. The hallways were dim and windowless with low-watt bulbs and cinderblock walls lumpy with generations of latex paint. The indoor-outdoor carpeting was stained and worn through. A leak in the ceiling had stained the cinderblock brown. It was startling to me, as I explained to my student guides, how the Lodges closely resembled the Soviet-era apartment buildings I saw in the Republic of Armenia. The students accepted my communist architecture analogy with grim amusement. There have been significant improvements to the Lodges in the past few years, but during my visits, they looked unimproved since the school's founding.

Dormitory Attachments

Students cannot become too attached to their dormitory rooms as all students must vacate all rooms at the end of each trimester, regardless of whether they have indicated (by registering or paying fees) they are returning to SIPI for the next semester. They must locate storage for their belongings for the weeks between trimesters, although they can stash small items in a storage room in the Lodge. There is a storage rental facility on the north end of campus, which some SIPI students use.

Relationships with dormitory roommates, as can be expected, run the gamut from friendly to hostile to complete avoidance. This might be in part due to individuals signing up for rooms, and subsequently finding that they are sharing a room with someone they do not know. SIPI students do not sign up to live with a particular roommate; rather they sign up to live in a particular room. Sharing a room does not necessarily lead to friendship. In fact, it might not even lead to conversation. If they want to room with a friend, they both sign up to live in the same room. "So, it's really like people not looking for good roommates, but looking for good rooms . . . They just let a person sign to a room. If they sign to the room, they get that room," explained a Sioux man, who also described living with roommates that he, in fact, never spoke with. He feels Native Americans are trapped behind a wall of extreme reserve. He thinks roommates at SIPI are almost unnecessarily cautious and self-conscious, a behavior he even saw in himself. In response to whether students make friends with their roommates, he said:

> When I try to say "hi" to my roommates, it takes a while. It takes a while. Probably, three weeks in order for them to really know who you are and what you do. And it depends on if they like you or not. I guess. If you're a good person. Trust, I guess . . . At times I felt like that I can get judgmental, about that person. Not outspoken, but in my head. Where I think, "This guy doesn't want to talk to me. I'd better leave him alone. This guy probably doesn't like me," you know. Just talk to him. I get all these ideas. I can't just say, "Hey, what's up?" Just speak up, you know? Because they're my roommates. Now I've been doing that. Lately, now, I've been doing that.

Mutual caution might truly be the best approach with some roommates. New, incoming students are required to fill out a housing questionnaire, but it did not seem to students that these questionnaires are actually used in pairing roommates. And while it is not unusual for students at mainstream institutions to complain that their freshman roommate is very different from themselves, the types of value differences students can see at SIPI are dramatic. These value differences can have both positive and negative results. A positive result is that students can learn about other cultures and become more accepting of difference. On the negative side, if students' values are tremendously different, they might clash on a regular basis over everything from academic goals to shared cleaning responsibilities. A few people related their experience of being housed with students who were not prepared for college or who were particularly messy and the impact it had on them.

Michael Little, a man in his late twenties, laughed as he described the perils of being assigned roommates whose value systems were at odds with his own. "The roommate situation is kind of crazy. I've had pretty good stories with roommates." Those "good" stories include students who glorified the criminal lifestyle. "No boundaries. If there were, they stomped right over them. So, I had three criminals that served jail time. Two juvie, one in state [prison] . . . So, they still had that mentality. Two of them got kicked out. One tried to come back again, and he got kicked out again. So, that's the roommate situation. Kind of crazy." When asked if these roommates would volunteer the information of having served time, he said, "They bring it up in their history. It's like they're proud of it. It's like a badge." Some students repeatedly find themselves in bad pairings with roommates, further intensifying the sense of instability students feel in their dormitory rooms.

A Pueblo man in his late twenties found that he had to adjust to living not only in the dormitories—in itself a new sensation—but also with roommates who were not a good fit. "It was a really strange place to me when I first came here. I never lived in a dorm facility before. I had to get adjusted with living with other people and sharing a room with different [people]. I know that was kind of hard to adjust to, at first. Until my roommates got kicked out two weeks after I arrived so I had the room all to myself! They didn't move people in after that. So, I was just having my own little space." Ironically, the bad fit described by these men and their roommates was mirrored in the bad fit between the former roommates and the school. The bright side of a bad fit is that academically motivated students might find their less motivated roommates evicted from their dormitory rooms, leaving them with a room to themselves. In fact, if a student is known for being particularly studious, they might find their more "party"-minded peers avoiding sharing a room with them.

On-Campus Activities: Crowning Ms. Frybread

The range of offerings for on-campus activities waxes and wanes with levels of funding, and interest and effort by the student body. SIPI hosts both culturally neutral activities (raffles, barbeques, and "Fun Days" in the quad) and more uniquely Native American cultural events on campus. The school has had several campus-based drum groups over the years. SIPI had a "Miss SIPI" competition much like the crowning of a powwow queen. The winner was featured on promotional literature for the school. Over the years, the school has hosted powwows in the gymnasium.

Campus career and college fairs also have waxed and waned over the years. Sometimes career and college fairs are massive events that feature booths from local and national colleges and a broad range of career opportunities. Other times, the fairs are so haphazard that students dismiss the offerings, such as the career fair in 2005. This event only offered job opportunities with recruiters from the military and the police. Several students bristled at the implication that, as one student told me, "Indians are only good for jobs where we get shot at." In response, the students organized their own career fair and invited a much broader range of exhibitors.

Other campus activities are smaller in scale yet are both celebratory of Native American identity and are fun for participants. These include Indian taco sales as fund-raisers for various school organizations, and as Lynae Archuleta describes, the Ms. Frybread competition. Lynae was delighted by the on-campus activities, and described participating in a wide range of them.

> A lot of people, when I was here, they used to like hanging out at the gym. And the SUB. Those are the main areas where they used to hang out. That's because [of] basketball. That's, like, the main focus. At the SUB, it was mostly because of pool tourneys. Going to movies. They had little activities. The activity I remember is the carving of the pumpkin.
>
> And the fry bread contest! [Laughing with delight] It would just be ladies that signed up. No males. All the girls will get all the ingredients, and they'll mix them how they want. Then they make the fry bread. Then the judges go into the little office. We had to lock the door. We had to try each of them. But they were numbered, so we don't say "Oh, that person . . . !" They even had the fryer and everything. They had everything ready for them. Whoever won got the title Ms. Frybread. That was the coolest thing! The frybread contest.

Not having a car makes some residential students feel trapped on campus, especially if they are not interested in sports. A young Navajo man told me, "After a while, if you don't have a ride, recreation can be a little boring a lot of times . . . There's not too much [going] on in recreation . . . Most students, I noticed, have their own vehicles, and they always want to go out at their own time. Not just wait for a certain amount of time at the SUB . . . And usually it's something to do with sports, you know. People are very active in [sports]."

School-sponsored activities for students are not value-neutral events, but rather are interpreted by students through their own lenses. Their interpretation can depend heavily on their age and life stage. Two interview participants—Kira Thomas and Richard Redgoat—described on-campus dances, but their interpretations of these events are vastly different.

When I asked Kira to give me a story about SIPI, she chose instead to present me with a montage of images. Kira sees the dances as social opportunities for students, and herself—a sort of budget fairy tale of romance and optimism. The context she describes is sweetly sad, as students make do with limited funds in their efforts to create a setting in which they will find approval among their peers. To Kira, the dances, their participants, and how they interact all act as a sort of shorthand for the meaning of SIPI.

> Montage experience one: Pathetic Valentine's Day dance. Trying to mimic a Valentine's Day dance in high school or something. A budget of $100 for decorations and refreshments equals pretzels and crepe paper and balloons and someone's [boom box] out of their room. That's your sound system. Maybe rented lights, consisting of one disco ball, in the SIPI SUB ballroom. Everyone's a wallflower except for five [people].
>
> Pathetic, pathetic, sad SIPI Valentine's Day dance. But everyone there is looking, and hoping, because it's Valentine's Day and because it's SIPI, and because the pressure's off . . . The expectation isn't so high physically [so] that the hope is even higher than it ever would be anywhere else. The reality is actually higher that you're going to meet somebody. That someone's going to look at you and *see* you . . . And watching people meet. And watching people dance. Desperately dancing. In the saddest way to contemporary American pop music . . . You're like, "I'm at SIPI! I'm at SIPI! This is a group of Indians. How does this play? What does it mean that a lot of these people might be traditional dancers? And this is contemporary pop music." [Kira injects an interesting cultural point here, by showing the intersection of Native American and European American cultural markers.]
>
> And then looking at yourself. You're also hopeful that you'll meet somebody . . . And you're this Molly Ringwald of SIPI, and you're having your moment. But it's at this sad, pathetic dance, with the [boom box] out of somebody's room. But there's still the magic.
>
> That is in essence SIPI. Even though it's a sad, pathetic [boom box], with fifty-cent crepe paper, and a sad, pathetic date, in comparison to the world. And maybe you being sad and pathetic and not in a prom dress. And you both not coming from a beautiful house. But you're finding magic between yourself and the place and the people around you. That's one moment of SIPI.

Kira's montage suggests that students hope to have a movie-perfect moment in an imperfect but earnest setting with their equally imperfect but earnest peers. Kira's image of "this sad, pathetic dance" is infused with hope. The hope of finding a romantic partner who sees past flawed external qualities becomes a metaphor for the hope, writ large, that is offered at SIPI. Kira is saying that while neither the school nor the students are perfect, they can have their own moment, their own opportunity, regardless of physical perfection, wealth, or funding.

In contrast, Richard Redgoat interprets the dances through a different lens—that of paternalism and a poorly meshed and dichotomous institutional culture. Richard is in his early thirties. He is Navajo, married, and has never lived on campus. Richard is a talented academic. Though quiet and soft-spoken, his peers respond naturally to his leadership qualities. He sets the academic bar high for himself in his classes, and without necessarily consciously recognizing his quiet leadership, his peers in turn push themselves to excel.

Richard did not come to SIPI to be nurtured or to develop a social life. He came to learn, to grow academically, and to move on. As a result, Richard interprets on-campus dances as representing one of the many dualities that he illustrates about the school. He is aware of, and displeased with, the contradictions inherent in the school's multiple institutional models—as he notes, "SIPI is a Native American, two-year, community college here in Albuquerque, but it's set apart from Albuquerque at the same time. It's a federal facility, so it's a bit different from what we think of what a normal college campus might be. I don't know how to explain that. It's a college atmosphere, but at the same time it isn't. There's a duality about it."

The duality to the school's institutional culture manifests itself in two ways, both of which posit students as little more than adolescents. School-sponsored activities such as the on-campus dances are, in his eyes, typical of a high school, as are the patronizing and time-wasting rules surrounding registering for classes (a common frustration that one student labeled "the SIPI runaround" and would warn new students about). Richard takes the end of school-sponsored dances and other changes as positive signs. "It's slowly changing. When I first got here, they were doing stuff like . . . some of the activities they had here. They had a dance here . . . a dance in the SUB once a month or every so often. There were things going on here that were on the high school level." Where he wanted a college atmosphere with institutional expectations that he would take responsibility for his own academic career, he was getting dances like the ones he attended in high school. The school was changing for the better, in Richard's opinion, but those moments of duality—of SIPI as both high school and college—were alienating.

The metaphor "SIPI is a high school" is derived not only from how students are treated, but also from how students themselves behave. Grace Nez suggests that it is the nature of student socializing and romantic pursuits that make SIPI resemble a high school. She said that SIPI feels like a high school to her "because everyone here acts like they're in high school. It's all about partying, friends, and finding a boyfriend or girlfriend. That's what I seem to see. I don't really see anyone here who's like, 'Oh, I'm here for school.'" Perhaps events such as campus dances reflect the administration offering students what they want, rather than imposing a belief that students are adolescents.

Students as Wards: *In Loco Parentis* and the Ghost Uncle

As Richard pointed out, students at SIPI are treated as if they are incapable of managing their own academic careers. Many describe glimpses into their own infantilization (being viewed, defined, and treated as children) either through how they are treated individually or in the institutional rules and structures that they answer to. Even the students who are most interested in registering for classes and accessing their own records are not allowed to do so. They are witnessing the holdover of the *in loco parentis* attitude held so dear by the Bureau of Indian Affairs toward students at Indian schools (who are, of course, usually children). SIPI students recognize that this dynamic is operating subtly in the background of their interactions with the school administration. Unfortunately, this undermines their preparation for matriculation to a four-year school because they are not receiving training in how to design a class schedule for themselves or how to register for classes. Over the years, I had former advisees call or come by to see me for help with their University of New Mexico class schedule.

There is frustration inherent in dealing with a patronizing and yet near-faceless school administration. A woman from a California tribe compared SIPI's administration to a "ghost uncle"—someone whom you always hear about and who has a huge impact on your life, but whom you have never seen. She noted that school administrators do not visit classes. She said that she was uncomfortable because she did not know who at the school was making the decisions that directly affected her life at the school and shaped her education.

The limits placed on SIPI students are not typical of the vast majority of colleges. The *in loco parentis* philosophy that was once typical of colleges throughout the nation was vigorously attacked in the 1960s and 1970s, and has steadily been replaced with the attitude that students are young adults needing educating, not aging adolescents needing supervision. The stance that SIPI students are overgrown or willful children who need to be treated as such is apparent both in word and in deed at the institution.

Several survey respondents noted what they perceived as an infantilizing tendency in the institutional structure of SIPI. For example, a Washoe man wrote that "the rules they [students] live by are kind of counterproductive. They say it's a college but still treat students like kids." Another man wrote that he hoped in the future "the rules and regulations won't be so harsh." A twenty-three-year-old Navajo woman from Kayenta, Arizona, succinctly described the school's underlying *in loco parentis* value system: "For some reason, we're treated like children. This is from dorm life to staff members. I wouldn't say the teachers treat us like children but more like the dorm aids [*sic*], librarians, etc." Students responding to the survey questionnaire repeatedly complained about the rules and the control mechanisms they faced.

Their comments have an historical precedent. Research done with female SIPI students, as well as their peers from the University of New Mexico and the Community College of Central New Mexico, shows that this frustration on the part of SIPI students is far from a new phenomenon (McReynolds 1997). The SIPI students interviewed for this research, conducted in 1994, complained about restrictive and controlling rules, and administrative refusal to consider students' input. "[Student] Senate input was rarely considered by school officials. [This] included a Senate request to change SIPI's closed campus policy. No changes were made in the closure policy, nor did the administration agree to engage in a dialogue about this matter. Wanda Craig complained, 'It's like a prison. You can't come and go when you want to or need to. They have to know when you go to the bathroom and everything'" (1997:83). Ten years after that research, SIPI students were still frustrated by the administration's refusal to participate in dialogues with them about students' concerns. It becomes quickly apparent in reading survey responses that the frustrations of earlier students are echoed in the words of contemporary students.

Treating adults like children shuts down the avenues for them to dissent. A Sioux woman in her twenties wrote, in response to a survey question, of how she would describe SIPI:

Unorganized. They want respect but don't give respect. [The administration] doesn't listen to your opinions and ideas. Treated like little kids even though this is a college. The only reason I'm still here is I want a degree and since I already start[ed] I should finish. If anyone ask[ed] me if they should go to SIPI I would tell them no . . . I didn't really think much of SIPI. My brother came here a couple of years ago, and he left because he didn't like it. I heard they treated you like a child, and he was right. SIPI is so unorganized. If they want more people (Natives) to succeed, they should not be so quick to kick them out.

Students recognize the *in loco parentis* quality of administrative decisions. Oftentimes, the rules that are applied to students while they are on campus run counter to their experiences as adults when they are off campus. Particularly eloquent about this dichotomy are the students in the focus group. They are all active members of the campus community. They volunteer for campus responsibilities, participate in the limited decision making available to students, and most important, are well versed in the policies that apply to student life. Students know they could be evicted from the Lodges, or experience other sanctions, based on how well they abide by the student handbook. But focus group members argue that while they are held accountable to rules of behavior detailed in the student handbook, the employees who hold them accountable do not themselves appear to know the rules. Autumn McWright said she often wanted to ask employees, "Do you even know the handbook?"

Focus group students are profoundly aware of the abridgment of their rights while they are on campus and that those limitations are not typical of other colleges. When asked to comment on the recurring metaphor of "SIPI is a prison," they had a strong reaction as the metaphor resonated deeply with them. Several themes arise in their discussion of "SIPI is a prison." They spoke about the campus security services, the fence that surrounds the school, the rules in the dormitories, the perception of SIPI by outside individuals (such as businesses located in the area around the campus), the rules against students entering the forest surrounding the Rio Grande, and as is universal at the Southwestern Indian Polytechnic Institute, the rules and regulations imposed on students.

The restrictions students face causes some students to act cautiously on campus for fear of angering an individual with power or violating a rule that would not be a rule elsewhere. A student in the focus group explained her timidity, "because there's really not a lot you can do on [SIPI's] campus that you can do on other campuses. There's a lot of restrictions. And . . . you're not sure if you're going to offend anybody or get in trouble." If students are walking on eggshells, unsure if they are going to accidentally violate some arcane and counterintuitive rule, how effectively will they attach themselves to the institution? Are cautious and fearful students the desired outcome of campus rules? Is there not a more positive position to put students in—one in which they participate in making the rules and consider them to be fair and age-appropriate?

The very fact that students routinely compare the college to a prison should raise red flags, especially for the school's administration. The prevalence of the metaphor in student conversation is disturbing. Even more disturbing should be the parallels students easily draw between the school and prisons. One person told a brief story of meeting a new student at SIPI and talking about SIPI with her. The student said, "She had actually gone to prison. She said . . . prison was better than the dormitories that we had here."

The dormitories were discussed further by the focus group, as two students described how a new rule limiting dormitory room occupancy to two students had improved dorm life and made it less prison-like. Jonah Nesbitt, a man in his twenties from a West Coast tribe who lives on campus, added, though, "It's still just like a prison, just a less [full] prison." Jonah continued in the prison vein when he listed positives of attending SIPI, then added: "The negative is that you have to, in order to get that [free education], you have to sacrifice a lot. And come to a prison. That's how I see it. I was talking to my friend the other day on the phone, and she's at the university I went to . . . for a year. And then I came . . . here . . . and I was telling her all this different stuff, and she was like, 'Oh, my goodness . . . You are in a prison. I'm going to . . . send you some care packages.'" Renee Verde added, "Sometimes it feels like people are trying to be your parents, especially when you don't need one. They still try, and it's just like, jeez! How do you be tactful and to let them know you have your boundaries? You have boundaries. These are your boundaries, don't overstep them. As a person. They don't treat you like people; they treat you like animals. They treat you like you don't know anything. They treat you like you don't have any knowledge, you can't think for yourself." The fact that the most motivated, confident, and successful students are made to feel like prisoners and animals by the treatment they receive from school employees indicates an acute and critical disconnect between the institutional goal of retaining and graduating students and student perceptions of their treatment at the school. It is almost as if there is an intentional effort to actively alienate students—or so they might suggest.

Students are not oblivious to the need for some campus rules to be strictly worded and strictly applied. An example of this is the campus zero-tolerance drug and alcohol policy. Students who are found drinking, drunk, or under the influence of other inebriates lose their dormitory privileges and, in some case, are denied access to the campus, depending on how egregious the violation. Students are aware of the culture of drinking on campus, and its negative repercussions, both for the individuals who participate and their peers. The zero-tolerance policy is in line with many other colleges. It is not the zero-tolerance policy per se that SIPI students reject, but the way in which the policy is applied.

Fair and reasonable applications of the zero-tolerance rules are applauded by many students. A Pueblo man insisted in conversation that living at SIPI had become much more bearable as the rules were more strictly enforced or, as he described it "since the Iron Wall has come down." Intriguingly, the strict enforcement of rules, to this man, was blatant (it was compared to a wall, after all) but he did not feel constrained by the changes.

Drinking, and its attendant behaviors, is seen by many students as one of the most negative aspects of attending SIPI. A survey question that asked students to name the negative aspects of the school generated several responses about alcohol use, including, "too many people drink and abuse alcohol," "people that choose to litter the campus with alcohol containers," "I see a lot of students who get caught for drinking and doing drugs. A lot of students hurt themselves," and "the students who party too much and give the school a bad name for other students who come to learn." Students are not arguing for the repeal of the zero-tolerance policy, because they can see the evidence of a drinking culture on campus, and they do not like its results. Instead, they want a zero-tolerance policy that appears fair and is applied reasonably.

Many students complain that the zero-tolerance policy is applied arbitrarily and inappropriately. Any student on campus deemed by staff to have consumed alcohol can be cited for violating the zero-tolerance policy regardless of his age, whether he was acting inebriated, or if he had consumed the alcohol off campus. This has meant students of legal drinking age, who were not intoxicated and who had not brought alcohol on campus, have been cited for an alcohol violation when they returned to campus. The student handbook describes smelling of alcohol as being in violation of campus policy (SIPI 2001:45). Unfortunately, according to students, the application of this rule has meant that dormitory matrons consider it appropriate to confront students who are sober and demand to smell their breath.

There is a delicate balance to maintaining a sober campus and treating students like adults. The need for this balance is reflected in the words of one student who, in describing the negative qualities of SIPI, wrote, "Students have alcohol/drug problems. Some rules are too strict to go by. As for the dorm, we're treated like kids." Rather than canceling itself out, this student's response implies that there must be a reasonable way to accommodate the students' need to be treated as responsible adults, especially in their living situation, while working to resolve addiction issues. Other colleges do this successfully; there must be effective models—not based on a parental and distrusting mind-set—which the school could emulate, thereby protecting students while also creating an encouraging living/learning environment.

Some students felt that the zero-tolerance policy ran counter to the need for experimentation that students experience in college. Darren Wingard, a Pueblo man in his thirties, complained about the zero-tolerance policy. Darren has a youthful face and demeanor that belie his age, and he is often mistaken for someone far younger, both by other students and by the staff. Darren is gregarious, opinionated, and friendly, and his commentary is punctuated by loud, good-natured laughter. He felt that the zero-tolerance rules kept students from "express[ing] themselves freely" because, while it is a college, "you just have to abide by the rules." He went on to note, though, that he was fairly adept at skirting the restrictions and had also learned how to use campus rules to his own benefit.

Nancy White expressed a concern that, by actively enforcing the zero-tolerance policy, administrators were denying students a very real opportunity test their own boundaries.

> I always had . . . and even still have mixed emotions about it—because I guess maybe two years ago if you'd asked me, I didn't always understand the zero-tolerance policy. I feel like a portion of the college experience, and that period of life in your early twenties, is experimenting and testing different boundaries. When you're a teenager, you test your boundaries with your parents and authority in different ways, but you're still in this safety net. When you become a young adult, you have new—new options. You're allowed to drink. You're allowed to vote. You're allowed to do things you weren't able to do before.
>
> I kind of think part of that is healthy, you know? Being able to test those boundaries, and say, "Okay, no, I shouldn't drink twelve six-packs of beer in a night and puke my guts out because that's gross and doesn't feel good." And so, part of me was always frustrated, because I think by telling students—I don't think it's okay to drink on campus, but if a student comes back to school and goes to their dorm room and

passes out on their bed, it's kind of their business. If they're a consenting adult, and they do that, I don't know—I don't really know if it's the school's place to say something.

Yet, her own opinion changed dramatically when she began spending more time on campus after getting a work-study job. "Now, working on campus, totally ... I have a completely different feeling about it. Finding a girl passed out in the bathroom, beer bottles in front of my car every day I come to school, and boys smoking dope all over the place. I had to break up a fight the other day between a young man and his girlfriend ... Later to find out he was drunk, and he didn't know what he was doing and by the time [they] went through the whole process and the cops got here, he'd forgotten what he'd done. Gave me a totally different frame of reference for that 'experimentation' and 'boundaries' and 'becoming a young adult.'" Gender is a significant factor in the enactment of *in loco parentis* control mechanisms. A twenty-seven-year-old woman from both a Northern tribe and a Southwestern tribe majoring in liberal arts wrote in response to the question "If someone asked you about SIPI, what would you tell them?": "I always tell them it is great. Most of the teachers are awesome. The higher staff [school administrators] need a little more open mind and need to really stop giving us lectures. We're all over 18 and what students do is what they do. Also that it seems the higher staff don't really care to listen to females in general and I find that a little unreasonable." This survey respondent points out the inherent contradiction in a situation where students are adults but treated like children. Her decisions and those of her female peers are seen as open to question by the administration, implying a systemic attitude toward female students. Ultimately, as an adult, her decisions are her own and not up for analysis or discussion by administrators, yet she feels that administrators make her justify her choices.

Mandatory Participation and Student Resistance

Another area of dispute between students and the administration—and one that students repeatedly liken to being in high school—are the mandatory assemblies they must attend several times a year. The assemblies are usually organized in response to visits by politically important individuals. SIPI's students, though, are notorious for not attending events they are not, in fact, made to. There are high stakes involved. Many of SIPI's important visitors represent federal agencies and the school is in a continual struggle to be allocated the appropriate amount of funds from the federal government. The administration needs student attendance and participation to validate the attention it is receiving from political heavyweights and to encourage new benefactors.

Students (and faculty) complain about mandatory assemblies. The major complaint from students is that these assemblies remind them of high school, and make students feel like children. (Faculty members complain about the loss of teaching time.) Student perceptions of college are that they would create their own schedule and manage their own time.

For most of my time at SIPI, students attended assemblies near the beginning of the trimester for a "student handbook orientation." These sessions centered on the belief that ignorance of the law does not preclude one from being held accountable to it, and the assumption that students, of their own volition, will not read the student handbook. These events resembled reader's theater, with faculty and staff reading portions of the handbook to students, and students grumbling restlessly as they are harangued with a list of restrictions and punishments, but virtually no privileges and rewards.

The most focused attention I recall students ever exhibiting at a mandatory assembly was in August 2001 at an assembly labeled disabilities awareness training for students. The campus community was gathered in the gymnasium, which was the meeting place for all large groups prior to the completion of the Science and Technology Building (which has a large, fairly well-designed, theatrically lit auditorium that now serves this purpose). Students and staff ranged out over the wooden bleachers that line the south wall. A German woman spoke to the students while seated on the varnished hardwood floor with a microphone set low in front of her. She was a victim of in utero Thalidomide poisoning, and she did not have arms. She was living in Alaska and made "Alaskan spirit dolls"—small clay figures outfitted in feathers, fur anoraks, and beaded necklaces, all of which she made herself, using her feet. Students were fascinated by her determination, and by her tales of her grim childhood, which she described as being filled with physical abuse and rebellion. There was none of the usual covert chatting or shifting of students in the bleachers, which causes the aging wooden benches and joints to screech and squeak, greatly magnifying even the smallest movements. Instead, students leaned forward in their seats, rapt and respectful, and lined up to talk to her afterward.

When United States Secretary of Education Rod Paige visited the Southwestern Indian Polytechnic Institute in April 2004, the administration was particularly concerned with guaranteeing a high level of student attendance. Instructors were required to cancel classes and reconvene them at the auditorium in the Science and Technology Building. SIPI was hosting a powwow the next day, so a Kiowa traditional dance troupe was in town. The troupe performed several dances on the floor in front of the stage. The troupe leader kept time on his hand drum while his eleven-year-old granddaughter performed a shawl dance. Six chairs were lined up on stage, with a podium between them. The visitors were taking a tour of the campus, and arrived later than the projected start time. People filed in over the course of several minutes, and when the Secretary began to speak, students were expected to sit still and listen, earning a displeased comment from the stage if they attempted to leave early.

There is an almost inevitable quality to students avoiding events for visiting political leaders. Knowing this has prompted administrators to impose a slew of student management techniques. If the event is during class time, faculty must cancel classes, escort students to the assembly site, and retake attendance. Administrators spread out across campus, keys in hand, and lock all doors, including those leading into the dormitories. Students are denied permission to return to their dormitory rooms. There are a range of efforts at bribery including raffling off items throughout the course of an event but requiring that students be present to win. These items are not exotic or expensive—however, many students have very little funding to cover even their most basic needs. As a result, students with few financial resources find themselves having to sit through an event in the hopes of winning basic toiletries such as shampoo or laundry detergent.

Commuter students are not held as rigidly to attendance at mandatory events as residents. Commuters can simply retreat home if they do not wish to participate. If a class is required to attend an assembly, commuters oftentimes can leave immediately after the allotted class period, claiming outside obligations, such as work or child care. Residents are far more constrained. This does not mean they do not find ways of resisting administrative efforts to force their attendance.

SIPI students show a range of resistance patterns when expected to participate in public and school-publicizing events. It is far more typical for students to avoid attending assemblies and other mandatory events, disappearing if they see a posted notice or attempting to peel off inconspicuously from the class if the instructor is required to walk the students to the assembly. The groundbreaking ceremony for the Science and Technology Building in May 2001 was the site of a massive effort of administrative control that was met with an equally massive show of student resistance. The administration was concerned that students would not attend the very public and politically charged events. No one asked *why* students would opt out of attending, nor was there an effort to understand student refusal to participate in on-campus activities in general. All campus buildings were locked, giving residential students and those without cars no place to absent themselves. The dormitories were locked as well, further reminding students how little control they actually had over their private spaces on campus.

Locking the buildings had some of the desired effect as students did, in fact, attend the event en masse. Attendance did not equal capitulation. More than two hundred chairs were placed in the sunshine in front of the podium on the lawn to the west of the administrative buildings. Campus visitors were scattered throughout the seating area, and the speakers repeatedly implored the students to come to the front and sit in the seats. Instead, students began gathering some distance away, under the shelter of a cottonwood grove. They were at the event but just barely. They were enacting the only form of resistance that was left—being present but not participating.

I have never fully understood why SIPI students routinely and actively avoid these events, as at many colleges the visit of a political leader would be considered an achievement. I came close to understanding student reluctance with the comment from the focus group participant who said students were treated like animals because they felt herded unwillingly to on-campus events. I propose some further possibilities to the consistent ennui and disinterest the majority of SIPI students' have shown at the presence of national politicians: Perhaps they believe participating in these events benefits only the administration, not the students; maybe they are interested in the results but disinterested in the process; and maybe they feel as if they are on display by the administration.

Campus Security Measures: Protection or Control?

Students register tremendous displeasure with campus security measures and security personnel. Campus security personnel are seen by students as being reactionary and hostile, more concerned with scrutinizing students than protecting them. Most of the security measures on the campus of the Southwestern Indian Polytechnic Institute are seen by students as mechanisms for maintaining administrative power, not for guaranteeing their safety and well-being. During a discussion with the focus group, one student pointed out that her favorite place on campus was the road, because it could take her off campus, which led into a discussion of the fencing that surrounds the campus. The campus fence is seen as a visual metaphor for control and constraint. From there, students segued into talking about the actual versus stated role of security personnel on the SIPI campus. The security staff is small, composed mostly of young men, and I have known of only one female security officer. Typically, there are three or four security officers to cover the entire week, day and night. This means that there is virtually no overlap of security personnel shifts, and oftentimes, daytime shifts are not covered. Security staff does not have the right to arrest but must simply hold violators (both students and unaffiliated campus visitors) until the Bernalillo County Sheriff's Office can send someone to make the arrest. The behavior of security personnel feeds directly into student usage of the metaphors "SIPI is a prison" and "SIPI is a boarding school."

Security personnel do not wear standard uniforms or weapons, but they do have handcuffs. They usually are distinguished by wearing a dark blue polo shirt embroidered with the SIPI logo and a utility belt. The school is small, and members of the community will eventually recognize each other from a distance. Over time, the security personnel become individually recognizable to students, and their utility belts serve as a marker of their position. SIPI, like all Bureau of Indian Affairs schools, used to have BIA police stationed on campus, but BIA police were permanently barred from all schools after the death at a BIA school of a teenage girl who was in on-campus police custody.

The fence around the campus, which can be easily climbed over in areas, is representative of the feeling of control but not protection. During the focus group, Jonah Nesbitt pointed out the fence where it was visible in an aerial photograph of the campus. He asked the other students if they knew of any other colleges that are fenced, and he named several schools that he knew of that were not. The suggestion was made that the fencing is because SIPI is a federal facility, and I suspect that this is a commonly supplied excuse. Surrounding a campus with fencing is not a universal federal educational policy. For example, there were angry reactions in February 2005 when an eight-foot-tall fence topped with barbed wire was erected around the historic Chemawa boarding school in Oregon. The barbed wire was quickly removed amid student protests, including comments that the fence treated students like animals (McCall 2005). Ironically, that fence, unlike SIPI's, had not been intended as campus security, but rather to surround a campus construction site.

Students were explicit in their assertion that security personnel are more interested in flexing their figurative muscles than acting in students' best interests. One student stated bluntly, "There's only one goal, and that's to catch you doing something wrong. It's not to protect you. It's not to make you feel safe. It's to catch you [doing] something wrong. That's why it feels like a prison." Even successful, rule-abiding students such as those in the focus group felt that the security personnel were patronizing. The actions of security personnel seem designed to emphasize that students are under observation. To students, because the administration is not allowed to search their possessions or bodies, security personnel are well placed to "catch" (a word used repeatedly by focus group participants in their descriptions of security staff) students for them. Jonah said: "I think it's also due to the fact that they still treat us as kids. Because we were going over an issue the other day about the security issue. To where security feels like . . . they're not here to protect us, they're here to catch us in violations. Because they're only here at night. And I think that's why they only have one entrance, because they want to catch us coming in." SIPI's security personnel serve as the face of the systemic institutional mistrust that students must answer to. Renee Verde supported Jonah's assertion by describing how it feels to pass through the campus security measures. She was adamant that, as Jonah said, the goal was to catch students, implying a punitive rather than protective role. Renee and Althea Running (both residential students) discussed an incident Althea had experienced a short time prior to the focus group. Renee said:

> And then when you come in and out of that security gate, it's like . . . you might as well be strip searched, dumping [Althea's] groceries out on the ground. Yeah, they had her groceries dumped . . . (Althea—"On the ground!") There's no probable cause for that! (Althea—"I was coming back from Target and he said he wanted to see what was in my sack . . . I bought cookies and whatnot.") You don't see it happening to staff. You don't see it happening to the cleaning people. You only see it happening to the students. I'd like to see it happening to the security guards. There's a lot of things that happen on this campus . . . [like we're] always doing something wrong, and that's not the case, that's not the case at all.

Focus group participants described a blatantly adversarial relationship between students and security personnel. Robin Hale also described bullying behavior by the security staff. In response to my question about why some students interpret SIPI as being like a prison, she suggested that they might be irritated by the zero-tolerance policy. Robin is a proponent of the zero-tolerance drug and alcohol policy, and feels that when students attend a land grant institution, they are in effect agreeing to abide by such institutional rules. This did not negate the fact that, in her experience, security personnel would egregiously violate standard legal procedure in their efforts to find a violation to charge students with.

Robin also saw the treatment students received as they entered or exited campus as making students, especially rule-abiding ones, feel like they were being punished. She added that another reason that students—especially those who had not violated the zero-tolerance policy—would define the school as a prison was their treatment at the hands of security personnel as they entered or exited the campus. Her description of invasive and legally dubious behavior further emphasized the hostility between security personnel and students. She added:

> Also, like the main gate area. They're only checking IDs, spot-checking IDs at night. Meaning they're only there not the whole night, but every once in a while they'd go out there and sit out there and wait for students. Well, this trimester they had closed one side of the gate. At night. So, people coming through would get their IDs checked. If you're leaving, you have to wait until everybody comes in, so that way they can get the IDs checked. And they were calling that—they were making this—they were saying this was a Homeland Security issue. They had that one side [of the gate] closed. They had the one you could come through to the school, and we've had a few students, where their vehicles were searched when they were inside the campus, when they were going to leave. That didn't make any sense because, why would you check a vehicle that's leaving campus if you're not looking for something? And not really check those that are coming in?
>
> [AK: Why do you think they're searching?]
>
> They're gonna find something. Yeah. It's the—they say it's having to do with the whole probable cause thing, where probable cause, if they see—the way probable cause is meant to be is if they see like a beer can on the floor [of the car] that would give them probable cause to check the whole car, and see if they [the students] do still have any alcohol. If they do, then they get written up. But what was actually happening these last few trimesters, they were just saying, "I need to search your car." [AK: Why?] So they could search for the probable cause, is from my understanding. And the way that a lot of students had gotten caught. With the Breathalyzers. They were forced to take the Breathalyzer tests. Well, from what our understanding was, even from last trimester, the security guards could not give a Breathalyzer

test unless it was okayed by the individual. But, see, the students aren't being told this. You can only be given a Breathalyzer test to prove your innocence. And they were using it to prove that they were guilty of being under the influence. I guess that's where they would say they feel like a prison. It's like that.

Robin's narrative illuminates the same blatantly adversarial and mistrusting attitude toward students that the focus group described. Student possessions were treated invasively, as were their bodies when they were inappropriately subjected to Breathalyzer exams. Breathalyzer exams were discontinued after these incidents came to light.

Worse yet, focus group participants expressed concern that security personnel reacted too little and too late to real issues of student safety. Brett Mann introduced the topic to the group by simply stating, "There was a person that was beat severely last Friday." I asked when the incident occurred, assuming it had happened late at night. Brett explained indignantly, "Lunchtime! At lunchtime! I was coming back from lunch and I saw the ambulance over there." Renee said construction workers on campus had provided the badly beaten man with first aid and called an ambulance. Renee noted that there were no security personnel on campus during the day, and said the matron in the dormitory did not know what to do in the crisis. Jonah added in frustration, "There's nothing here ... for the student that was in jeopardy. There is no emergency call box on campus [one has since been added] ... There's only security here at night. And you know they're only here to catch us in the act." The students' feelings of being mistrusted frustrated them. But their belief that their physical safety was in jeopardy made their petty humiliations by the security personnel even more upsetting.

Students are describing a powerful theme of institutional distrust. That distrust can even shape a former student's memories of the school. John War Horse told me that he had spoken with a man who graduated from SIPI in the 1970s. This man told John there used to be a jail on campus—the ultimate symbol of control and distrust. Even though the thought of a jail on a small college campus seems ludicrous, the suggestion was too provocative and disturbing to leave unexamined. I asked two individuals who had long-time associations with SIPI about the "jail." They were both adamant that there was never a jail on campus. It is possible that the speaker was misremembering one of two buildings—the guard shack or the abandoned adobe house immediately to the west of campus. The house is on private land and apparently had bars on the windows back when there were walls. For this graduate to conceptually turn the guard shack (with its intended implications of protecting the school, not punishing students) or a small abandoned house into a campus jail implies that he felt, even though he was thirty years gone, there was a high level of distrust and control of students by the institution.

Autumn McWright, who also participated in the focus group, usually described the school as a network of support and a resource for self-determination. She had to resort to negative metaphors when describing campus rules and security personnel. When asked what kind of home SIPI was, Autumn responded that not only did she not see it as one, but that "Some people might call it a prison." When asked why, she specified, "You have to follow rules... I don't find that it's a prison, but sometimes it does [seem like one]... the whole matrons thing. I find that the guards, sometimes, they act like it [is a prison]... [They tell you that] you can't do stuff just to be macho or something."

Students complained about several forms of institutional oversight, yet there was surprisingly little comment by students about the installation of security cameras throughout the campus. The cameras are motion-activated, and permanently record everything they witness, even though much of the footage is of wildlife activity and people walking to their parked cars. Initially, the cameras were intended to be used exclusively outdoors. Eventually, security cameras were to be installed at the guard shack, the boiler room, and the back doors of the dormitories. There was no mention of interior dormitory spaces being monitored. Ultimately, cameras have been installed over the entire campus, and I was told this includes cameras trained on the halls in the women's dormitory, so that women complained that they could no longer wear robes or towels from their rooms to the showers. Additional cameras were planned for several interior spaces, including lobbies, hallways, and public areas. Even the most benign or private act on campus is now both open to security scrutiny and made part of the permanent record.

Meaningful Campus Places

Campus locations and features are weighted with meanings. Many of the meanings assigned to these places are shared among students, implying a culturally assigned value rather than a value based on individual experiences and preferences. Some locations are entirely positive, such as the gymnasium, the library, and the Bosque (riparian forest) along the Rio Grande. Typically, outdoor locations are viewed more positively than indoor ones (excluding the campus fence). Several locations and features are seen as physical representations of the restrictions and unfair treatment experienced by students, and references to these places are used in constructing negative metaphors about the school (such as "SIPI is a prison"). The dormitories, the security guard shack (and its accompanying turquoise steel gates), and the campus fence are all symbolic of unreasonable rules and patronizing institutional values. Oddly enough, the one building on campus—the Hogan—that was intended to have the most positive meaning for students is a site of conceptual conflict and is seen as synonymous with a disregard for the feelings of students of many tribes.

Outdoor areas offer students the most flexibility in claiming the school as their own. Students feel proprietary over outdoor areas for several reasons: With the size of the campus, many of these sites (on and off campus) are difficult for campus personnel to keep in view; outdoor areas do not have the level of rules and regulations attached that most indoor areas do; and they are accessible at all hours of the day and night. The picnic benches in the quad and the parking lot outside the dormitories are central meeting areas. Regardless of the weather, students utilize outdoor areas, even if this means brushing off snow or braving a buffeting by grit-filled spring winds. The significance of the picnic benches as a social hub is immediately apparent, even to new students. Before or after classes, students congregate in the quad at these benches. On the first day or two of classes, students who have just met sit or stand around the benches, quizzing each other about their names, tribes, and hometowns.

The parking lot outside the Lodges—for most of its history, a rutted dirt patch without marked parking spaces—is also a meeting area for students. Men and women who want to see each other, but do not want to do so under the watch of their peers in the dormitory lounges, friends picking up dormitory residents to go out to various Albuquerque hotspots, and those who simply want some relief from the rules indoors all congregate in the parking lot.

During an overhaul phase of the campus, the open field across from the dormitory parking lot was spruced up with a picnic table and volleyball court. Xeriscaping with plants native to New Mexico's desert environment was added, delineating that space from the rest of the unimproved fields. In conversation with a fellow employee one day, I wondered out loud about the attraction of the parking lot. He said he had shared my curiosity about what students did all day in the parking lot and volleyball field. One day he joined them, and to his great surprise, and disappointment, he discovered that, as he put it, they did *nothing*. I took this to mean that students would rather sit outside in the cold, barely interacting, than be indoors, under the scrutiny of staff. Clearly, our curiosity was shared by some students. An interviewee described receiving a tongue-in-cheek introduction to the campus in which her guide explained sarcastically that "all the cool people" hang out at the volleyball court. She marveled, "I do see people there, at all hours of the night. Even if it's midnight and it's zero degrees out. And I'm like, 'What are you doing there?! Why are you sitting under this tree on a bench in the middle of the night?!'"

Off-campus outdoor places also attract students. Locales along the Rio Grande or in fields surrounding the campus have attracted students since SIPI first opened. One place that students spoke about was known as the Hickey Spot. This area was apparently consumed by encroaching development. For students who want to stay closer to home, there is one consistent "party" spot, the slowly melting adobe house directly over the western fence on private land that might have been mistaken for a campus jail. I always presumed that its attraction was ease of access to the dormitories, especially for those students who did not have cars. Known as the Sugar Shack, the house disintegrated before our eyes, and the last portion I remember still being somewhat intact was the tiled floor. It is easy for students to access the house. They simply walk out of the dorms, across a swath of parking lot and dirt field, and step over the fence, basically climbing into the house. Because they are physically off campus—although only just—their behavior does not get reflected in campus crime statistics. A female student was brutally raped in 2006 in this area immediately outside the campus fence. It was counted as an off-campus offense.

Another attraction of outdoor spaces is that they are often more comfortable than indoor ones, especially in light of the age and decrepitude of SIPI's heating and cooling system. This monstrous beast fills the majority of a building on the south end of campus by the dormitories. It pushes hot or cold water across the breadth of the campus, which is riddled with aging pipes. It is a struggle to maintain a reasonable temperature throughout the campus. The system breaks down fairly often, and students cannot open the windows in the dormitory. Students routinely suffer through the results of these breakdowns, with cold showers in winter and suffocating heat in summer. The collapse of the air-conditioning is particularly hard for female students, as they are not as comfortable as males in moving outside to sleep (even going so far as to camp in the Bosque).

My strongest recollection of student use of outdoor areas occurred on a snowy morning soon after Thanksgiving one year. The snow was unusual for the time of year and for Albuquerque because, rather than melting off as soon as it touched the ground, it began to accumulate. Slowly, layers of powder settled all across campus, gently erasing harsh lines and bright colors. High overhead the skeletal arms of the cottonwoods accrued teetering piles of snow. The sun was hidden behind clouds, making the sky glow. Students began trudging across campus for their early morning classes. What they did not know, and the staff slowly came to realize, was that the aging hot water pipes that crisscrossed campus and provide the heat to the classroom buildings were leaking underground in different areas on campus. The temperature in the General Studies Building—one of the farthest from the boiler room—began to drop to meet the temperature outside. The greensward south of the building was buried under a thick layer of snow, but thin rills of steam escaped the cover and wisped into the air. At the base of the steam sat an ever-expanding puddle of melted snow and steaming water. One of the hot-water leaks had been found, lending a smoky and otherworldly appearance to the lawn.

Students made their way to their classes, collars pulled high. A few had not scanned the sky prior to leaving the dormitories and, unknowingly, had simply worn T-shirts in the frigid air. They all hustled to get inside the buildings quickly, not realizing the inside was almost as chilly as outside. The temperature in the classrooms dropped steadily over the next two hours, and students and staff wore their winter coats indoors. As the temperature sank to the low fifties, a snow day was declared. With a combination of glee and surprise, the students piled back out of the classrooms. Instead of fleeing back to the warmth of the dormitories, though, they began to play.

Snowballs were thrown between opposing camps, students laughing and dodging and teasing each other for their terrible aim. Three students went behind the building to find a source of pristine snow and built a ragged snowman. Soon, they had cannibalized his parts to fashion a pile of snowballs. They competed to see who could score more snowball hits against a fire hydrant sitting nearby in a sliver of lawn. Scattered across the open areas, other students stood with hands tucked in pockets and faces tipped skyward, simply enjoying the feel of the snow tickling their faces. It was not a day for metaphors, for protests against paternalism, acts of resistance, or accommodation. Some days at SIPI, like this one, were simply about being young, in college, surrounded by friends, and suddenly receiving the gift of a day to play.

Mealtimes are another time when students come together. Trays and dishes cannot be taken out of the cafeteria, so virtually all students—resident and commuter—pass through the cafeteria to eat. Typical to college cafeterias everywhere, the seating rules at the cafeteria are unspoken but quite rigid. You do not sit with people you do not know, unless invited or unless they are of parental age. Over the years, several introductory cultural anthropology students did participant observation projects in which they mapped the rules of cafeteria seating. Seating rules at SIPI seem to diverge from other colleges, where seating may be based on shared classes or shared dormitory space. At the Southwestern Indian Polytechnic Institute, the occupants at a table oftentimes come together because of shared tribe (unlike most true TCUs, where everyone in the cafeteria would most likely be from the same tribe). From there, students might narrow down their tablemates based on their reservation hometown. For his map, one young Navajo man reported that, if a tribe had only a few representatives at the school, then students came together based on region instead. He noted that students from different Oklahoma tribes sat together, listing Cherokee, Choctaw, and Creek students all together at one table. He was unsure if it was shared culture or shared region that drew these students together, or possibly both. Simply attending a college with other Native Americans does not guarantee that students know much about each other's cultures, and occasionally, their peers are deeply uninformed. (I experienced this firsthand when a teenaged student from a nearby pueblo raised her hand in response to a reference I had made in the cultural anthropology class, and asked, "What's Chickasaw?"— a watershed moment that prompted me to pursue resurrecting and restructuring the Contemporary American Indian Issues class—long untaught, but still in the course catalog.)

The Hogan

The Hogan is another meaningful campus place. It is a lovely building set slightly apart from the main administration building. The groundbreaking ceremony in May 2001 took place in the area in front of the current entrance. An Apache medicine man blessed the site. Participants in the groundbreaking stood in a semicircle facing the Sandia Mountains on the eastern edge of Albuquerque. The two New Mexico state senators flanked the school's president, and on cue they all plunged their gold-plated shovels into the sandy soil.

The Hogan has the most attractive interior space on campus, making it the de facto meeting area for visiting dignitaries and guests. It is easily visible to campus visitors, and its landscaping is distinct from the rest of campus in its use of desert plants and chunks of bright red sandstone. The eight-

4. A view of the back of the Hogan, dwarfed by the Science and Technology Building in the background. The Sandia Mountains appear in the far background on the left. Photo courtesy of the author.

sided building has windows set into every other wall. Each window provides a different view of the campus and its surroundings. Through one window are framed views of the Sandia Mountains and the Science and Technology Building, erected after the Hogan. Visible through another is a stand of cottonwoods and the distant campus greenhouses. The third window offers a sliver of the entire campus and framed in the fourth are the administration building, gymnasium, and lush lawns. The Hogan is oriented to the east like a traditional Navajo dwelling and faces the Sandia Mountains.

The soft scent of pine permeates the Hogan, and outside noises cannot penetrate the thick log walls. From the outside, it appears much lower to the ground than it actually is. Upon entering, a visitor notices that the ceiling rises in a peak high overhead to the top of a massive central support beam. Dangling from the ceiling are white power cords and hanging fluorescent lights, which all inject a corporate feel to the raw, lightly sanded log walls. Donated artworks in a variety of media line the building. A galley kitchen in the back is flanked by restrooms. The restrooms add a contradictory architectural touch, as the generic laminate restroom fixtures are bolted on to log cabin walls still weeping sap. Hand-carved tables and chairs are arranged symmetrically around the center pillar, lending a Southwestern feel that is only slightly offset by the fluorescent lights. Meetings, retreats, institutional training sessions, and other administrative events regularly take place in the Hogan. Virtually none of these events, though, include students. In fact, students are rarely invited into the Hogan, and have to enjoy it almost exclusively from the outside.

What would first seem to be a meaningful place for students is a site of significant emotional and interpretive conflict. Navajo students can look to the Hogan, as focus group participant Cecilia Ervin did, as a comforting symbol of home and community. Cecilia is a shy, soft-spoken residential student, and she finds other students to be unfriendly and unpleasant. She derives emotional comfort from the presence of the Hogan on campus, but she is saddened by the fact that she cannot actually enter the building. She was gently teased by the other focus group members, who called the Hogan her special place as if she were nursing an unrequited crush. They also pointed out that, no matter how comforting or meaningful it was, because students are not allowed free access to the Hogan, she (and students like her) can only derive limited comfort from it. She can only utilize it by looking at it, or thinking about it, not by actually being in it.

At the same time, for students from other tribes, this building implies the unfair privileging of Navajo culture and values over that of all other tribes represented at the school. I, like other employees, had long thought that the Hogan was a positive or value-neutral place. My first awareness of the conflict students feel about it occurred when I mentioned to a class that I had just attended a meeting discussing how to turn the Hogan into a museum space. The reaction was swift and negative. One student, an older man from the Midwest, said that he thought any campus museum at SIPI should focus only on Southwestern tribes. When I asked him to clarify why he felt the school should take such a narrow perspective, he pointed out that the choice in the building design already reflected a narrowness of perspective. The Hogan is a Southwestern building design; hence in his mind, it was only intended to benefit Southwestern tribes. He went on to suggest that traditional buildings from other tribes be erected around campus and dedicated as museums to those tribes. Another student, a woman in her twenties from a local pueblo, said that, in fact, the Hogan should not be a museum to Southwestern tribes but instead only a Navajo museum, since the traditional *hogan* building is not used by other tribes in the Southwest. Many of the non-Navajo students in the class agreed with her. Surely, the alienation felt by non-Navajo students in the class was not the intention of the administrators when they made their design choice, but the resulting fractionalization was real and was deeply felt by the students in my class.

Ultimately, there are two core conflicts occurring around the Hogan: The first is that for non-Navajo students the building represents the unfair privileging of one tribal culture over all others, a very real quandary in a school that is meant to serve more than one hundred tribes. The second dilemma is that for students who do feel an affinity for the building, they are routinely denied access to it, reminding them that even the symbols of home are regulated and controlled.

In Loco Parentis and Life in the Lodges: It's Like Living with Your Parents

Much of the daily life of a SIPI student centers around the dormitories. Fully more than half of the student body lives in the SIPI dormitories. Even for those students who live off campus, the dormitories are a social hub where friends meet up, study groups gather, and romantic partners might see each other for the first time in the day. How the dormitories function, and how they are perceived by students, is extremely informative when considering students' experiences on campus.

The dormitories are the site of constant, subtle conflict between students and the staff. Conflicts arise over the nature of the dormitory rules, the uneven or patronizing way the rules get applied, and the lack of student recourse to complain about them. Conflict between students and the administration of the school, and complaints about the treatment of students, have been a continual feature since the school opened. This does point out that the school's corporate culture has been consistent over the years as the current conflicts are often about the same issues as those that frustrated students in the past. The Southwestern Indian Polytechnic Institute is nearing the end of its fourth decade, and yet students and administration are still struggling over issues such as students' rights in the dormitories and mandatory student work details.

The tensions between students and administrators have led to at least two large campus sit-in-style protests. One protest in April 1975 drew AIM activists to the campus "in protest against the accumulating complaints against SIPI" and treatment of students by staff (Davis 1998:238). Another major campus protest took place in 1993, including student sit-ins and attention from the news media.

The ongoing trend of conflict between students and SIPI's administration arose in interviews done soon after the protest (McReynolds 1997). One informant said, "I feel like I have to get out of here as quickly as I can because you don't know what they [the administration] will do next, like with the protest last year. We did everything we could in a nice way, you know, we tried to state our problems so they would listen . . . They said we were ungrateful children who made demands about things we don't know about" (McReynolds 1997:73).

There have been bitter conflicts between students and the school administration over the dormitories from SIPI's earliest days: "SIPI students also criticized . . . the policies regulating dormitory life. Judy Fragua (Jemez Pueblo) and Lillus Brooks (White Mountain Apache) complained that the administration was not sufficiently involved in student life. Since SIPI failed to schedule any recreational activities on weeknights and weekends, students often drank and smoked in their dorm rooms. In response, SIPI administrators adopted stricter rules. Resident hall directors [matrons] ordered windows sealed shut. Instead of respecting students' privacy, dorm staff knocked on doors only once before entering rooms" (Davis 1998:237). "At the time of this research, there was a curfew on students. The exterior dormitory doors were locked by the dormitory matrons at midnight. Students were required to knock for admittance, and matrons were not obligated to let them into the dormitories" (McReynolds 1997:75–76). Students who were considered troublemakers for having actively participated in the protests were routinely locked out of the dormitories.

The rules have not changed much. During the research period for this book, matrons still had the one-knock rule. Lighting or burning anything in the dormitories was a violation of the student handbook guidelines. Unfortunately, the practical result was that students who wished to burn sage or other traditional incenses faced punishment for doing so, an abridgment of their ability to observe certain traditional religious practices.

Considering the longtime condition of the dormitories, the ease with which dormitory matrons enter students' rooms, and how often the students must vacate their rooms, it is unsurprising that students feel a sense of impermanence in their housing situation. When asked what kind of home SIPI is, a few students scoffed, stating that the dormitories, and by extension SIPI as a whole, is little more than a place to store themselves and their belongings while attending college.

There are weekly room checks, during which matrons enter students' dormitory rooms to inspect the condition and cleanliness of the space. Blame for grime and clutter is not assigned individually, but equally to the group residing in the room. Tidy students find themselves forced to act as housemaid to slovenly roommates. A room that repeatedly fails its room check for being messy or dirty can potentially lead to a tidy student's expulsion from the dormitories along with his or her messy roommate. Tidy roommates become anxious about living with someone who might cause them to lose their dormitory room, because losing housing privileges is akin to losing a full scholarship to college.

A classroom full of students raised the issue of room checks during a discussion one day. They protested the subtle—and not-so-subtle—favoritism they witnessed in the dormitories. The class insisted egregious violations of room cleanliness standards were ignored if the room belonged to a preferred student. Several of them insisted they knew of, or had themselves experienced, instances of such blatant favoritism. For example, shoes left on the floor of one room merited punitive detail duties and in another room obvious filth went unpunished.

Darren Wingard, a Pueblo student who is slightly older than average, and who lived independently prior to attending SIPI, said that living at SIPI was strange. Darren was an extremely social, outgoing individual who knew most students on campus. His dormitory room served, by his design, as a hub for socializing among students. In explanation of his "strange" comment, he said: "The environment. The living situation. It feels like institutional living. I mean, it feels like a correctional facility or something. I mean, with the . . . bathrooms and communal living . . . I hate to say this, but I was in jail . . . last trimester when I was caught for DWI. And it just reminds me of jail sometimes. It's like, wait a minute, something's familiar here! I was only in there for like seven hours, but that was an experience and it kind of reminded me of that." Like several other interviewees, Darren pointed to SIPI's rules as directly contributing to students' negative perceptions of the school. He also told me, "I've heard a lot of negative things about SIPI . . . Especially with the rules and everything." He explained further that he had made friends with people at the school who had left, and that he remained in contact with those friends. He tried to explain the perspective of the people who left: "You just have to abide by the rules. That's one thing, a lot of people don't agree with the zero tolerance, you know. Because it is college, and they like to express themselves freely. But it's kinda hard to do here, you know, when we have zero tolerance and all that. Rules enforced." Later in the interview he told me: "I think if SIPI had a lot less rules, it would make it feel more like a college than an institution. A place where they have to come in, be perfect. Because nobody's perfect! Nobody's perfect. Everybody makes mistakes. I'm pretty sure a lot of these people who work here made a lot of mistakes—some mistakes, you know. We all learn from our mistakes, but here they try to kind of enforce that you've got to be perfect. Do this all the time, you can't do this. I think that's where a lot rebellion comes from."

Part of the institutional feel at SIPI stems from the fact that it is a federal installation. From Darren's story, it appears that, by living within the confines of the school, students fear administrative censure would be supported by the full weight of the federal government. Darren told me of a student he was helping: "I know this guy who's got a problem. But he doesn't want to speak out. He's afraid of the matrons. Okay, this is something that's happening at the dormitories currently. Something that affects him. I'm not going to say what it is. It affects him on a personal level, but he's afraid to approach the appropriate person. [AK: Is he worried about retaliation?] Yeah, yeah. I think that's what a lot of students are fearing. This is a government institution. They do have a lot of rules. They're [students] afraid to speak up because of what might happen to them. Or something. I don't know. That's just the feeling that I get from a lot of these students." Few students worry that administrators at Generic State College will find a way to punish them for speaking out or that the federal government would take notice of them. For students afraid of retaliation, their conceptualizations of the school are intimately tied to the fact that it is a federal institution. They are also making an indirect reference to the hand metaphor described earlier in the book—some students fear the large governmental hand that hangs over them.

Yet paternalistic attitudes toward students can reach absurd levels as, during a staff meeting in 2001, employees were told that the new, federally mandated emergency campus evacuation plan might require them to drive students home. When asked what distances were involved, an administrator responded that if employees had to drive a student home to Montana, then they would be required to do so. Remember, students at the school are all legal, and legally competent, adults. Further, during the same meeting, employees were told that during an emergency students would be locked on campus until they officially checked out or created a huge fuss, whichever came first.

Gender again plays an important part in student experiences on campus. Women complained not only about being ignored by the administration, but also about the excessive management they faced in the dormitories. According to two students who were interviewed (one female and one male), women are more closely watched and carefully controlled than men. Lynae found that her movements in and out of the dormitories were constrained. She said that when she first started attending SIPI in the late 1990s, female residential students were required to sign in and out of the dormitories when they left campus. "When I first got here, they had us sign out. If you go home for the weekend. Or, off campus. You had to sign this little paper that says you're off [campus]. The time, then your name, and then your destination and what time you'll be back. When you come back, you sign back in again. I don't know if it's still there, but you do that. And we're like, 'Huh! That ain't cool!'" Men were not required to give any sort of accounting for their whereabouts or plans, let alone an accounting as specific and detailed. Darren concurred with Lynae. He told me:

> The women's dorm is a lot more strict than the guys'. The women have to come and knock on the door after twelve o'clock . . . whereas the guys' dorm is constantly open. The doors aren't locked. So here [in the women's dorm] they're really gung-ho about control. Controlling everything.
>
> It's kind of like going back home to Mom. I don't think it's necessarily right . . . This is a community college. People know the right from wrong. They should be allowed to feel for themselves that specific right. But when you have people controlling, like [a] military base, who comes to the door, at what time—specific at what time—I think that's wrong. Like going back to high school years. When your mom told you to be home at a certain time. Knock on the door just to come in the door.
>
> You're constantly being supervised. I think that really bothers a lot of students, because you don't get that kind of treatment from the guys' dorm. You're allowed to come and go as you please. Just like you should be treated in the adult world.

Darren and Lynae's comments make it clear that while all students encounter a certain amount of paternalism on campus, female students experienced far more restrictive control mechanisms than male students. I was told that the men's dormitory was never locked, whereas the women's was locked at night, requiring returning students to show their school ID cards. Campus urban legend has it that locking the women's dormitory was in response to past experiences of inebriated male students accidentally wandering into the women's dormitory, thinking it was the men's.

Apparently, oversight of students is not so strict that dormitory residents are necessarily recognized as such. Grace Nez told a particularly funny and telling story about an experience she had in the dormitory soon after moving on campus. Grace is a bright, academically talented woman raised on the Navajo reservation. She expresses affection through teasing and her sarcasm cuts through any pretense. She feels, and seems, out of place at SIPI as she is more confident and academically prepared than the majority of her peers. She has attended a four-year college (and lived in the dormitories there) and many of her insights come from her comparisons between the two types of institutions.

> That the dorm matrons look at you like—I mean, I live in the dorms now. I was in one of their little TV rooms within the dorms. I was in my pajamas, I had my glasses on, no shoes. My books spread out and I was watching TV and one of the dorm matrons said, "Are you a student here? Can I see your ID?" And I was like, "Are you serious? Yeah, I hang out at SIPI in my pajamas at eleven o'clock at night just for the hell of it!" I was like—I don't know, I was like "Are you serious?" and she was like, "I need to see your ID!" And I was like "Let me go to my room and get it then." And she's like, "Okay, never mind." And I was like, "All I had to say, I had a room? Or what? Innkeeper?" It was so weird! It was eleven o'clock at night! And I was just out there, doing my homework, and because I was watching the baseball game. And I couldn't believe she asked me that! Do you live here in the dorms? [sarcastically] No! Obviously, if I had been a friend of somebody and I was just there, I would've had my clothes on! And someone else would've been in the room with me!

The Lodges are single-sex facilities, one of the ways in which the school exhibits a cultural lag from mainstream institutions. Opposite-sex students cannot visit each other's dormitory rooms. Instead, they must meet in the dormitory lounges. Students can be punished for being in the "unauthorized" areas of the opposite sex's dorm, known as "unauthorized visitation" (SIPI 1998:16), or for bringing an individual into an off-limits area, known as "in the private living area of the opposite sex" (SIPI 1998:16). Engaging in sexual activity on campus is also expressly prohibited by the student handbook, which describes this proscription as having derived from tribal leaders and students' parents "who have expressed strong feelings about such acts taking place anywhere on campus" (SIPI 1998:16), regardless of students' status as adults. These three types of violations (sexual activity, visitation, being visited) are considered major violations and school administrators reserve the right, detailed in the student handbook, to suspend students from school (SIPI 1998:15). They are listed in the student handbook ahead of more socially disparaged violations such as "self-destructive behavior" and "contributing to the delinquency of a minor" (SIPI 1998:17)—both also defined as major violations. Stranger still, sexual activity and visiting the opposite sex in the dormitories are major violations (meaning offenders risk expulsion), whereas stalking is only a minor violation (SIPI 1998:15), which at most can lead to SIPI probation or mandatory counseling (SIPI 1998:18). This sex segregation has been a source of conflict from SIPI's earliest days (Davis 1998:237). The pathologizing of consensual sexual activity between young adults is, at best, naïve and parental, and at worst, an invasion of students' personal lives.

Dormitory Work Details: Only Parents Assign Chores

Mandatory work assignments, known as "details," are an area of continual conflict and tension between students and the school. Detail assignments in the late 1990s and 2000s were done in the dormitories, typically involving the cleaning of common areas. All dormitory residents are expected to do details. Additional detail duties are assigned as punishment for students whose infractions in the dormitories warrant censure but not eviction. In SIPI's first decades students were required to do detail labor in areas around campus in addition to cleaning the dormitories (McReynolds 1997:74).

The assignment of cleaning details resonates with the BIA's history of using mandatory student labor to offset the costs of operating federal boarding schools. Students are aware of this history, which serves to support the metaphor "SIPI is a boarding school." Many of them have heard their parents' and grandparents' stories of working for their schooling—willingly or not—and they are reminded that while they are in fact attending college, they are still in the Bureau of Indian Affairs educational system.

Tension over details is long-standing. Research at the Southwestern Indian Polytechnic Institute undertaken in the mid-1990s describes the conflict: "From the student's perspective, the dormitory management and environment exemplified SIPI's bureaucratic control. Similar to the boarding schools of the 1900s, SIPI depends on student labor" (1997:74). That conflict is still active and tension-filled, for several reasons. Details offer uncomfortable parallels to Bureau of Indian Affairs boarding schools, alienating students from their educational experience at SIPI, and making them feel like children. Details also make students feel as if they are children being given chores by their parents.

An older commuter student from a local pueblo, who had attended a four-year college prior to entering SIPI, said, "In the dorms, from what I hear, you have to do your work details, and help clean, and do this, and do that. It just feels like there's a real [im]balance, like they're the parents telling you what you need to do, when you need to do it." She described details as being representative of a larger, institutional stance of treating students as dependent, incompetent, and childlike. She added, "I don't think they see students as adults. I think they see them as people who need to be told what to do."

Grace Nez had moved onto campus just a few weeks before our interview. Prior that she had lived off campus, and before that had attended a four-year college out of state. Her perspective on SIPI was shaped by her varied college and academic housing experiences. Living at SIPI was a practical, financial consideration. She compared living on campus to a kindergarten-through-eighth-grade boarding school on the Navajo reservation that she visited as a child. "That's how it feels here with the whole room-check thing. They do it every Thursday. At a real college, they don't do that sort of thing. And they have details. I never had a detail at [out-of-state liberal arts college]. I had someone come and clean my bathroom. That's when I was living large!" She made further comparisons between living in the dormitories at SIPI and dormitory life at the small liberal arts college that she had attended previously. "I mean, they have the details here where people have to clean the bathrooms or the showers. They have to vacuum stuff. They have dorm meetings. The way they set things up. When I come in at twelve, I have to flash my ID again because the doors are locked."

The majority of Lynae Archuleta's experiences in the Four Winds Lodge were positive. Her dormitory room was cozy and she had a close family member as a roommate. Her dealings with the staff, though, prompted her to describe the dormitories using the metaphor "SIPI is a parent." During her recounting, she was able to laugh with honest humor at her experiences, including the blatant favoritism other students experienced. While she does conceptualize some of her experiences with the dormitory staff as having a family-like feel, she sees those experiences as being representative of only the most restrictive and controlling aspects of living at home, as a child. She said:

You still have a mom or a dad watching over you, at the dorms. That's probably where, I'm thinking, they say SIPI's cool but it sucks. Is because when you are out of the dorms, you're actually an adult. Everybody treats you right. But once you go into the dorms, the matrons—especially the little one that's the highest ... She took care of us, right [sarcastically]. She was the one that was like the little dog, the little pit bull. You couldn't do nothing wrong. When she's not there everybody's like, "Ahh" [imitates relief]. Same thing with the matrons. Some of them were cool, and some of them weren't. The ones that were more friendly were the ones who worked with students for a long time. They were kind of more laid back. They'll just talk to you to tell you not to do that again. But I think the main thing is they still want to kind of treat you like little kids.

Student complaints about details had three main themes: (1) It is unheard of at other colleges for students to be required to act as janitorial staff, to the point of cleaning toilets used communally; (2) details as punishment resemble the types of community service punishment required by court systems, creating a negative connotation to their labor; and (3) assignment of detail duties is arbitrary, unfair, and entirely contingent on who are the matrons' pet students. Lynae spoke of her frustration with detail assignments with a playful jab at the unfairness of the process: "Right away they give you details. I didn't really care for details. Some students didn't have details while others had it. I don't think it was equally distributed, the assignments. Some students would get it once in a long time. There were other students that would be assigned details almost every other week. It was like [laughing], 'Hey! Do I clean good or what?!' It was like you knew you were being picked on. That's the part that really sucks." Details are an arena of conflict and power dynamics that get played out daily, weekly, and in the most intimate spaces, such as students' dormitory rooms. The assignment of details emphasizes power disparities between matrons and students, emphasizes the preferential treatment of some students, and encourages outright resistance or more subtle forms of student protest.

While leading a cultural anthropology class discussion in 2003, our topic of gender construction and power dynamics in prisons resonated with students in an unexpected way. One older student raised his hand and announced that the same power dynamics seen in prisons are at play in SIPI's Lodges. I asked how he meant this comment, and he told me (corroborated by the majority of the class) that students skip doing their detail assignments as a subtle but real form of protest. The assignment of detail duties, and the standards by which cleanliness is judged, were seen by students in this class as being unfair and arbitrary. In fact, he insisted, students who were tidy at home would become slovenly in the SIPI dormitories as a way of resisting institutional power, as represented by the matrons and detail assignments.

Not all students found details to be offensive. A student who entered SIPI after separating from the Marine Corps acknowledged other students' complaints about doing details. She thought that students who compared SIPI to a prison were most likely responding to detail duty. She felt she had little to complain about since, she pointed out, unlike cleaning duties in the Marine Corps, at SIPI she never had had to get on her hands and knees and scrape built-up wax off the floors. "Picking up a vacuum or wiping things down, it's not a big problem for me." She knew of a student who never had had to do chores at home and others who thought by leaving home, they would no longer be responsible for cleaning.

Efforts were routinely made to address drinking on campus and refusal to do detail duties. I attended a mandatory dormitory meeting at the Four Winds Lodge in which these issues were addressed. Virtually every female resident was in the room. They were required to attend the dormitory meetings or risk expulsion from the dormitories. I was excited to be there. They were not. Their faces, at best, reflected boredom, and at worst, frustration. Even students who I knew to be perpetually cheerful sat watching, affectless.

An elderly dormitory matron stood next to the council president, as if trying to impart a sense of seriousness to the proceedings. The matron wore a walkie-talkie, which blared messages between security staff. She began to harangue the students over the noise of her own radio. The students tuned her out but kept their closed faces turned to her. The harangue, and the crackle and mutter of the security radio, imparted a vaguely hostile and militaristic energy to the proceedings. What could have theoretically been a positive, dynamic meeting of all the female residents became a tense scene of enforced attendance.

The two main concerns addressed by the dormitory council president were the violations of the zero-tolerance policy and students not fulfilling their detail duty obligations. The dormitory council president lifted a clear garbage bag filled with liquor bottles and informed the students that the bag was from a dormitory room. Students had been caught drinking in their rooms and were evicted that same day. She pointed out that dormitory matrons had the right to enter a student's room anytime they wanted. There was no safe time or place to drink. Therefore, she asserted, do not drink in your dormitory rooms or risk losing your college education. The response was silence. Drinking in a zero-tolerance dormitory on a zero-tolerance campus seemed to me to be an almost desperately risky act. As an act of resistance, the only damage done was to the academic careers of the students who were caught. Was the possibility of transgressing under the noses of dorm matrons too tempting? Were students actually seeking to be evicted? Whatever the result, drinking alcohol in the dormitories as a protest against the school's rules and in effect arranging to get caught was a Pyrrhic victory at best.

The dormitory council president went on to inform the gathered women that several students had been neglecting to perform their cleaning detail duties. It quickly became apparent why some students were resisting doing their mandatory cleaning details. The dormitory council president impressed upon students the need to dispose of biohazardous materials properly. Students doing details were finding used feminine sanitary supplies on shared bathroom counters and in showers, even though there were trash cans nearby. The dormitory council president noted that these students were potentially endangering their peers as, "there is AIDS on this campus." Disposal of these items was an ongoing struggle. One has to ask in what other setting would such deeply personal items be left for other people to handle? It runs counter to women's typical behavior in other public settings, and as several students had expressed concern about witchcraft in the dormitories, potentially put these women at spiritual risk as well. If their actions are a form of protest or acting out, they were simply victimizing their peers, who would be punished if they refused to complete their detail assignments.

Internalizing the Rules

Colleges have rules, whether students agree with them or not. Students at the Southwestern Indian Polytechnic Institute obviously could not reject all of the school's rules wholesale. Sometimes, though, students acknowledged that they followed rules that they did not like or agree with. They caught themselves in surprising moments of obedience even when they knew they were not being observed.

During the focus group, Jonah Nesbitt expressed his frustration with having to abide by a range of unfair rules, including attending mandatory meetings, then found himself veering into uncomfortable territory. He said, "We've got to do all this stuff; we've got to do all that. But that comes with, I guess, free education." He paused, startled by his own statement. "I have that mentality to where I'm already making excuses. You know, 'They treat us like this, but we're getting a free education.' That's how we've become. I don't want to bring up the B-word, but brainwashed, you know what I mean?" Students at the Southwestern Indian Polytechnic Institute, especially the highly motivated ones, are aware that a cost-free education comes with strings attached. As Jonah's statement points out, there is an awareness that bending to the system in order to follow one's own goals could have the unintended consequence of erasing one's own boundaries. Jonah was shocked with himself to realize that he was proposing agreeing to being treated like a child or ward because it allowed him a free education.

Grace Nez described students' sense of obligation coupled with resentment and an awareness of history. "They're not paying very much for it, and they're getting what people would have to pay a lot for. I mean, our instructors are always telling us how much our textbooks would cost if we were actually going to a real college, and the fact that we're getting it for free. I think they [students] like that, but at the same time they feel it's—they feel obliged to the government, for like, 'Oh, thank you [sarcastic tone] for doing this for us. Thank you for supplying our free books.' At the same time they kind of feel a little bit of anger towards that just because of the history, I guess. From what their elders have told them. Stuff like that." Cody Daniels, from a Midwestern tribe, also raises the issue of absorbing institutional values to the point of losing a sense of independence. Cody is in his twenties. When he wrestles with a dilemma, he can seem intimidating and intense. As soon as he relaxes, he shows a playful and self-deprecating side. Cody knows virtually everyone on campus. He is involved in a range of socially conscious activities and refuses to back down to patronizing behavior.

Cody feels tremendous affection toward SIPI, which is evident in his demeanor during the interview and in his words. He sees many positive aspects of the school, such as the social and cultural connections he has made to other students and his ability to fulfill his educational goals, but he is not oblivious to the systems of control. Cody describes several ways that students unwittingly absorb SIPI's institutional culture and organizational rules. Not only did he come to feel that he was being managed by the school—through the institutional emphasis on time and rules—but as evident in the story that follows, Cody also sees himself and his friends as having internalized SIPI's rules, such as SIPI's zero-tolerance policy.

> I remember the first time I had my own apartment. [It was] me and my friends. Somebody knocked on the door. I was sitting at my own kitchen table in my own apartment. It was the first night there. We were all glad that we could do what we wanted. I actually hid my beer. I told the guys to hide their beers, because we couldn't do it—can't do

it in the dorm. It was my own apartment, and there wasn't anybody who could tell me anything, and somebody knocked on the door and I instantly hid my beer! Like I couldn't have it. They laughed at me. I wasn't the only one that did it in the room! There were four or five other people that did it!

While Cody found himself laughing as he recounted this tale, it is also evident that he marvels at the very fact that he and his friends have become so well trained by the institution. Even in the privacy of his own apartment, well away from the SIPI campus, he was startled to find that he and his peers reacted as if they had done something wrong. All the students present in his living room had adapted to the knowledge that their dormitory rooms were easily entered by dormitory staff. Cody and his friends had so completely absorbed the belief that, while students at SIPI, they had no control over their personal space that they carried over this conceptualization to their lives off campus. They found themselves responding to control mechanisms that were not present. Relevant here, too, is the way that student resistance was so immediate and unconscious. Cody noted that he and the other students hid their beers in preparation for an invasion of their privacy. They were aware they had been subjected to regulatory practices while living in the dormitories, and they had internalized the significance of being caught, hence the hiding of their beers. These students, though, did not adhere to the *value system* implied by the imposition of this regulatory practice; they just followed the required behavior.

Cody also was struck by the almost Pavlovian response that he, and other students, developed not just to the authoritarian-sounding knock at the door, but to the clock. Cody was uncomfortable as he described becoming totally acclimated to living by a schedule imposed by the institution. He realized that he had begun to unquestioningly comply with a set of values or standards that he did not share. Much of what he described could have been said of a Bureau of Indian Affairs boarding school. He said:

Here you get institutionalized. You get so used to the clock. You get so used to doing things, it gets so routine. When I worked for my brother, I used to eat lunch. But you don't eat lunch at noon or one. You eat lunch whenever. When you're hungry. But here, you know you have to eat between eleven thirty and one or else you'll have to wait till five. And you have to eat between five and six before the next day. You know, if you don't have any money, your life is set by that particular clock.

On the weekend students know that from ten to eleven thirty is brunch and from four to five thirty is dinner. So, a lot of people get hungry [because they are dependent on SIPI providing their meals]. When I was staying with my friends, it was getting on—eleven thirty, noon, and I was getting hungry. I knew that the fridge was just right over there, and it was weird that I was actually getting hungry and I ate at specific times.

Cody's narrative closely resembles that of a student from a historic boarding school as she described her first meal at the school, with students approaching their chairs to the sound of one bell, praying at the sound of the second bell, and eating at the third (Zitkala-Sa 2005:32–33).

In addition to the way that students have, in his opinion, adjusted even their appetites to fit SIPI, Cody Daniels also discussed a form of student compliance that he felt led to student dependence. "As far as the independence that people have at any college, if you have an appointment . . . it's your problem. You know, if you need a ride to the airport, you need to ask your roommates. You got to call a cab. But here they've got that mentality that, 'We'll give you a ride to the clinic. We'll pick you up. We'll give you a ride to the airport. We'll pick you up—bus station, train station.' It's kind of like the same BIA mentality that Indian people can't take care of themselves, but they provide those services for us. I think it also makes you institutionalized." To Cody, SIPI fits the same set of characteristics common in Bureau of Indian Affairs schools. SIPI is paternalistic because it is run by the BIA. The BIA as an agency creates dependence. Boarding schools created dependence. Therefore, SIPI is a BIA boarding school. Cody rejected the metaphor of "SIPI is a prison" because of the simple fact that students attend the school voluntarily. It was illogical to him that students acted as if they were coerced into attending rather than acknowledging that they had chosen to attend college. He noticed how some of his peers treat attending class as an onerous responsibility. He noted that he sometimes found himself falling into that mind-set: "I hear students complain, 'I hate to go—' or 'I have to go to class.' They make it sound like it's so hard. I catch myself every now and then, saying 'I have to go to class,' but if you just think that you have to go to every single class and have an attitude where you don't want to be in there, then you shouldn't be there. You shouldn't be here." He added, laughing at his own, and others', attitudes, "You actually chose to be here, so go to your classes." He told me that he knew students hated the rules but that they needed to adjust. When Cody conceptualized the negative qualities of SIPI, he focused on the subtly coercive practices—the practices that he found himself following unconsciously and unwillingly—rather than the more explicit modes of control.

Conclusion: Success in the Face of Distrust

It becomes quickly clear that, while students find a way to succeed at SIPI, there are multiple institutional characteristics that are frustrating and counterproductive. Residential students face more rules and intrusions than commuters—whose experiences with administrative management policies are more typically associated with issues surrounding their academic careers.

The college experience of attending the Southwestern Indian Polytechnic Institute is hardly a mirror for the experiences students have at contemporary mainstream institutions. And SIPI students are oftentimes resentful of those differences. They know what "college" is supposed to be like. Students see themselves repeatedly rendered powerless in their interactions with staff, assigned chores as if they are still living with their parents, and constrained by unfair rules that even the school's employees do not fully understand.

Students see control mechanisms in a range of aspects of the school— the rules, the handling of students, even the architecture. One anonymous survey respondent described the school using multiple negative metaphors that shared the theme of "SIPI is a system of control." He wrote, "SIPI is almost like a correction facility. We have no windows in the dorms to open. Teachers treat students like little kids." His issues seem, at first, to be disparate, as one complaint focuses on control through architecture (inoperable windows) and the other on prevailing parental attitudes (treatment of students). Both, though, share the quality of illustrating power and restriction.

The cultural values of the Bureau of Indian Affairs also shape the metaphors that students use in conceiving of the school. SIPI students who use metaphors of control see themselves as being distrusted from the outset much like students attending the BIA school at Santa Clara Pueblo described in chapter 3 (Swentzell 1997). The minute they step onto campus, with its fence and guard house, they are reminded of how distrusted they are. Nor are they surprised by that distrust, aware as they are of SIPI's place along the timeline of Bureau of Indian Affairs educational institutions.

Jeremy Bentham's model of the Panopticon, a perfect machine for overseeing those requiring correction and control, provides a lens for examining student perceptions of SIPI. Bentham's prescription for schools is based on the idea that students, like inmates in penitentiaries or asylums, need constant supervision. This oversight guarantees order, and ensures that the overseen behave in a fashion deemed acceptable to those in charge. Bentham felt that the most effective form of his system would arise when the individual incarcerated within it began to internalize his own oppression, and reenact his oppressor's regime because he thought he might be watched and "not being able to satisfy himself to the contrary, he should *conceive* himself to be so" (Bentham 1791:3). When Cody and his friends found themselves automatically hiding their beers at the knock on his door, they were enacting this type of training that Bentham saw as being the ultimate goal of the Panopticon.

Cody's example of following SIPI's rules when he was no longer living on campus, and Jonah's worry of having been brainwashed, point to their awareness of having been inculcated into the school's institutional values, possibly at the expense of their own. Cody found his experience bleakly funny, while Jonah was genuinely disturbed. Either way, the reality they both experienced and described support Foucault's argument that by internalizing his own control, the individual who is watched by representatives of the institution makes it even easier for the institution to control him by keeping himself in check (Foucault 1977:202–203). Cody and Jonah were arguing that this was indeed the case for them and their friends.

A college that makes its students feel watched, and even brainwashed, is not likely to maintain a bond with alumni. Nor, it seems, would that school be particularly successful in retaining students, if it were not for its extremely low cost. When students throughout the course of the school's history complain about being patronized, ignored, and constrained—even going so far as to "remember" a campus jail—there are fundamental problems with the campus culture that must be addressed.

While students can be, and are, successful in the face of a patronizing institutional culture and controlling rules, it behooves the school's leadership to find ways in which students can become true participants—as capable and competent adults—in the system of the school. In light of students' articulate and illuminating explanations of their frustrations at the institution, it is clear where changes need to be made and how beneficial those changes will be.

Any suggestion that students at a college feel like prisoners or animals is profoundly disturbing. Yes, students at mainstream colleges complain about the rules. (TCU students do not appear in the literature making similar complaints, but that might simply be a factor of the writers' editorial choices.) But the sheer number of student complaints at SIPI (as evidenced in the interviews, survey responses, classroom discussion, and casual conversation) points overwhelmingly to a substantial and fundamental failure of the school. There are successes, such as when they learn about their culture and the cultures of other tribes from their peers. In the classroom, students are exposed to new ideas and ways of thinking, and develop confidence in their own intellectual abilities. But through their interactions with the larger power structures at the school, students are learning that they are devalued and dismissed and that in the administration's eyes (since the rules are designed and implemented at the administrative level), students must be contained, lest they cause damage or chaos. How can a college function successfully, retain students, engender loyalty both in current students and in graduates, if the core philosophies of the school debase the students so intensely?

It would be a productive starting point in addressing student concerns to have a neutral, or pro-student, individual engage students who use the metaphor "SIPI is a prison" to list the parallels they see. While it is obvious that students are not, for example, locked in their dormitory rooms at night, their interpretation of certain campus experiences or rules as being prison-like and excessively controlling provides an obvious, and actionable, starting point for campus reform. In addition, there need to be systems put into place that guarantee action is taken on student concerns.

Frustration with the institution does not prevent students from building strong emotional and social ties to their peers. In fact, the everyday frustrations and constraints they experience with the school bureaucracy might even serve to strengthen their bonds to their peers. And those bonds are, in fact, quite strong. So strong that, to some students, SIPI is a reservation.

6
SIPI Is a Reservation
Family, Friends, and Mentors

There are multiple positive metaphors students use when describing SIPI, many of which center around the personal relationships they have built. Students say "SIPI is a haven" because it provides a microcosm of Indian Country, free of externally imposed racism, and surrounded by the larger metropolis of Albuquerque. Or some say, "SIPI is a family" because of actual kin on campus or pseudokinship ties that they build while they are there, ties that make them feel emotionally supported and accepted for who they are as individuals. Other students use the metaphor "SIPI is a reservation," and go on to describe the many qualities the school shares with their home community. Ultimately, all these metaphorical descriptions hinge on a shared sense of caring, support, and safety from the outside world.

It does not appear from students' stories that SIPI is as much the creator of these ties as the context in which the bonds are built. Students are creating a personally meaningful social space, and where this occurs is less relevant. Any similar type of institution—one that attracts young Natives from across the country—could potentially be the setting for the same types of metaphors.

Metaphors of Home and Family

The Southwestern Indian Polytechnic Institute is, in many ways, a family affair. Many students have actual family ties to the school, including family members who previously attended, or even were attending SIPI while they themselves were there. Others had kin who worked at the school. In the 2002 survey, 33 percent of the students listed family ties as one of their top three reasons for attending SIPI. Family narratives about SIPI can be positive, such as Kira Thomas's memories of her father participating in league basketball in the SIPI gym, or Nancy White visiting with an older relative. They can also be negative, such as Autumn McWright's uncle warning her of drinking on campus or Michael Little's cousin telling him that SIPI was "pretty rough," including stories of beatings and stabbings among students. True family ties exist prior to a student's attending the school. But for students who did not have family members on campus, the school can still come to resemble a family. Family can mean the sense of safety and acceptance they experience in their interactions with their peers, the role they play for each other, or it can refer to the more mechanical aspects of daily living, such as sharing meals and living together.

Community Mothers

While many younger students might see the school as resembling a family because their peers resemble siblings, for older students the family dynamic takes an interesting form, and a wholly unexpected one. Female students in their forties and older are unofficially appointed to a parental role by their younger peers. Put simply, oftentimes to their surprise, older female students are valued as elders by younger students. It is common at mainstream institutions for older students to feel alienated from their peers. Two of the women I interviewed said that they had had misgivings about returning to college, given their ages in comparison to the other students. Yet older female students at SIPI are generally treated with respect. Their advice is sought by their younger peers, and they find themselves providing a caring ear or experienced counsel, sometimes to students they do not even know. Yvonne Kee (Navajo), Isabella Begay (Navajo), and Althea Running (Sioux) spoke of the respect they are accorded by their younger peers, which none of them had anticipated when they entered the school.

Yvonne Kee's experience of attending SIPI in her forties is shaped quite positively by the fact that, as an older Navajo woman with college-aged children, she is treated with considerable respect by her student peers. Yvonne is a friendly and somewhat retiring woman who excels in all things artistic. She has a positive outlook and eagerly tries new experiences. Yvonne had been hesitant about returning to school. She told her daughter how nervous she was, worried that students would be dismissive of her because of the age difference. "I was telling my daughter that I'm not going to fit in, and that, oh, I'm going to be pushed in the corner and forgotten. 'I don't think I'll fit in. I don't think I'm going to be comfortable,' and she says, 'Try it. You'll never know till you try it.'" Her daughter's encouragement helped to prepare her, but she still was very nervous when she first entered SIPI.

I mentioned to her that I had heard older students are treated respectfully by younger students, and she responded, "I've experienced that, and I wasn't ready for that! I just feel like I'm a grandma, and I don't have any grandkids yet! I always get, 'Here! Here! Sit over here!' . . . 'Do you want coffee?' 'Are you cold?' Or stuff like 'How are you doing today? Are you doing all right?'" She had not anticipated being so valued, perhaps because she was expecting a college experience more on par with mainstream colleges. All her worries turned out to be unfounded, and she said of her experience of returning to college, "It was different. Different from what I thought. Positive. More positive." The value placed on elders, happily, allayed Yvonne's fears about returning to school as an older adult. She was not "pushed in the corner and forgotten," but learned that she was valued, which gave her the confidence to take full advantage of the educational opportunities available at the school.

The respect that younger students accord their older peers is an expression of a significant Native cultural value—respect for one's elders. For younger students, women like Yvonne might represent a supportive adult figure who has the added benefit of not being allied with the power structures of the school. Yvonne, and her older female peers, have the same class assignments and deadlines as everyone else, yet they also have more and broader life experiences than traditionally aged students. Because they attend classes with younger students, they know what attending SIPI is like, but they also have the wisdom of experience and self-knowledge that allows them to put life in perspective for their younger peers.

Isabella Begay's fears about returning to school were assuaged much like Yvonne's. Isabella is a Navajo woman in her forties who looks much younger than her years. Isabella decided to return to school at her children's urging. She is a kind woman who exudes a sense of calm. She challenged herself academically, but did so in a low-key way. Isabella's experience at the school was closely tied to her treatment by her peers. At first she was apprehensive about coming back to school. "It was very uncomfortable, just because I felt like I was older. I felt like, 'Oh my goodness, all these young kids!'" Isabella spoke of how difficult it was to decide to return to school in her forties. I asked her if younger students intentionally made older students feel uncomfortable. She said that, "It's just something that older students feel. Coming back to school. I feel that way. I feel like, 'Gosh, I should have done this twenty years ago.' When I was going strong, I should have. But you know, I decided to have . . . a family." Returning to school as an older student was a life-altering choice, one that she found to be an exciting challenge. She told me, laughing, "At forty! It isn't fun going back to school at forty! Hard on the back!" Her worries about being an older student meant that she was at first drawn to other older female students because of their shared experiences. They felt an almost instantaneous bond among themselves. They would greet each other and motivate each other. She told me, "When you see somebody around the campus, 'Hi. How are you? Where are you from?' And then, they're feeling like, 'Oh my goodness, I don't know if I can do this. I decided to come back to school.' And I'm going, 'You know, if I can do it, anybody can do it. You can do it.'" The mutual support among older students perhaps led to them encouraging their younger peers in turn.

Isabella, like Yvonne, did not anticipate being categorized into a maternal role by younger students. She began to realize that, as younger students became more comfortable with her, they were placing her in this role. Unlike the younger students who often feel shy about meeting their peers (or their roommates), Isabella felt, "It's easy to get to know the younger students." In fact, getting to know them began to take a ritualized form. When she met younger students, they routinely asked her two questions to establish her identity and decide how they would interact with her. First, they asked if she was a residential student. When she imitated someone asking that question, her voice lifted in a hopeful lilt. The students she spoke with seemed to want to have a maternal presence in the dormitory but one that lacked the potentially punitive power inequality found in interactions with the dormitory matrons. She was also routinely asked, "How old are you?"

She explained that she would immediately respond, "And I'm going, 'I'm forty-two.' I'm not ashamed of my age. I usually tell, 'I'm forty-two, and I have to keep coloring those grays!' But anyhow [other students respond], 'Forty-two! I can't believe you're forty-two! I thought you were in your mid-thirties!' or something. And there are some young guys that sit [hitting on me], and [I respond], 'Nope! I'm married!'" Isabella said after going through these ritualized questions, she would start to develop relationships with her younger peers. Most of these friendships have a parental or mentoring quality. Like the Sioux student who described developing a trusting relationship with his roommates, Isabella described her mentoring relationships as being built on trust:

> It really takes talking to the students and making them trust. Establishing that trust between you and the younger students. Then I think they look at you like a role model. I have two young men that . . . one

was in my math class, and the other was in my anthro and English. They're bright! They've looked at my work and said, "You need to do [correct] this." But they're lazy. They don't want to do any work. I'm going, "You need to do this tomorrow. It's due." I say, "It's easy. It's easy." And so they're going, "Okay!"

It's funny, when I'm in the Learning Center [the campus tutoring center] and they're going, "Did you do your proposal? Did you do your [homework]" and I'm going, "Yeah, this is all you need to do. Just go back there, and if you know the subject, you should be able to whip it out in no time. Get it out in no time." And with math, "It's okay, this is all you need to remember. It's just repetitious."

From Isabella's description, the students she mentors are competent but unsure of their own ability. She encourages them to do their coursework but does not have the power to direct them to do it. Her encouragement provides them with a feeling of support, like a parent, yet she is unlike a parent in that she lacks the coercive power to demand they complete their assignments. I asked her, "Do you think the fact that you're kind of watching them helps [motivate them]?" In response, she told me: "I know the one guy, he pulled through English. The other one, he dropped out of math and English. He said, 'Ah, I'll just take it over.' I said, 'You're so bright and young, why are you doing this? You don't want to just . . . that's the second stone that you're gonna set up for yourself. You're repeating, repeating. Get it over with. Then it's like anything else. When you were young, your parents told you to do your chores. Get it over with and you're done.' And he said, 'Oh, goodness. You really sound like my mom!'" No doubt she did sound like his mom. But from her description, that was exactly what he was seeking in their friendship—a maternal figure to push him to succeed. Her status as that figure shaped her positive experience at the school and the high level of acceptance she enjoyed among her peers.

Students' metaphorical conceptualizations of her as a parental figure ("Ms. Begay is a parent") are contextual. In situations where she provides guidance or encouragement, she is slotted into a maternal role. When she herself needs academic assistance, students simply see her as a peer. She made a point of telling me how instrumental one younger student is to her own learning and academic success. She characterized this other student as "a go-getter." Her friend does not need Isabella's mentoring, and as a result their relationship was not based on the model of mentor/protégé or parent/child. They are peers, providing mutual support.

Isabella's relationship with her go-getter friend is in contrast with the relationship she has with the two young men she described. To them, *she* is the academic star, the go-getter, and as such, she serves as a motivator and a form of academic parent. She noted that they are both intelligent and have in the past provided her with academic guidance and editorial assistance. They do not come to her to teach them the material, but rather to have her encourage them and perhaps even to chastise them a little. The young men value her input and are respectful of her support. (One wonders if they, in turn, conceptualize SIPI as a family owing to her influence.)

Althea Running's experiences with younger students is somewhat different from that of her peers. That difference can be in part due to the fact that she lives in the dormitories. She, like Isabella, speaks of being seen as an informal mentor for younger students. She says she likes to find an empty table in the cafeteria and wait to see who joins her. Sometimes she shares meals with students that she already knows, and other times she is joined by complete strangers. (It is extremely uncommon for younger students who do not know each other to share a table and talk to each other.) Althea said she asks so many questions that she is practically interviewing the other students at the table. She is curious about their tribal cultures, where they are from, and the traditional crafts their tribe makes. Althea also speaks of mentoring a younger friend through difficult times.

Unfortunately, she also has had experiences in which students make it clear they are uncomfortable having older students on campus. She said she overheard two younger students complaining, "We're all young and we're in college. We're supposed to have fun but we've got these old people walking around." If younger students see an older woman as intrinsically parental, then perhaps they were interpreting her presence in the dormitories as like having a parent in their midst, constraining them through her mere presence.

These women also shared an important characteristic—they were all raised on their tribe's reservations. For students who were experiencing homesickness or culture shock after having left their reservation, these older female students, who themselves come from traditional backgrounds, represent several things. If a younger student is from the same tribe as one of these women, she can represent their actual home, tribe, and community. If a student was raised on a reservation but not the same one as the older female student, she might simply represent the concept of a student's reservation home. Lastly these women represent the successful transition to college for students who have left a small, insular, rural community. They are role models as individuals who were raised on the reservation and successfully integrated into college.

The older female students had initially been fearful of returning to college after hearing stories of the alienation of non–traditionally aged students. Ultimately, though, they found a level of acceptance by their younger classmates at SIPI that surprised them and pointed to a core value at the Southwestern Indian Polytechnic Institute that differs from a mainstream institution—older students being valued as elders and peers.

Native American Identity and Peer Acceptance

Younger students speak of being nervous about entering the Southwestern Indian Polytechnic Institute, but for an entirely different reason than their older female peers—for many, they have never lived or worked in a Native American milieu before. They do not know what to expect when they get to SIPI, where they will be surrounded by other Natives, and they are nervous about it. Nerves oftentimes give way at the realization that they are now in a unique locale, one in which they can explore their own racial and cultural identity, and learn about the tribal cultures of other students.

Attending SIPI can offer students the chance to learn about a previously unclaimed or unexplored cultural or racial identity. Students are at times surprised by how willing their peers are to accept them as individuals and, for those seeking to learn about their tribe's culture, to educate them. Native American identity cannot be reduced to simple matters of tribal enrollment or blood quantum, and in fact, identity can be, and is, constructed from individual and community concepts of race, ethnicity, tribal identity, tribal history, tribal membership, Certificate of Degree of Indian Blood (commonly referred to as CIB), family, fluency (or lack of fluency) in one's tribal language, traditional tribal religious beliefs, regionalism, or other factors. To reduce Native American identity to a simple marker or label does not do these complexities justice. For some students attending SIPI, who were not raised among members of their tribe, or any tribe, and who simply did not know where to start in their search for cultural knowledge, attending SIPI can effect a sort of individual ethnic renewal—a process that can include "acquisition or assertion of a new ethnic identity by . . . adding to an existing ethnic identity repertoire, or filling in a personal ethnic void" (Nagel 1997:10). Students at SIPI can incorporate that ethnic background into their larger identity for the first time and into their interactions with their peers. They are exposed to fellow students from a range of ages, and they develop a sense of their cultural identity in relation to other Natives both of their generation and older.

The Southwestern Indian Polytechnic Institute does not teach culture, per se, although many students have commented to me that they came to the school to learn about their culture. Native American language classes are limited to at most three trimesters of Navajo and a Distance Education experiment in which Choctaw was offered to SIPI students for a brief time via satellite feed from Oklahoma. Native American studies courses, including tribal law and Native American literature, are offered, but these are not classes on specific tribal cultures. SIPI does offer a setting that shares a benefit of attending TCUs: "Instead of creating an alien environment, tribal colleges are providing a neutral ground where students can be themselves without having to make choices that are detrimental to their wellbeing. Tribal colleges have created places where students can appreciate and make sense of their experiences without abandoning their culture" (Soldier 1997:3). SIPI provides the setting or context for students to meet and learn from their fellow students who share their tribal backgrounds.

The fact that SIPI's corporate culture, curriculum, and core values are not based on any one tribal culture, nor does the school promote any specific tribe's history or values, creates a context for two important developments for students. First, the lack of cultural specificity at SIPI means students get exposed to a range of different tribal cultures and histories. Through this exposure they then gain an understanding of other tribes' worldviews, value systems, and histories. From there, they can begin to conceptually place themselves within the context of a larger, intertribal Native American community and identity.

The survey questionnaire from 2002 included the questions "Has attending SIPI affected how you see yourself as a Native American? How?" This prompted some wonderfully evocative responses. "SIPI has changed my view of Native Americans. I now see a bigger spectrum, [a] wider variety of culture. I've learned much about other tribes and people," wrote a Navajo man who planned to become a visual artist. Another student wrote, "It has made me feel even better about being a Native." Attending SIPI leads to a sort of multicultural, multitribal exchange that is unlikely at either a mainstream school or a TCU that is dedicated to one tribe's culture. The bonds between students of different tribal backgrounds shape their own perceptions of a larger, more general Native American identity.

A Navajo woman in her twenties who grew up both on and off her reservation described learning about her own culture at SIPI and learning about shared Native American issues as well. She said, "I found out a lot about myself here . . . found out a lot more about my culture. A lot more about my language. And a lot more about my history. Versus going to school in the city, where you're exposed to nothing but the American way of doing things. There is a big difference between tribal law and business law. Law in general. A lot of differences. When you go into tribal things, it's a lot about customs and traditions . . . The way I grew up, it wasn't a whole lot about that." Her education was academic and social. She came to see clear distinctions between Native American and European American value systems that she had not explored before.

Another woman said that she had changed because attending SIPI had made her more open-minded about other tribes' cultural values, and that they "think different ways, they all practice their traditions different ways." While she gained an understanding of values that were shared among tribes, she was also pushed to adopt a culturally empathetic viewpoint. She learned to be sensitive to other tribes' taboos, while she also learned to honor her own tribe's rules. Attending SIPI meant, for her, a type of immersion that showed her the "big picture . . . this broad spectrum of all these other tribes." The intersections and divergences between her personal beliefs, those of her tribe, and those of other tribes fascinated her. She saw commonality, but learned also to see difference as valuable.

There is a second benefit of SIPI's lack of cultural specificity for students who are ignorant of their own tribe's history and culture. If they attend a TCU dedicated to that tribe specifically, they potentially face marginalization from their peers and the institution. (For example, one survey respondent had written, "I feel sort of dumb when people ask me easy questions about my heritage.") SIPI students can participate in their tribe's culture as much or as little as they feel comfortable with while at the school. Ignorance of their tribe's culture at SIPI does not alienate students as much as it creates an opportunity and a motivation for them to learn.

The benefits of attending an all–Native American school are not always centered around cultural exchange. It can mean, at its simplest, that students feel like they fit in. As one student wrote, "It is nice to attend class with people who look like me," and another wrote, "People feel comfortable attending school with their own kind." Feeling comfortable might not be equated with personal growth per se, but feeling they are in a safe and accepting environment might in turn make them more receptive to learning about other tribes.

Not all students saw SIPI's all–Native American student body as advantageous, as, for example, one Navajo man wrote that he felt more comfortable around people other than American Indians. A twenty-four-year-old man expressed dismay because, as a result of attending SIPI, he said he "became more aware of prejudices toward white people, which I do not like because not all white people are bad." Others felt that their peers needed to be exposed to the larger world outside their reservation and SIPI. One writer equated the two by writing, "I think they need to realize there's a bigger world out there than SIPI or their reservation." SIPI's quality as a haven can backfire, marginalizing students from the larger community beyond the gates of the school.

Robin Hale, who is enrolled with a Southwestern tribe but has more cultural experience in a different tribe, spoke of having culture shock when she first entered the school. She was near graduation and open to analyzing her experiences at the school when interviewed. Robin was raised several states away from where her tribes are located. She said she had never lived in areas with high numbers of Native Americans, and she had not participated regularly in her tribes' traditional events. Robin had worried about being accepted at SIPI by her peers. She admitted that she had been a bit of a loner when she first got to the school. Initially she was not sure where she fit, embarrassed by how little she knew of her tribal cultures. She was aware that some students attending the Southwestern Indian Polytechnic Institute rejected the Indianness of students who had been raised off their reservations and who did not actively participate in their tribe's culture; Robin, though, found acceptance with her roommates. "[I]t's been good because my roommates, they haven't teased me. They haven't said anything like that." To Robin, teasing is a way for students to mark their peers as less Native. She received more than simple acceptance, as her roommates took her under their wings and began to teach her about her culture. Teasing students is divisive and counterproductive because it serves no purpose other than to further alienate students from their culture. She said, "I have seen the other students go through that [teasing]. Where they don't know what their traditional stuff is and they're teased because of it. I think that's what really keeps them back from wanting to learn." The openness her roommates displayed in teaching her created a safe setting for her to explore her culture.

Delilah Park, an Alaskan Native, was also motivated to learn more about her tribe's culture after having witnessed her peers at SIPI participating in and celebrating their traditional cultures. Delilah did not feel the need to be accepted by her peers because, as a commuter with clear educational goals, she was not attending SIPI to create a social life. Delilah's situation was a bit different from Robin's because Delilah was not in a position to explore her culture while attending SIPI, owing to its significant distance from her tribal community. After having spent years in the company of students who were fully fluent in their cultures, she came away with a strong sense that it was time for her to learn about her own. When asked how she had changed since attending the school, she responded:

> I've become a little more interested and aware of the fact that I need to study my culture... It never really was something foremost in mind, of saying, "I really need to study my ancestry. I want to learn more about it," because I was never really exposed to any of it. Now, being here is like, so many people come into this, and they've got their traditions, and they've got their beliefs. They've got a heritage, basically. And I want that... I want to be able to develop that. I want to be able to research that. I want to find out. It's going to be difficult because of the long distance. I mean, if I was from anywhere down here, in the lower forty-eight, then I would be able to find someone, as far as an elder or a mentor that would be able to teach me some of these things and share some of these things. But the distance, I think that's going to probably be the biggest obstacle to overcome.

Like Robin and Delilah, Nancy White had a cultural epiphany through her interactions with her peers at the school. Attending the Southwestern Indian Polytechnic Institute allowed her to experience a level of deep acceptance from other Natives of her generation. At first glance, Nancy does not appear Native American. It is difficult and frustrating for her that people, especially people off campus, do not realize she is Native. In fact, she has gotten so used to it that when she first arrived at SIPI, she felt that she was not truly a part of the campus community. I asked about why she felt she did not fit in and she told me:

> It's just that period where I felt I totally didn't fit in and thought I'm never going to be like "these people." That's weird to say. Like the other students. But in the last few years I have had this transition of thought. It seemed that it was okay that I live in both worlds. It's probably better for my people, to be in both worlds. Because I have the ability to speak in settings where they may not be heard. That's powerful. To me, that's very powerful. It's heartwarming. I guess in that sense, some-

times SIPI can feel like home. There's an understanding of things that have been part of my family and my life, that non-Indian people sometimes don't get. I never related it to my Indianness, until after I came here and went, "Oh, that's where this comes from! That's my cultural script! That's what that is, right there!"

Nancy found that her peers at the school accepted her. Their acceptance allowed her to develop her identity as a Native American woman without feeling constrained by outsiders' assumptions about identity and appearance. While working with another woman on campus on a project to improve a program for SIPI students, Nancy found herself struck by the accepting tone of the conversation.

We stepped outside. She said, "I think that's fine that everybody has this opinion about this thing, but I don't think they understand that these are our people." She's talking to me like I needed to identify that, that these are our people and I have, and she has—like she has a greater, vested interest in helping our students at SIPI.

So, I guess I realize that I'm recognized by the other Indian people on campus as an Indian woman. Then my perception changed about it. And now it's weird because at that point when she said that to me, I had to look at the people on campus who weren't Native and go, "They're different." That was bizarre. I don't know if maybe that was the point when I fit in.

Nancy's experience with being accepted by her peers was life-altering. It enabled her to shift her thinking about herself and develop a fuller sense of her ethnic identity. She even came to see some of her most basic life values as deriving from her Native identity, a realization that might not have come if she had not been both immersed in an all–Native American student milieu and also freely accepted by her peers.

Acceptance by one's peers at SIPI is not guaranteed. Students can find themselves on the receiving end of a judgment that they are not Indian enough or are "too white." Whiteness can be ascribed not only if a student has light skin, but also if she was raised off her tribe's reservation, she chooses not to or does not know how to participate in traditional tribal culture, or she does not speak her tribe's language.

Language use and comprehension are often used both by Natives and non-Natives as an indicator of how assimilated into European American culture an individual is. Early into the trimester in the Contemporary Native American Issues class, we would discuss issues of identity including language. True fluency was rare. Typically, in a class of twenty students, three could claim fluency in their tribe's language, which we usually defined as being able to generate fluent speech and engage in adult conversation, including telling and understanding jokes. A few others were passively fluent (understanding most of what was said to them but not being able to respond in the Native language) or could speak at the most rudimentary level, which we likened to speaking like a toddler. The vast majority did not speak their tribe's language, and they were often frustrated that they were labeled as less Indian for that lack. A woman I spoke with expressed frustration that, because she had not been taught her tribe's traditions, she was looked down upon. She asserted that rather than label her negatively, shouldn't her choice to attend SIPI and her subsequent efforts to learn about her tribe's traditions indicate her true identity?

An Alaskan man complained that there was a lot of racism on campus directed toward students with lighter skin. He had had no previous experience with the attitude that skin tone directly correlates with cultural adherence and identity. While being called "white guy" was not a daily occurrence for him, he found that it was more common than he had anticipated. "Where I'm from, back home, everyone's got different bloodlines running through them," he noted, and then pointed out that his peers' ignorance and hostility probably derived from having been exposed to so few other cultures. A Navajo woman told me in frustration that there is a lot of self-segregation on campus, partially because of shyness, but also because of students' judging their peers' "Indianness." An Alaskan woman said other students assumed she was joking when she told them she would be attending SIPI because, she said simply, "I look too white." She was told several times that her listeners would "believe it when they saw it." That phrase is a coded way of saying not that they doubted whether she had the wherewithal to attend college, but whether she would pass muster as being "Native enough" to be accepted to attend the school. Once they saw her on campus to attend classes, she was seen as being validly Native, as approval from SIPI's admissions office was a validation of an individual's identity as Native American. In this instance, the school, as a branch of the Bureau of Indian Affairs, was viewed by students as being more credible in defining her racial and cultural identity than she was, even though—or perhaps strangely *because*—the college is a branch of the federal government.

Acceptance to the school, though, is only the first hurdle for student acceptance by their peers. The Alaskan woman described overhearing a student who had been told she was too white by another student in the dormitories. She said, "I know that there is a bias as far as the way that people view me sometimes, too. But I think that everybody's kind of gotten over that." Perhaps it was by getting to know her that her peers accepted her identity. She did note that she often gets odd, questioning looks from other students, who then ask for her tribal affiliation. Telling them is enough to stop the odd looks.

Concern about being accepted because of one's appearance was not just based on whether one looked phenotypically Native, but also on other physical characteristics. John War Horse is an older man whose body bears the results of a physical injury. It was this injury that, John admitted, made him worry that his peers would reject him. Instead, he found that students did not define him by physical limitations, but instead saw all of his facets. John, a devout Christian, developed a strong religious and social community while at SIPI. He spoke of the emotional ties he built with other students, including those ties that grew out of being accepted for his true, individual self. He made good, solid friendships that continue to this day, and he feels that he was accepted for himself, neither because of nor in spite of his injury. He was, as he told me, simply "John War Horse, SIPI student."

John includes the school's administration on his list of supportive individuals. The school made some necessary, but previously unheard of, accommodations for him. No other tribal college that he knows of had made similar ones for students with physical challenges. Those accommodations, John feels, are what tipped the balance toward his success at the school. It is both the all–Native American social setting and the support and concern of the administration that made John feel at home and helped him to succeed.

John reveled in being surrounded by other Native American people. He felt the other SIPI students made up a large, multitribal family. He appreciated the chance not only to be immersed in a Native American community, but to also be accepted for who he is. "I'm very grateful. Grateful because . . . I felt I belonged there . . . When I first came to SIPI, I was kind of scared because I had never been around so many Indians, in one place, at one school. After I broke through that initial impression, it was exciting. To go to school with your own people around . . . It wasn't too hard to build friendships. I had to prove myself to no one." A few months after I interviewed him, I ran into John at an event on the SIPI campus. He told me that he had been thinking more about my questions, and he told me a story of his first Thanksgiving dinner at SIPI. It was at that dinner, surrounded by his peers and reminded that those peers represented tribes from all over the country, that he realized that SIPI students are a family. His family.

Food and sharing meals with peers had emotional significance to Nancy White as well. She used the idiom of food to characterize her kin-like experiences at SIPI. Nancy described SIPI as being like a home to her because, just like at home, "I'm always fed here. Always fed here." Her reference to being fed highlights the meanings of food within families and communities. John L. Phillips notes that in his own research with the Cheyenne River Sioux community, "Food not only represents a connection of people to nature, but of people to people" (Phillips 2003:30). How does Nancy know she is in a family-like setting at SIPI? Because kin feed you, and when she is at SIPI, she is fed. The act of receiving food signifies her bond with the school and her peers. By feeding her, the individuals who gave her the food are indicating their acceptance of her and inviting her into their social web, their temporary SIPI family. At the same time, they are creating a reciprocal relationship where she will be expected to return the favor. For John War Horse, it is the gathering together for a shared meal—Thanksgiving no less!—where he realizes he is participating in a type of family with the other Native Americans sitting at his table. Seeing his peers gathered together for a celebratory meal marked their unity as a type of family. Darren Wingard spoke about the significance of food in his social relations. His strong friendships and constant social activities center around food. Oftentimes, socializing is initiated by individuals coming to his dormitory room and asking him if he is cooking anything. Darren uses the act of cooking for and feeding other students as a method for building ties with them. For Darren, making food for other students is an expression of his concern for his friends and dormitory neighbors. For John and Nancy, the acts of being fed and eating together metaphorically represent what a family does for its members. These kin-like ties helped them to conceptualize their emotional ties to other SIPI community members.

SIPI Is a (Metaphorical) Reservation

It is common among students, and employees, to make the metaphorical comparison of "SIPI is a reservation." To define the school as analogous to a reservation is to make a complex and subtle series of comparisons. A linguistic note—if an individual says, "SIPI is *a* reservation," she means it shares similarities with a "typical" reservation. If she says, "SIPI is *the* reservation," she is saying that it epitomizes a reservation.

Comparing SIPI to a reservation implies that the school community, much like a reservation community, is a type of extended family with shared history and cultural values. (One student summed up the nature of a reservation as: "A lot of culture. A lot of *my own* culture. Not very many people.") When students conceptualize SIPI as a reservation, they are referencing qualities of family, home, haven, but also shared cultural values and a sense of community. There are multiple subtle subtexts to the metaphor of "SIPI is a reservation." In its most positive sense, it can mean they feel like they are in their home community, surrounded by their own people, safe from an uncaring or racist non-Indian outside world. It can also be an allusion to the mutual support students share during difficult personal times. For a few students, "SIPI is a reservation" means safety from the responsibilities and rules of the outside world, defined by one student as "outside those gates." Students who compared SIPI positively to the reservation are making a reference to the strong social, cultural, religious, and familial connections found in reservation communities, the shared cultural values, and the feelings of support and acceptance they find in their home community. "SIPI is a reservation" has negative connotations, too. In its negative sense, students are referencing qualities of reservations such as boredom, high crime, gossip, and federal mismanagement.

The grounds of the Southwestern Indian Polytechnic Institute physically remind many students of a reservation. When asked why students might refer to SIPI as a reservation, one student responded immediately with, "The way it looks! I would say that. The way it looks. I know they are trying to do the improvements [on campus], granted. But it does [look] like a desert reservation. It looks like a desert reservation. It really does." Lack of funding accounts for part of the run-down quality of the school, but some students see their peers' lack of respect for the campus as a factor in its condition. I was warned away from visiting any rooms in the men's dormitory as it was described as being disturbingly ill-kept. Student litter and refusal to keep up the campus upset their peers and contributed to their negative perceptions of the campus.

A Navajo man from Canyon de Chelly saw multiple similarities between SIPI and a reservation. When asked how he would describe SIPI, he wrote, "The rez. So many similarities everywhere, but that's expected." Temptations and potential missteps are everywhere but "SIPI is good to you if you know what's up . . . It's not for everyone. You have to know yourself before you know how to live here. You meet so many similar characters here that remind you of people back home. Whatever tribe you represent, you will always find a piece of home here. Other than that, SIPI is the rez. I see the same things back home that I see here, like the alcohol containers scattered. The mentality to have fun is always switched on." This writer assumes there is a universal quality to his peers' experiences of their home communities (he also assumes that his peers come from reservations, rather than having grown up in cities). There is both comfort and dismay at the school's similarity to the reservation. There is also what he describes as the "good times" mentality that "constrains" SIPI and lends itself to alcohol bottles strewn about the campus.

Grace Nez announced that SIPI looks like the reservation because it is "so desolate." She laughed mischievously throughout her description. She told me, breaking into peals of wicked laughter:

> I mean, you see places around SIPI, like the Rio Grande, across the fence, and there's grass. It looks so nice and neat. Then you come to SIPI and it's like dirt, weeds. Buildings look kind of run-down. I mean, the only nice place on campus is the Science and Technology [building] because that's the newer area. It looked kind of like the reservation, because on the reservation, that's how things are. Things are very run-down looking. Sandy. I mean, look at their football field! It's not a field! [It's] two field goals. 'Football field.' And the track is like a tractor or something dragged a little circle around the poles. It's not really a field.

It is almost a cliché, she added playfully, having to look "over the fence to the grass. It's always greener on the other side, right?"

Employees of the Southwestern Indian Polytechnic Institute also look around the campus and proclaim it a reservation. Early in my time at SIPI and on a particularly hot summer day, I stood with another employee whom I had not yet met. We were on a cement apron that surrounds a classroom building. We were peering into the high weeds after having been warned of an increase in snake activity. She turned to me and said that SIPI really was a reservation. When I asked why, she shrugged and said, "The snakes."

Her analysis was later deemed inaccurate by another coworker, who scoffed, "SIPI isn't a reservation."

"Why not?" I asked.

"No stray dogs."

To that individual, snakes can be found anywhere, but "rez dogs" are unique to the reservation.

Grace found another similarity to the reservation in the insularity of the students. She says she depends on the Internet to keep up with the outside world since the school does not offer multiple newspapers. Students seem content to satisfy their social life entirely among their peers on campus. She found herself living on campus but socializing with friends in Albuquerque as often as she could. As her visits with them begin to wind down, and she prepares to return to SIPI, she and her friends engage in banter about her having to "return to the reservation."

The insularity of the school is emotionally satisfying to many students. Students know they will be buffered from the harshness of the world "outside those gates." "SIPI is a reservation" means that SIPI students know they are in a safe and recognizably Native American place. Being at SIPI means being safe from racism and prejudice that they might experience in the non-Indian world. Kira Thomas described SIPI as a haven because it mitigated certain social pressures she had experienced in non-Native American settings. She spoke of the relief she felt at SIPI's academic and economic standards, which allowed her breathing room while she attended. SIPI was less academically stringent than other schools. A hardworking student, she felt "[i]t was a vacation. I could still feel like I was being productive with my school work, with an A, but still have a little more free time. The pressure was off, so I could relax, and enjoy myself."

Along with the lessened academic pressures is an easing of social pressures. Wealth and very narrow, very culturally specific ideals of beauty or fashion are often used to define individuals in school, but SIPI students do not expect their peers to spend a lot of money on their clothing or cars. Intriguingly, this is in contrast to research with children on Pine Ridge Reservation, where teasing about clothing was so pronounced they became fearful of attending class (Wax and Wax 1964). Kira feels her peers share her economic background and, therefore, do not place much emphasis on wealth or European American concepts of conventional beauty. Rather, to be successful, a student simply needs to cultivate an interesting or amusing personality. Kira insists, "Funny is key. Funny is absolutely key. If you're funny, it doesn't matter what you look like. And for a large part, it didn't matter what you looked like on campus." The value placed on personality is liberating for her, providing a "vacation from self-inflicted pressure." She explained, "It did feel like there was some kind of unity like, 'We're all poor. We understand.' . . . That's the unity factor I gravitated toward, so it was nice . . . Picking on another SIPI student about . . . not having the best clothes and the best car was like picking on yourself because you're pretty much in the same position.

You would make fun of it, but you were making fun of yourself in a kind of way."

Shared life experiences and value systems, especially for those students who were raised among Native Americans, make SIPI a supportive place. Their peers not only understand their experiences, but have quite possibly experienced the same issues themselves. Needless to say, college students at mainstream institutions also support their friends in times of need. The difference here, though, is in both the amount and the level of crisis in SIPI students' lives. Poverty, ill health, violence, alcoholism, and all manner of social chaos regularly touch their lives. In order to understand the magnitude of crises (health, financial, social, familial) faced by SIPI students, it is not useful to describe the "typical" student at a mainstream school. SIPI students, and TCU students in general, come from a population in the United States with a far greater amount of health and social crisis than average. Poverty rates among most Native American tribes are extremely high (25.7 percent) compared to the general United States average poverty rate (12.4 percent) (Ogunwole 2006:12). The tribes that utilize SIPI the most, the Navajo Nation and the Pueblos, have the second and third highest rates of tribal poverty in the United States, with the average poverty rate of 37 percent for Navajos and 29.1 percent for Pueblo people (Ogunwole 2006:12).

Health statistics among Native Americans point to particularly high rates of several life-threatening illnesses. Some of the diseases that regularly affect Natives are becoming less common nowadays in the general U.S. population, such as tuberculosis. In 2005, the Native American tuberculosis rate was seven times that of European Americans and in 2006 there was an increase in cases (U.S.D.H.H.S. 2007). Type II diabetes is epidemic, diagnosed in an average of 16.5 percent of the Natives who are served by Indian Health Services, with rates of 29.3 percent in southern Arizona (NDEP 2008). If students at SIPI are not facing these issues themselves, their family and friends back home most likely are.

Even individuals who escape the ill health common in many Native American communities struggle with depression and despair. Suicide rates for Native American adolescents are more than three times the national average (APA 1999). For example, Zuni Pueblo in New Mexico had one of the highest rates of adolescent suicide among Native American youth (APA 1999). Native American women face a horrifyingly high rate of sexual assault that is more than 2.5 times the national average. The vast majority of reported assaults (86 percent) are by non-Native men (Amnesty International 2008).

Drugs, especially methamphetamine, have become commonplace on some reservations. Twenty-five percent of the babies born on the nearby San Carlos Apache Indian Reservation have tested positive for methamphetamine (Marquand 2006). Forty percent of the violent crime in Indian Country is associated with meth (NCAI 2006:2). There has been a 64 percent increase in domestic violence reported by tribal police (NCAI 2006:2).

Many students try to leave these problems behind when they come to the school. SIPI, then, can be a kind of haven for students—sometimes it provides emotional respite for them because they know they are surrounded by people who understand their problems or who have faced those same problems themselves. Other times, SIPI is an actual, physical haven from the violence they fear in their home communities. Several students—mostly male—spoke about attending SIPI as an escape from the problems, drinking, and social disorder that they were being pulled into back home. Unfortunately, while the students are away from those problems, their family members are not. A crisis at home often cannot be ignored, and many students find themselves trying to deal with family problems while they are at school. (Violence itself is not entirely left behind either. In one of the first courses I taught at SIPI, all the male students in the class had injuries on the same day—limping, bruises, black eyes, even broken ribs.)

Perhaps having peers who have shared so many of the same types of problems leads to slightly better retention of students in crisis—they know they will be emotionally supported by their peers and might not feel the need to leave school. Cody Daniels saw the supportive environment among his peers as defining a safe place, set apart from Albuquerque proper. Cody was raised on his reservation in a Midwestern tribe, and described SIPI as providing a sense of approval and support that he recognized from back home:

> So, that's ... why I feel a little bit safer, or you feel a little bit more comfortable here. Even when I stay at a friend's house over the break, we're all Indian people in the house, but then it didn't seem comfortable for some reason. I was comfortable, physically. Mentally, and maybe even socially, you could say that I felt kind of out of place. As soon as I was back here, I seem to sleep better and I wasn't real nervous. Even though these people were my good friends. It was kind of different.

It is common to hear students say that they left their reservation to avoid certain social realities—peer pressure, drinking, violence—only to find those issues arising in a similar fashion (and in some cases, they say, generated by the same people) when they arrive at SIPI, as several of the survey respondents did. Cody put a different spin on this by suggesting that students have in common certain experiences from living on reservations, and that made SIPI emotionally safer and more inviting. SIPI students can, to some degree, assume that certain cultural values, experiences, slang, and modes of interaction are both understood, and appreciated, by their peers. They are well aware that they cannot make that same assumption if they were to attend a mainstream institution.

These relationships are not derived from SIPI specifically, nor do they incorporate institutional qualities or practices. Rather, they are tied to the people and develop parallel to, not in conjunction with, the institution. Lynae Archuleta said SIPI was "homey," in large part because, to her, it resembles her tribe's reservation, a small, tight-knit Pueblo community in New Mexico where their culture, language, and religion create powerful bonds between individuals and families. For Lynae, to compare the school to her reservation is a high compliment.

> It's like, you come from a reservation, and you come here into a city, but it's like you're still in a reservation. Because of all the other Natives. We have our own little cliques and stuff like that. Like a little family . . . I guess it's just common stuff. Like little slang words or jokes. People come together when there's powwows here on campus. Everybody's all into that. I guess basketball. Basketball's like a big thing over here . . . You've got that home base, with all the Natives [at SIPI]. It's like the reservation because it's a community of Indian people, and you had the basic common stuff. Understanding of each other, because of where you come from. It's not really reservation-like but it's [a] reservation, within a city. I guess you could call it an urban Indian thing.

Ultimately for Lynae, the relationships she shared at SIPI define her experience there. These include the ties that she already shared with her sister, the connections she felt from being in an institution with a population composed mostly of Native Americans, and the encouragement she received from faculty, all of which helped her to find a place there.

The Southwestern Indian Polytechnic Institute is a reservation for Sioux student Dallas Wicke. For Dallas, a reservation is a type of haven. Dallas feels that SIPI saved him from bad choices and a wrong path in life. Dallas grew up on several reservations in the Midwest, including his own. He had family in Albuquerque, and when he decided that he wanted to change his life, that familial connection provided the means for him to leave the reservation and take the risk of attending SIPI. I asked Dallas what had motivated him to attend SIPI, and he responded, laughing at himself throughout the interview:

> It was not motivation! It was like I was telling my friends—not that I don't want to go to SIPI because . . . back at home I used to be a party animal. I used to party all the time. So if I go to SIPI, it's just a party school. So, "I'm not going there. I don't want to—I'm doing it here, why should I go there?" But one day I was desperate, you know, to move off the reservation. It would help my—help me quit drinking, help me quit partying, and all those other things. I was desperate. I was willing to take off with anybody, you know? And one day my—when I thought I was stuck on the reservation for another four months and then my aunt finally came up and asked me to move in with her. So I was like . . . She's from Albuquerque. So I'm like "Yeah! I'll go."
>
> In my mind, too, when I told her, I was thinking of getting back into school. But I thought school had already started . . . I didn't know anything, so when I moved down here, I had three days to pack up and leave. I remember that bit, so I left. When I came down here, I felt that school had started—started in about a week. So, I had one week to get all my stuff. So, I did everything, rounded everything up, and I got accepted. So, I got in and do completely fine, and then I started . . . and then I—I was sober for two months. Not drinking. And my GPA at midterm was a 3.8, and I was just so happy here, because I'd left the reservation.

Dallas sees the reservation as both his home and a source of temptation to make bad choices. He would not be able to fully redirect his life and reject his former ways if he had stayed at home. He decided to come to SIPI in an effort to change his life and leave his old patterns behind. When I asked him what characteristics helped a student to fit in at SIPI, he responded, "Someone belong or not belong? . . . Well, at least you're Indian. It's like a little reservation. People feel comfortable. When you know . . . your people [are] around you, and you can relate to them, I guess. And you know that you feel comfortable, and you know that they are going through the same things that you're going through. I think of race, racism, and how—just, how some people in the world view us sometimes. Negatively. And I think that's what brings us together at SIPI . . . But then I just see the desires that separate

SIPI Is a Reservation

each other. Separate us at SIPI." I asked him to expand on his assertion that SIPI was like a little reservation, and he said:

> You know, it's like [his home reservation]. You get in trouble with the cops, it doesn't go federal. It doesn't go state [jurisdiction]. Unless it's a serious murder. But here on campus you just get kicked out. You aren't going to jail unless something serious happens, and unless they call the cops. You know, if you're really intoxicated, call them in. But, I guess, it's kind of like that sense.
>
> Because it's free, too. I mean, people look at it as free. You get free room and board. But then when you go outside the gates, then you know you have to pay. Pay rent. It's almost like a reservation. You know, you get free hospital, free medical care. But then, when you're off the reservation, you've got to pay for medical care. You got to pay for the bills. You got to pay for the doctor who's going to do surgery on your knee, you know. So, that's what I see. [AK: Is it like home?] Yeah. It's kind of like home. Yeah, I think it's like home. Almost like home. Just different tribe groups, I guess.

Dallas explained further that students at SIPI become almost too comfortable there. He says some students eventually become fearful of leaving the school. He added that the tendency to settle into SIPI grows out of fear of going "outside the gates" and he added, "Kinda like home or the reservation."

The theme of students feeling so safe at SIPI that it leads to student dependence arose in the interview with Cody Daniels as well. Cody sees SIPI as closely resembling a reservation because of the strong emotional connections between individuals, and the sense of safety and separation from Albuquerque proper. One way that students perceive SIPI as being "the rez" was in the way that they are protected from the consequences of their own actions, as a sort of free-flight zone, a home base. Cody Daniels explained:

> It seems like students, if you're doing something wrong or if you're out raising hell or whatever, you can come back to SIPI, and once you get past the gate, you know you're safe. You just have that feeling like you're back on the reservation. You're going on and off the reservation at times. [AK: Why did they feel safe inside the gates?] Mainly because a lot of time a lot of the law enforcement agencies can't go

178   Chapter 6

onto the reservation. Here at SIPI, APD [Albuquerque Police Department] and Bernalillo County [Sheriff's Department] have jurisdiction but more than likely they [Albuquerque police] won't come on campus without Bernalillo County [sheriffs] with them. It's really weird because we're federal property and we're under the federal jurisdiction of the BIA and we're in the county of Bernalillo. That means they can respond.

The classic issue of police jurisdiction on tribal land arises here. Much like reservation lands, jurisdiction on SIPI campus is unclear and contested, implying that SIPI's federal nature is like a form of tribal sovereignty. Interestingly, Cody also points to one of SIPI's major institutional contradictions—is it part of Albuquerque, the federal government, or Indian Country?—as being confusing not just to students but to city and county government as well.

Cody reiterated the point that several other students made, which was that the people at SIPI provide psychological comfort for students. He said, "The minute you get back here, you feel comfortable. Just seems that way . . . Because you're amongst your own people. You're amongst all Native people. No matter what happens, what goes on, there's always some relationship, or correlation where whatever happens in your life . . . there's always somebody here who's been through the same thing." Cody went on to explain that after a recent series of family crises, he was heartened when several students who had experienced similar difficulties approached him to let him know that they, too, had gone through such times. As Cody made clear, the shared experiences and values allowed him both to draw comfort from his peers and to come to an understanding of the larger meaning of his experiences. He was relieved to be among peers, as "it was really different to get the perspective of it. Lot of Indians . . . believe that things happen for a reason and that there's some reason why it happened. You know you look beyond the issue and try to find out what it means and how it's going to impact you." Not only could they provide support but his peers also help him to come to an understanding of the deeper meanings of his experiences.

Sharing cultural values with other students provides Cody with a basis to evaluate his situation within a culturally familiar context. He believes that shared cultural values and shared experiences give students a sympathetic peer group in which they can find support, as if they were still in their home communities. However, being away from home did not completely alleviate the social ills students attempt to leave behind. As the following quote shows, SIPI may function as a supportive environment for students to escape problems at home. A male student in his mid-twenties explained to me:

> I was also with . . . friends that wanted to try to quit drinking, quit smoking and stuff. I mean, I shouldn't say I'm a really good role model when it comes to that stuff, because I like to go out and have fun, too. But there are some students here on campus that really do have a drinking problem.
>
> Everybody knows that one of the number one factors in Indian Country is drinking. So, here everybody has that same kind of mentality [to try to quit drinking], or they came here not only to improve their lives, but their family and their own people.

Sadly, they might have simply been leaving one maladaptive environment for another. "They know that when they come here, drinking is so prevalent . . . [yet] a lot of them say they come here to get away from it. But then again, you're also amongst a bunch of other Natives, and you get away from that problem and come to a different environment. A so-called 'college' environment and being on your own, it's more prevalent."

Institutional Support

The supportive aspects of the school are not confined to peer-to-peer interactions. The school's administration, faculty, and staff all can help shape students' images of the school as a caring and supportive environment. Several students spoke of the positive impact that faculty and staff at the Southwestern Indian Polytechnic Institute had on them. Generally, faculty and staff were described in positive terms, although negative descriptions of individuals were sometimes mentioned in order to highlight the nature of the positive relationships. Students speak of mentors who guided them through their intellectual and personal growth, and interactions with employees who supported them and shaped their experience of the school.

At a time when she was in desperate need of a change in life course and a place to live, Kira was able to attend SIPI and live on campus. In response to a question about what type of home SIPI had been, Kira at first had difficulty articulating her perspective. After several long, thoughtful pauses, she found a metaphorical description that summed up her campus experience.

She likened living at SIPI with two types of abstract kinship: the relationship one has with the parents of good friends and also the relationship that one might have with concerned stepparents. She said:

> SIPI was a good place for me. It was a comfortable—I don't want to say comfortable . . . I guess I would say it was equivalent to living in the back room of a friend's parents' house that [weren't] gonna get into your business. But that had a bunch of very stringent rules, and you knew you could break those rules because there wasn't much supervision. But you just knew you shouldn't. Because you could mess up a good thing. So, that's what it felt [like].
>
> I guess it was the same kind of relationship where it doesn't feel like, as a student, you're SIPI's priority. Even though you're SIPI's student, you're SIPI's stepchildren. You're on the back burner. Kind of 'Keep quiet. Follow the rules.' You can break the rules, but as soon as you break the rules, like a stepchild you're gonna be cut off, twice [as much]. You're gonna be punished, twice as much as a regular child of that parent would . . . But there isn't a regular student of SIPI to really compare yourself to [meaning there are no SIPI students who are equivalent to the institution's "real" children]. That's what it feels like, when you're living here on campus. If your stepparent didn't abuse you and provided, it's an okay relationship. It's an okay place to be.

Kin, or pseudokin in Kira's example, are neither suffocating nor particularly invested in the individual. Interestingly, in contrast to Kira's perception of SIPI as a type of home, when I chatted with Kira's mother, she said she did not see SIPI as a home. She told me: "No, I think it's just sort of like a home away from home back then . . . I never looked at SIPI as a home. I sort of look at SIPI as a stepping-stone, foundation to other things . . . It was just something that we passed through, when we were younger, without really planning our future. We just sort of [said], 'Okay, let's do it!' and we did it, and never thought much about it afterward. Just the fact that my husband got his skills, got a job, and decided to stay [in Albuquerque], it made a big difference in our lives." Robin Hale sees SIPI as an avenue for overcoming negative stereotypes about Natives. If someone were interested in attending SIPI, she offers, "I would say where do you want your life to lead? Do you want it to lead this way, or do you want it to lead to a better way of living, to get yourself out of that rut? So that you wouldn't be looked on as another Indian with problems."

When she was asked to sum up SIPI, Robin responded by saying, "I would say . . . the faculty and staff." For every positive example of a supportive faculty or staff member, Robin would refer obliquely to ones that were equally unhelpful or untrustworthy, in order to highlight her positive experiences. All in all, though, Robin sees SIPI as pushing her to grow and improve herself.

At one point during our interview, Lynae Archuleta made comments that equated SIPI with a type of home. I asked her to expand on those comments by asking her if SIPI was a kind of home for her, and if so, how did it fit that category. She paused to answer the question and musingly repeated, "Home." She went on to tell me: "It was good. I was safe here. That's all I can say is I was safe. I never felt like I wasn't safe at all. [AK: Physically safe?] Physically, spiritually, and mentally. Because with Natives, that's what we're really more concerned with, the spiritual realm. I really felt spiritually safe here. Because I guess, my soul was—my spirit was just calm here. It was just like, okay. Like, you felt, I guess, loved here. I don't know. My spirit was always calm here. I never felt scared. I was always calm here." Spiritual safety and emotional safety went hand in hand for Lynae. She spoke of the confidence that she gained through attending an emotionally and spiritually safe school. "I was not afraid to try something or do something. I remember going to other places, and I'd be all like, 'Ohmigosh!' [sounding nervous]. Over here, I never felt that. I was always calm here. It was a good home! In the spiritual way. It was just safe. All around, it was just safe."

Conclusion

The ties between students at SIPI help to motivate, support, and educate them. It is an important facet of the school that there are members of so many different tribes on campus. SIPI is a safe place for students to explore their identity as Natives, and their specific tribal identities and histories. Literature on Native American student success often notes the value of students having strong emotional connections to others at the school. For example, Reyhner and Eder note that "the results of a study of a successful mission school in Alaska indicated that a key factor in the school's success was that teachers and other school staff took an interest in the lives of their students" (Reyhner and Eder 1989:6). Cankdeska Cikana Community College, a TCU in North Dakota, factored the importance of family ties into their educational model, proposing that the school should act as a member of the community, respectful and supportive of students' responsibilities to their families (Rousey and Longie 2001). Terry Huffman (2003) shows that for students raised on their reservation, such as Cody, Dallas, and Lynae, college can serve to support their identity as Native Americans. Residential students can come to feel the school is a type of home (and others are equally blunt about SIPI simply serving as temporary housing during their education). At a mandatory student meeting in January 2001, a student leader exhorted her listeners to view the school as a home and take responsibility for it accordingly. She said, "Your instructors aren't going to set up fun things for you to do. This isn't their home. This is your home," to which several students responded affirmatively.

The theme of a school community acting as a surrogate, or temporary, family runs through much of the literature on early Bureau of Indian Affairs boarding schools as well. Perhaps because of the alien and lonely nature of those schools, children attending them found ways to support their emotional needs through the connections they made with their peers. In a related vein, teachers in boarding schools saw themselves as having a familial role in relation to their students. In the autobiography of Essie Burnett Horne, the authors take pains to note, "As a teacher, Essie became more of a parent figure in a constructed family of students who spent all year at the school, just as she had experienced the familial support of Haskell as a child in the school family when she was a student there" (Horne 1998:61).

In this way, too, SIPI resembles a TCU as those schools also generate discourses of relationship and kinship, as discussed in detail by Rousey and Longie (2001) in their analysis of retention at Cankdeska Cikana Community College. The authors note that the school must manage to retain and teach students who, on average, enter the school at an eighth-grade academic level and must leave at the level of a college sophomore (Rousey and Longie 2001:1495). This must be undertaken in conjunction with helping students to deal with major social upheavals including extreme poverty, unemployment, and substance abuse. The authors assert that the school personnel realized that the only way to improve retention rates is through taking a "holistic" view of students as "situated within a history, culture, and nuclear and extended family" (Rousey and Longie 2001:1496). This means to, in part, support students and their families through policies and procedures that acknowledge a student's role in their family and community. In addition, though, TCU personnel are so intimately tied to the local community that they are aware of personal problems that a student might be dealing with, even knowing if a student has died (Rousey and Longie 2001:1502–1503). This level of intimacy between schools and communities is not what SIPI students are speaking of, though. They are instead speaking of trying to create that same level of community and emotional connection, but without the benefit of an institution based in a community, nor one that sees its core role as being one of support rather than one of control and contradiction. These students are speaking about connections made, not *through* the school, but around, inside, or in spite of it.

Many of the students that I interviewed talked about being accepted by others at the school, sometimes in contrast to their expectations. Older women found themselves being treated as valued elders. Other students who feared not fitting in (such as Nancy White, John War Horse, and Robin Hale) found that they were accepted, in a way that they had not experienced outside SIPI. John, for example, found that it was his personality and values that defined him to his peers, rather than the physical challenges that make up only a part of who he is.

Nancy White made references to each of the three relationship discourses. She had family members at the school when she was young, she found acceptance as a Native American woman, and she felt that she was treated like family.

Kira Thomas framed SIPI two ways—as a place that served as a backdrop to her family's own history, which she has inherited through their stories, and as a safe haven from experiences in a European American–dominated school system that made her feel demeaned and disregarded. Kira applied kin and relational metaphors to several aspects of her experiences at the Southwestern Indian Polytechnic Institute. First, she saw a familial dynamic when she was given a place to live on campus. She also spoke of being in a set of relationships and interactions where her individual positive attributes helped her build social ties. Friendships were formed based on personality, a sense of humor, and kindness rather than being based on wealth, beauty, or race. Lastly, she felt supported by not having to overachieve as a response to racist assumptions imposed from outside her community.

For Cody Daniels, Dallas Wicke, and members of the focus group, SIPI closely resembles a reservation, for both the good and the bad. Cody and Dallas see SIPI as having the supportive and protective qualities of being on one's reservation, surrounded by kin and friends, and protected from making dramatically bad choices. Cody described his sense, like Kira Thomas, that his peers understood his experiences, as many of them had experienced the same type of events in their own lives. He knew he could turn to his fellow SIPI students and receive a receptive ear and a supportive response.

Dallas saw SIPI as not only providing a safe haven for students likely to make youthful mistakes, but also as a haven from the youthful mistakes he had made back home, prior to attending. SIPI provided him with a network of friends who shared his religious beliefs, and who encouraged him to avoid partying.

Isabella Begay, Yvonne Kee, and Althea Running did not need SIPI to fulfill the role of family in their lives. Nor did they attend SIPI with the intention of creating pseudofamilies, as they already had families. In fact, Isabella and Yvonne both said they were cautious of attending and spoke of wanting simply to be accepted by their peers. They found they were categorized as surrogate mothers/respected elders by their younger peers. While the respect they received as older women was culturally appropriate, it was unexpected. The surrogate parent role was mutually beneficial—older women were appreciated and treated with respect, and younger students, both male and female, could look to these women for advice, motivation, and emotional support.

For many students, regardless of their frustrations with the school's rules and parental attitude, SIPI provided a safe and accepting setting for them to learn about themselves, further their education, prepare for a four-year college, and escape from a potentially threatening outside world. For those students who planned to move on to a four-year institution, that safe setting also trained them to navigate through a complex and bureaucratic academic system, like those that they would face at other colleges.

7
SIPI Is What You Make It
Academics, Administration, and Working Around the System

The Southwestern Indian Polytechnic Institute is, at its most fundamental level, a community college. It shares certain qualities with other community colleges, such as the need to remediate students, small class size, and individualized attention for students from faculty and staff. Students in surveys, conversations, and interviews use the metaphors of "SIPI is a stepping-stone," "opportunity," or "what you make it," usually in reference to the possibilities offered by the institution because of its low cost and educational offerings.

Classes are typically offered from 8:00 to 4:30, and are usually 55 minutes long. College-level classes follow the typical Monday–Wednesday–Friday or Tuesday–Thursday schedule. Adult Developmental Education classes usually meet five days a week, lending support to the metaphor "SIPI is a high school." In recent years, there have been more efforts at offering evening classes but many residential students avoid them, for fear of missing dinner at the cafeteria. The classes are small, as the majority of the academic (non-technical) classrooms can hold no more than twenty-five students. Members of the campus community, especially faculty, eagerly awaited the completion of the new Science and Technology Building, assuming the classrooms would be larger than what was available in the older buildings. The classrooms in the new building are no larger than the old, and some are noticeably smaller. The state-of-the-art laboratories replaced aged and rickety portable buildings that sat in the middle of an unpaved parking lot on the far eastern edge of campus. The labs, though, only hold up to sixteen students. There is no redundancy in faculty. In Liberal Arts, for example, most classes have only one qualified instructor on campus. This means, for example, that, with only sixteen seats per science lab, there was a dramatic increase in the number of laboratory sections that each science instructor had to offer.

Students must take a minimum of four classes in order to be considered full-time, and only full-time students can live in the Lodges. All full-time students, regardless of whether they are a resident or a commuter, can eat in the cafeteria for free. If they are dropped from a class for any reason, such as excessive absences (students can miss no more than 10 percent of class hours), they run the risk of being evicted from the dormitories as well. Like a mainstream college, SIPI has a portion of students who are attending not so much for their education as for their social life. For these students, attending classes becomes the necessary step to maintain the benefit of virtually free housing rather than seeing the classes themselves as the benefit of attending. This off-kilter cost-benefit equation was brilliantly explained to me by a fellow faculty member one day as I puzzled over why some students act as if attending class is a chore. It was at SIPI that I was introduced to a term more typically applied to prison recidivism—the lure of guaranteed housing and food known as "three hots and a cot."

Accreditation, Academic Rigor, and Student Attitudes

SIPI, like its tribal college counterparts, had to find the means to secure accreditation, and like many TCUs, did so by making agreements with a local university. The agreements between schools can cover the hiring of adjuncts, transferability of classes, or as in the case of "Home College," create an alliance to assure consistency in student record keeping and course certification (Tierney 1992: 121). It is in this fashion that SIPI contracted with the University of New Mexico's Division of Continuing Education to hire adjunct instructors. These alliances can be problematic, but SIPI is able to avoid one significant hurdle faced by TCUs—that of creating an organizational structure that honors the founding tribe's cultural values while satisfying accrediting bodies (Tierney 1992). SIPI's nature as a federal installation and its intertribal identity mean that they are already designed along federally approved guidelines, and in addition, they do not need to satisfy any particular tribal culture. SIPI received the highest accreditation possible from the North Central Association, the accrediting body that the school answers to. I suggest that this is in part because SIPI does not wrestle with the same internal philosophical conflicts between tribal culture and European American college culture. The philosophical conflicts that do occur are instead between European American institutional models—community college, boarding school, federal installation, with just a bit of TCU thrown in.

The alliances built between the University of New Mexico and the Southwestern Indian Polytechnic Institute signify the validity of SIPI's course offerings to some students. Students had a positive reaction to adjunct-taught classes. Unlike students at mainstream institutions who might see adjuncts as not being "real" professors owing to their temporary status, SIPI students interpreted having adjunct instructors as further proof of the value and rigor of their education. (And it would be hard to argue that adjuncts at SIPI are "temporary" as several adjuncts taught there for years.) A woman from Naschitti, New Mexico, appreciated SIPI's small classes with "UNM and TVI teachers." Knowing that adjuncts were hired through the University of New Mexico meant, for students, that they were getting university-level instruction, rather than simply BIA or SIPI schooling.

College-Level Teaching?

The metaphor "SIPI is a high school" derives from several factors. As described earlier, it can be a reference to how students feel they are treated by the administration and how students themselves behave. It can also serve as a commentary on the level of teaching at the school, the quality of coursework expected of the students, and students' own academic efforts. Doubts about the value of their education are not unique to SIPI students as TCUs in general are also viewed by potential students with some skepticism. Native American students do not always have a positive impression of the academic expectations and requirements of tribal colleges. In William G. Tierney's research, Native American students who chose to attend a large university described their rejection of their local tribal college as based on "aspir[ing] for the best" education, and because tribal colleges were "for people who can't do real college work" (Tierney 1992:115). The TCU students he interviewed expressed concern that they were not being adequately prepared to fulfill university-level academic standards. A student told Tierney, "I'm not sure . . . if the classes here are hard enough to make you ready when you go away to a university. The classes at the university were a lot more intense. There is more information given every day" (Tierney 1992:125). SIPI students, especially those who had previously attended a four-year college, shared the concern of Tierney's informants.

SIPI students and their TCU-attending peers are concerned about how prepared they will be to enter a university. Students who were successful in their smaller, community-based school might not matriculate well, realizing that their TCU (or SIPI) instilled counterproductive values in them. Students from another Native American–serving educational institution were surprised and dismayed to realize how the lenient TCU culture they came from left them unprepared for the expectations of a university (Brown 2002).

Aware as they are that the Southwestern Indian Polytechnic Institute does not have a reputation of academic rigor, several students felt obliged to explicitly note the ways in which SIPI is, in fact, academically challenging. Michael Little spoke highly of the classes and the academic societies available to students. "I enjoy the classes. I think they are pretty quality. They're quality classes with good instructors . . . Class-wise, I like the programs. I really like the programs. They weren't here when my cousin came down here in '95." If a student who was interested in attending asked about SIPI, he would tell them, "There's lots to do. Lots of good classes, good programs, good student organizations. If they want to get involved, they can get involved with PTK [Phi Theta Kappa—the community college honor society], AISES [American Indian Science and Engineering Society], or Student Senate or anything like that. It is not a bad place. It depends on what you want to—basically the old cliché, you get out of it what you put into it." To Michael, students who, like himself, sought an academic challenge at SIPI could easily find one. Other students assert that SIPI's classes must be obviously college level because it is easy to transfer SIPI classes to universities within the state, the adjuncts are drawn from the local university, and these students can point to their own intellectual growth and effort.

Faculty Expectations and Student Responsibility

The effort (or lack thereof) that students put into their schoolwork and the expectations that instructors have for them go hand in hand. Complaints about faculty leniency are paired with complaints about students who do not take their classes seriously or who haggle for deadline extensions. Arlene Padilla described that situation at SIPI. Arlene was raised in a local pueblo and came to SIPI in her twenties. She has a gentle demeanor and she often takes it upon herself to assist students with disabilities or difficulties. Arlene's previous attendance at a university informed her view of SIPI. She values the smaller class size of SIPI, comparing it to the intimidating size of classes at the University of New Mexico. She added an interesting corollary to her comments by noting, "At SIPI, you know, small classrooms. You get helped along the way. Sometimes I think helped a little too much along the way."

She explained further that, from what she had witnessed during her time at SIPI:

> It's either done for you or not done for you at all ... like with classes here, classes that I've seen, this still feels real high schoolish ... They're always telling you when your homework is due ... that kind of stuff. And I don't like that ... I think students get caught up in that. Some, when it comes time to do something on their own, they don't know how to do it ... Scholarships and things like that. I'll find any ... scholarship and apply for it. One of the ones I went to apply for, AIHEC Student of the Year, there were only two or three of us who applied. I don't think they [other students] go out and take that initiative. They're still in that mentality of "Well, they'll tell me when I need to apply" or that "I guess if I really needed it, they'll tell me that's something I should go for" ... I think [SIPI employees] see them [students] as people who need to be told what to do. Because there's some instructors who make guidelines, "This is what we'll go by," and that's fine and all good. But then there'll be a few students who push and say, "Oh, c'mon, can I turn it in later?" or whatever, and the teacher says, "Okay." They don't see them as adults and keep them [to limits].

It appears from Arlene's comments that overmanagement of students in turn creates student dependency. Unfortunately, in her experience, students could not count on help being consistently offered.

Instructor lenience was a chief complaint of several students who describe SIPI as being like a high school. Arlene's first impression of the school was that it was geared specifically to high school students. The only information she had heard about the school prior to enrolling was regarding the campus summer programs for high school students, like Upward Bound. There was no comparable effort to advertise SIPI's college offerings.

Grace Nez felt that the combination of students' unmotivated attitude toward their schoolwork, combined with faculty lenience, lent SIPI the aura of a high school.

> Just the attitudes people have toward their high school. Like, in high school, you always had the teacher who would give you the extension on work. They'd say this paper's due here, and when that day came, there would be students who'd say, "Oh, I didn't have time to do it

and blah blah blah." They'd make up excuses. That's how I feel it is here, at SIPI, sometimes. Not too many people take it seriously. I've heard one student say that to me. They're like, I became a procrastinator here, because I always know when they say it's due, it's not going to be due. Because there's going to be a majority of students in the class saying, "I didn't have time to do it. I don't have the assignment finished." And then the instructor gives them an extension. I guess the whole—I guess that's how it feels like high school. They're given extensions. They're given extra chances. Whereas when I was at Fort Lewis, it was due this day, and it was that day or else you had a zero. That's how I felt.

Grace commented that SIPI does not feel like a "real school." I asked her to elaborate on this viewpoint. She shared Arlene's frustration with the students who do not take responsibility for their own academic success and with the faculty who indulge this irresponsible behavior. She said:

I guess it is a real school. It just doesn't feel like it to me. Just like I said, because the instructors are so lenient towards the students. They practically hold their hands and you wouldn't get that at a real college unless you made the effort. Unless you sought out your instructor and said, "I need help with this. I don't understand this. Help me understand." Whereas here someone doesn't understand something from the homework and the professor will use the whole class period just to explain something that he taught the day before, when people should've been taking notes. They should've been doing the examples. Obviously they didn't do their homework, and now we're wasting a day going over that. Whereas they could've come in on the instructor's office hours and said, "Hey, I didn't understand this. Help me with this." You know? I guess that's what makes it feel like not a real college. It feels like a school, but a high school. It just doesn't feel like a college just because of the mere fact that the students are not seeking the help when they need it. [AK: They're not taking responsibility?]

Exactly. They're not being responsible. They're not being very independent about it. If I have a problem with something, I always go find the instructor and ask them, "Hey, help me with this" or "I tried to do this problem, can you explain what I did wrong?" In my class, I've heard some of the other students say, "I don't have to do the reading. He's going to go through it all anyway." But at the same time, he's going through it all because nobody did the reading, and therefore, he answers his own questions. The students that do read the stuff try to help out but I don't know.

Even for students who enjoy the school's lenient qualities while they attend, it is not unusual for a matriculated SIPI or TCU student to regret the lax deadlines and easygoing attitudes they had previously appreciated. In one study, even students who were certain that they would recommend their TCU to friends and family as a helpful stepping-stone to a four-year college described their former faculty as too lenient (Brown 2002:67). The most common forms of leniency were in faculty not holding students to deadlines and a tendency not to cover all of the required course content (Brown 2002:67–68).

A man in his twenties from Alaska described a self-defeating process of resistance he witnessed among his peers. In their efforts to reject being controlled, he told me that, "Supposedly, some people don't want to be seen as a good student here, but I don't know if it really hurts or helps your [sense of belonging] . . . but it seems kind of like high school. People don't want to be seen as some kind of teacher's pet type of thing." If students see SIPI as an offshoot of the federal government, perhaps being a good student is seen as a form of selling out. Lomawaima (1994) described the delicate balancing act of loyalties and accommodations that students made at Chilocco Indian School so as not to get a reputation as a sellout, thereby betraying one's peers. Perhaps this is a pressure students at SIPI also feel? Students are supposed to want to excel, yet to do so could mean becoming complicit in their own repression (or as Jonah described it, becoming brainwashed).

Academically motivated students speak about the peer pressure they experience not to excel. In conversation one day, a student mentioned that his roommate asked to be reassigned because the roommate did not like that student's constant studying. AIHEC sponsors a yearly conference at which TCU students participate in a wide variety of competitions. These include events such as the Knowledge Bowl, in which students are quizzed on Native American studies topics, competitions in traditional storytelling, men's and women's basketball, and traditional hand games. The 2004 SIPI's Knowledge Bowl team complained to me and the other coach that they were being heckled by the members of the SIPI men's basketball team for "taking up room" on the bus driving them out of state to the competition. They were told that basketball was an acceptable way to represent the school and competition over academic knowledge was not.

Self-Esteem and Academic Growth

Attending SIPI changed students' life course but it also changed their self-perceptions. Their self-esteem and confidence levels increased as they were encouraged by faculty mentors and gained academic success, sometimes for the first time in their lives. They are individually encouraged and focused on in the small classes and they recognize they are more than one small cog in a very large machine. A central goal of tribal college educators is the support and validation of student intellectual effort. Tierney found that faculty at one TCU explicitly stated, "Building self-esteem is a big part of our mission to provide education to students . . . I not only teach the content of the course, but I concentrate on building their self-worth" (Tierney 1992:123).

Clayton Griego, a Pueblo man in his thirties who came to SIPI for a career shift, also speaks of acceptance at the school. He makes it clear that, unlike his younger peers, he has not needed the school to provide a home or social life, as he is married and commutes to SIPI. He attended the school with a family member, and his extended family has a long history of attending the college. Those family connections, though, are not the most important part of his experience. Rather, he spoke of the acceptance and encouragement he received from his instructors. He spoke of the confidence the faculty instilled in him, describing in detail one instructor who gave him confidence. This individual would tell Clayton that he was capable of doing whatever he wanted. Clayton went on to finish school at a university and entered into a career that required him to feel comfortable with voicing his opinions and meeting new people. He said, "If you don't participate [in classes at SIPI], you really lose out. Being able to speak up in class, and learning how to do that here, helped me at [the university]. I'm not afraid to be a part of a bigger university where I'm really a minority." He said that he would remember the instructors the most because they provided "my base for what I'm trying to do . . . Sitting with them, talking. Listening." The high level of acceptance he felt at the school made him more extroverted, which benefited him professionally. "Now I have to be able to go up and talk to people that I wouldn't normally walk up to . . . I've been able to get past being that type of Indian who just sits there, watches everything go by . . . Now I'm participating." The support and approval Clayton received during the course of his education helped prepare him to succeed in a setting that was more competitive, and less emotionally supportive, than SIPI.

It was important for students to know that they were noticed. A female student described instructors who she felt were particularly active in supporting students. Rather than viewing each student as simply one of many, as they might at a college with hundred-person classes, the instructors at SIPI are invested in each individual. "They want to know what's going on with the student if they notice a change in their performance. They talk to them about it." A student failing, especially one who previously did well, is worthy of notice, concern, and intervention. SIPI instructors share this quality with TCU instructors.

Instructors at the school focus on the individual, their skills, personality, and interests. That individualized attention means that students feel they will not simply fall through the cracks, because their instructors would seek them out to counsel them. Attending a mainstream school means being lost in the crowd, even for extremely bright and academically motivated individuals such as Michael Little. Michael had attended a large, mainstream college, and although he found the work easy, he also felt like part of a faceless horde. At SIPI, he valued being known as an individual, and said, "I like a lot of the instructors better than when I tried the University of Alaska. I was just a number there. At least here I'm getting one-on-one attention and the instructors know me by name. And by sight. They aren't, 'Oh, who are you?' They certainly know who I am."

Individualized attention in the classroom also means that students feel listened to. A young Navajo man from Greasewood, Arizona, described the interaction in the classroom as "almost one on one," and a young Navajo woman from Jeddito, Arizona, noted that "the instructors listen to you." The small class size and the personalized attention make taking the first steps of a college education safer and less intimidating. Someone who would not immediately succeed at a larger school can attend SIPI, build their academic confidence, and move onward and upward from there. Several students mentioned the goal of Harvard and Yale, in relation to SIPI, saying that the school provides the necessary first steps to set someone on the path to larger, more prestigious schools.

A graduate insisted, "If you want to know about academics for individuals, I would say, SIPI's a great place to start. Bottom line. Great place to start . . . If you want to go to Harvard, if you want to go to Yale. If you want to go to UNM. If you want to go somewhere else. Start! If you don't know what you want to do, but you know you want to go to school, start at SIPI. Take one semester. One very small step at a time." Community colleges allow students to practice the skills needed to succeed in a four-year institution, and students at the Southwestern Indian Polytechnic Institute were attuned to this. A central skill that several of them spoke of was the process of developing confidence in themselves and in their intellectual efforts.

When I asked her if she had changed as a result of attending SIPI, Lynae

Archuleta spoke of the relationships that she had with faculty while a student. These relationships were catalytic to her personal growth and construction of her identity as a student. I asked her to explain how she had changed and she told me:

> I should say I got out of my shell. I talk! I'm not as shy as I used to be when I first came here. And I have more confidence, self-confidence, in pursuing higher education. I'm not as easily put down [like if I were] at other schools, like [disparaging tone], "Oh, you're Native," and stuff like that. It's like, I'm proud!
>
> I guess it's because of the instructors that I had, like you, and stuff like that. It's you guys encouraged me to, "Hey, it's your mind . . . We're not basing [our perception of] you on your skin color." And that's what I liked when I was here.
>
> You guys went for our mind, rather than our color of skin. That's what I liked a lot. You guys encouraged us. That's the one thing that's stuck out, most of all. Over here, the instructors were pretty cool. Really encouraging.

Her relationships with faculty nurtured her, helping to shape her identity, self-confidence, and self-perception. Like Clayton, Lynae's experiences in the classroom set the stage for her later confidence in herself. She felt safe, encouraged, and valued by the faculty. The emotional support she received allowed her to develop her sense of herself as a student.

Sharing ideas, and gaining the confidence to talk about their opinions, is a benefit of attending the Southwestern Indian Polytechnic Institute. Kira Thomas saw multiple opportunities in the classroom to broaden her knowledge and understanding of Native issues:

> SIPI again is another place where you can be in a classroom, talking about contemporary Native American issues, and have the most representatives from various Indian nations across the country, and have an age range of eighteen to eighty-five, and talk about your issues. Talk about the issues in the book. Or talk about the issues laid out, yet it's coming to you slowly that you're talking about your issues, each individual's issues. You're debating and arguing about the issues stated in the book, and maybe somebody will bring in their own expertise. Which is amazing! Which will counter the book, or support the book. Realizing that this is the only place in America where this is going to happen, and it's all free!

Autumn McWright also described how she grew intellectually at SIPI. "I'm more open-minded to other things. Usually I wasn't, but somebody told me something, and I believed it. Now I have my own mind, or something. I think for myself. Before, I don't know... Issues, like the contemporary Native American issues, I was never taught that. Now... my mind's open. It's broader than it was before." Autumn is arguing that her open-mindedness stems specifically from her classes, rather than just through her exposure to peers from different tribal cultures.

In Loco Parentis in Academics and the SIPI Runaround

The attitude of *in loco parentis* is apparent at every level and in every system on the campus. It surfaces in classrooms, too. The central institutional philosophy that students need to be protected—from themselves, from others, from the outside world—plays out in expectations placed on faculty. Finding ways to guarantee respect for and adherence to the multiple belief systems of the different tribes on campus leads to some unusual pedagogical dilemmas. Some of these dilemmas are quite clearly a result of trying to honor tribal beliefs. Dissection presents one of these dilemmas. Certainly, high school and college biology and zoology instructors have found themselves having to adjust their curricula to address students' discomfort with the dissection of mammals in class. There is a similar problem at SIPI—what animals are appropriate to dissect? Not all tribes assign the same significance to a species. A student who is a member of one tribe might be profoundly disturbed to dismember an animal that is spiritually meaningless to another. I was told of administrators having to work quite hard to find an animal that was common to biology classes and easy to purchase in bulk but to which no tribe assigned any particular meaning. Frogs and toads are not an option as they have religious significance to some tribes. The solution turned out to be the staple of biology classes throughout the country—the fetal pig.

An example from my own experience also seems illustrative. Students, not faculty, are in the best position to decide how to integrate their spiritual beliefs with material taught in the classroom. An instructor cannot assume that all members of the same tribe subscribe to the same value system, nor can they assume that all students know and participate in their tribe's traditional religious beliefs. Yet at the institutional level, there is a protective attitude that the school will make those decisions for students. I saw this situation directly when I submitted an internal application for funds from a large grant SIPI had received for the teaching of science. I requested funding to purchase skull models and models of stone tools to use in the classroom. My request was denied. I was told that the funding committee was concerned students would be offended by the models. Traditional Navajo people—the majority of SIPI's student body—have taboos about handling or viewing human remains. Two individuals stated that I, as the course instructor, was obligated to guarantee that students did not come in physical or visual contact with bone models. Further, they argued that I was responsible for teaching students this taboo, regardless of whether their tribe held this belief and regardless of whether they themselves did. Eventually, I was able to purchase the items. At the beginning of each trimester, prior to using the models, I would inform students that we would be handling plastic models of bones. In the course of teaching over many years, I had only one student choose to step outside during those lessons. This is not to imply that this individual was the only student who adhered to their tribe's traditional religious beliefs. Rather, my students interpreted the material as they found appropriate, and I, their Armenian American instructor, did not have to parent them nor did I instruct them on their own cultural values.

Staff did not trust that students would or could take charge of their academic careers, and intriguingly, students trusted the staff too much to fulfill their needs. Administrative decisions betrayed both a distrust of students and a worry that if students were not kept occupied, they would sabotage themselves. An example included the very short-term decision to go to a four-day class week, with Fridays being reserved for class preparation and committee meetings. The plan was scrapped for the next trimester with little input from students or faculty. It was decided the institution was obligated to keep students busy five days a week or they would get into trouble by having three-day weekends all trimester long.

The paternalistic attitude is apparent in the process of control that one student called "the SIPI runaround." Unnecessary bureaucracy, obstructive administrators, impenetrable red tape, and the wasting of students' time all contributed to students' frustration. In response to the question of what advice she would give incoming students, Nancy White said, "Don't get discouraged initially. Because, you're going to get . . . a little bit of runaround. I used to always call it the SIPI runaround. You have to go from this person's office to have this signed and they're going to tell you to go to so-and-so's office, and that person's not going to know what you're talking about and send you to another office, and you'll end up back where you started, and you'll feel like you're not getting anywhere . . . [T]he good majority of people on this campus I think really want to see students [be] successful. I'd basically tell them not to get discouraged because it can be really discouraging." For students who preferred to actively manage their own academic career, the high level of supervision they experienced was frustrating and offensive. Richard Redgoat, a Navajo man from Shiprock, expressed his frustration with the system. He acknowledged that, in some cases, limiting the access of students to their own records might prevent unprepared students from making devastating scheduling mistakes. For students like him, the SIPI runaround was a tiresome flashback to high school. The paternalistic view was most apparent to him when he was attempting to register for classes. He said, "You're running around, back and forth on the campus everywhere just to get permission to do something. When we're registering, we come in here, see your counselor, register for the courses, . . . check your grades, and go down to the head of the Liberal Arts Department and get their permission." For Richard, the SIPI runaround was just another symptom of not being fully in control of managing his own academic career.

There are multiple ways that students' control over their educational careers is co-opted. Students are often not given copies of their own records. Faculty advisors are expected to keep all of the student's relevant materials on file. And oftentimes, they do not ask or expect students to keep copies of their own records. Even those students who wished to have copies of their records have to request them from their faculty advisor, rather than automatically receiving a copy. Students are not allowed any access to the registration database, even if it is simply to check their grades. All access to the registration and grade check functions is in the hands of staff. Students are allowed only three official transcripts per trimester and are not allowed to have additional transcripts, regardless of whether they offer to pay to offset the costs. Students become utterly dependent on their advisors, having to check in with the advisor on whether they are close to completing their courses and which courses they still need to take. Many advisors stopped giving students the list of the classes required for their academic program, assuming they would lose them. The result is that well-organized students could not plan out their schedules on their own nor could they plan particularly far into the future. They become dependent on the accuracy of their advisor's records. Students leaving SIPI to enter a university find a rather rude surprise when they arrive at the other school—they are expected to choose and register for their own classes, check their own grades, and keep track of their own academic progress. SIPI's policies that serve to maintain docility also serve to undermine students' ability to matriculate smoothly to a four-year institution.

I also regularly found that less motivated students would routinely lose or forget to update their course completion list. It was not uncommon for students to neglect to pick up an updated transcript or ask for a printout of their grades. These are self-defeating behaviors, because each faculty member has multiple advisees to keep track of, and a student who does not keep his own records might not know which classes he needs to retake or how close he actually is to graduation. Quite soon after becoming an advisor, I handed the "goldenrod" copy of a quintuplicate form to one student. She looked at me with bewilderment and said, "Is this for my [long pause] records?" as if the need to keep her own copies for her records was a delightfully foreign, but very adult, experience. Someone once told me that he felt since records are kept on Indians by so many government agencies, students do not save their records because they have come to expect that someone somewhere must have another copy of their paperwork.

Chris Clerk, an Alaskan student, expressed frustration with capricious decisions made by indifferent administrators. Chris is insightful, with a dry wit and a strong sense of the ridiculous. He is particularly frustrated not simply because of the obstacles he faces in attempting to complete administrative tasks, but worse yet, the fact that those obstacles grow out of a complete lack of awareness on the part of staff. "[I]n general, I find the school is hard to work with, a lot of red tape or whatever. A lot of having to deal with various people who hold various positions, who seem, in some ways, like they could care less about how—how things go for me. But then their decisions weigh rather heavily for what I do." Chris is not describing an administrative system that makes him feel supported. He is describing unconcerned bureaucrats whose decisions have significant ramifications on his life, but who themselves care little about the impact. Worse yet, he describes a system—a college—specifically designed to serve students as they fulfill their educational goals as being profoundly unconcerned about that exact thing.

His perceptions, and the perceptions of many students, are in direct contrast with the self-perceptions of several administrators. Over a six-month period, in informal conversations, three different administrators unequivocally asserted to me that they see themselves as advocates for students having conflicts with faculty. They did not claim to act as unbiased mediators. They saw themselves as standing up for students when dealing with unfair faculty members. This self-perception, while emotionally validating to these administrators, proposed that students and faculty have an adversarial relationship, which is patently not the case. There is a conceptual disconnect between student and administrator perceptions. The administrators posit themselves as advocating for students, but against whom? Faculty, apparently. Students saw faculty, especially their academic advisors, as acting on their behalf in opposition to an adversarial school administration.

Sometimes students simply must do things for themselves. Students who are successful academically are often successful at negotiating institutional barriers because they have to be. A common metaphor used by students is "SIPI is what you make it." Several students gave examples of ways in which they "made" the school, or rather "remade" it into a functional system for themselves. This could mean refusing to accept a refusal, or through the use of intellect and wit, reframing an interaction with an individual who represents the school's authority. Kira Thomas feels that institutionally provided opportunities come with strings attached. How, during one episode of bureaucracy, she negotiated those strings, worked her way through the school's bureaucracy, and influenced policy change all point to a student who saw SIPI as what she could make it into.

Kira provided a dramatic view of the frustrating and inconsistent red tape at SIPI through her description of her last-minute efforts to enroll and live on campus that resulted from a bureaucratic problem with her previous school. The power in this narrative is in her description of the series of impediments that she overcame. Not only that, but her efforts instigated a change in SIPI policy. She reshaped the school to fit not just her own needs but her perceptions of what SIPI could be. She described what she considered to be a fundamental characteristic of the school, an unspoken, but powerful, requirement that students remain aware of their low position in the power structure on campus.

> As a student, you can run into some very negative people. You can run into negative students—that's easy. You can run into negative employees. Your first experience, which is parking . . . and asking questions—"Where is the administration building?"—could really turn you off! If you make it past that, then going to administration and trying to apply, that could really turn you off, too. If that didn't turn you off, try the SIPI food. If that didn't turn you off, try to register for class! So, all those can get in your way. And so if you show any inkling of cockiness in any of those processes, the door's gonna shut in your face. You've got to be humble. It's like that scene in Harry Potter, where you're trying to approach the hippogriff. If you don't bow first, if you don't humble yourself first, before this magnificent creature, the creature's gonna attack you. If you show any slight inclination of overconfidence, then you're just demolished immediately.

Kira used humility tactically. If humble persistence would allow her to achieve her goals, then she would utilize that as a way to get the door to crack open. She sees the institutional power structures as both a supportive (lifting upward) and an oppressive (pushing downward) hand to illustrate the types of obstacles that students must overcome in order to succeed at the school. I asked her if the hippogriff she described was the hand holding students down that she had described earlier in our interview. "Absolutely the hand! It's gonna knock you down. It's the analogy of crabs pulling each other down. You can't immediately reach for the top. You just have to go with the flow. If someone says 'No,' that's fine. Smile and thank them. And try to knock on another door. Try to talk to somebody else. Because there are good people at SIPI. It's really hard to find them sometimes, depending on which day, what time. When you do find them, they'll help you, and SIPI can become a tool. SIPI is a tough nut to crack. If you can—if you have the persistence—you're rewarded. So, that's one of the various walls at SIPI." In this paragraph alone, Kira uses several metaphors, equating SIPI with a crab bucket, a tough nut, an oppressive hand, and a tool. Kira shows quite explicitly that, for her, SIPI can be seen through many lenses and that the school can also be what she chooses to make it.

Kira's description of her difficulty in finding employees willing to help her turned the relatively mundane problem of dealing with an unresponsive bureaucracy into a heroic challenge. She does not feel that students could simply turn their fates over to the school, as the institution is more obstructive than benevolent. It is instead a place filled with hurdles, walls, hostile peers who attempt to undermine each other (crabs in a bucket), bureaucrats, and barriers. She uses her ingenuity to leap over or dodge around the obstacles she runs into. She is so effective doing this that she even manages to help remove one of these barriers permanently by encouraging a policy change.

> But I needed a place to live. I needed a place—I needed to continue school... I said, "What can make it happen?" [An administrator] told me essentially how it's gonna run, so I took that with a friend of mine, we ran all over town, and made it happen. It all ended up one day, I heard "no" a thousand times. "No" from everybody. Even though if I took twelve hours here at campus, [due to the glitch] that I would not be able to stay in the dorms. There was no way... I can't live in the dorm. It's impossible...
>
> At that time I had the prospect of, "Oh, I can be on the street." And

I still want to keep my grades up. I was an honors student. I got to figure out a way. And it all came to me. Where do you go next? Who was the top of the top? The president of SIPI. I ran into the president of SIPI's office, and I asked [the secretary], "Can I see the president?" She said, "No, the president's gone all day." I said it's really important. She said, "No, the president's gone all day."

So, I sat outside [on the] couch, and I waited, and I came back. She said, "No, even if she does come back, she's busy." And I was like [realizing], "She's going to be back today!" That was the last day to do all the paperwork, and the last day for me to decide if I was going to disenroll... I was upset, went outside, cried. Figured it out. Came back in. The president actually happened to walk by me. And I ran into her office, past [the secretary]. And the president was like, "What's going on?" Just like a movie. I was like, "Please let me talk to you. I just need five seconds of your time. I'm a ... student." She said "Okay [to the secretary], I'll talk to her." I talked to her. I pled my case. Told her who I am, why I'm different, why I'll succeed ... and she said, "Okay." She looked at me for a long time! And she said, "Okay," and that opened the door. Made my life a lot better.

But there are other people on the route to that. I was running around. People told me get this paper from here, go back to B, get this paper from here. I ran into [an administrative assistant]. I didn't know who she was. She didn't know who I was. But she told me to sit down, and she made phone calls, so I didn't have to run around. It was amazing. Yeah ... there are some doors. But it's really hard, and you've got to sit and wait and cry and then come back again, in order to, sometimes, navigate through SIPI. Yeah, but it was worth it. SIPI is kind of a tough place.

In Kira's story there was a range of behaviors that she found herself having to manage from being actively helped to virtually ignored. These multiple modes of treatment forced her to try to find the means to understand a system that can be helpful and unhelpful at the same time, which she does by utilizing discourses of agency and self-reliance. Kira attempted to work within the chain of command. It was not until she saw that her efforts would be stymied by the bureaucratic mentality that she chose to sidestep the proper procedures and push her way in to speak directly to the president. Her brash confidence (or her panicky self-interest) allowed her to speak as a peer to the president, rather than as a child to an adult. In the process of selling her case to the president, she converted herself from faceless student to active participant in her own education and experiences at the school.

SIPI Is What You Make It

By positing the school as a resource, students acknowledged that there is a certain amount of bureaucratic labor necessary for them to maximize their time at the school. Students become quite talented at negotiating the labyrinth of bureaucratic inertia and administrative roadblocks. Many become involved in on-campus activities, participating in student government and joining campus clubs and organizations, such as Phi Theta Kappa. SIPI's many contradictions simply create opportunities for these students to mold the school into whatever they need it to be. Successful students see the ways to utilize the school to their best advantage and, with a strong end goal in mind, are able to jump the institutional hurdles that make success difficult for some of their peers.

Metaphors of agency and self-reliance were the ones most commonly used among the academically successful students that I interviewed. This is not to imply that students using discourses of family and haven were not academically successful. Simply, more of the successful students spoke of agency and self-reliance.

The metaphor "SIPI is what you make it" is particularly powerful in relation to the other metaphors used by students because it suggests the force of student will, the infinite flexibility of the institution, and a type of meta-metaphor. It is the most definitive statement of student agency.

Ultimately, making one thing into another is both the act and the goal of a metaphor. With this metaphor, though, the speakers are taking the concept of metaphor one step further. They are not simply constructing a metaphor around the school to make it less confusing by comparing it to something more easily understood. Students who see SIPI as what they make it are saying the school is a blank slate. Rather than needing to use a metaphor to make it less confusing, they are effectively arguing the school is not confusing, but simply waiting to be shaped (by them) into something.

"SIPI is what you make it" emphasizes the speaker's will, suggesting that the institution is infinitely malleable. The speaker is powerful, in that he can reconstruct the institution to satisfy his needs. Individuals using this metaphor, though, are also recognizing and revealing their awareness of their own agency. They are conscious of their act of making the school into what they want it to be. They are performing an act of self-will—they are ignoring how others see or define the school (including administrative and institutional views), they are creating a definition that feels most authentic to them, and then they are applying it.

Making SIPI into whatever they want is an act of dehistoricizing the school. They are aware of the school and its history, and are setting that knowledge aside in order to utilize the school as they see fit. In some cases, students actively ignore their families' wishes and advice in order to attend the school because they know what they are going to make it into.

Michael Little had every reason to avoid attending SIPI. All he had heard prior to attending and during visits to a cousin were tales of violence, excessive drinking, and mayhem. During his time at the school, he went through a string of roommates as several of them were expelled from the school. Yet he could see past the violence and excesses, and reframe the school in terms of what he wanted from it, and how he intended to use it. He entered the school with specific academic goals, achieved them, enjoyed his time on campus by participating in clubs and events, and graduated. To students who saw the school as a prison, Michael wanted to point out how, in the long term, restrictive rules were not relevant—"Hey, you live within the rules, you get your education, you move on, then you can live your life." Focusing too much on the frustrations of the institution diverts focus from the benefits of attending.

Some students view SIPI as a malleable resource. When they describe the school, they use metaphors of self-determination, such as "SIPI is an opportunity," "SIPI is a stepping-stone," and "SIPI is what you make it." When students see SIPI as an opportunity or as what they make it, they evaluate their experiences on the campus through the lens of their own self-will. Their interpretation of SIPI is more functional and less emotional than that of their peers who use negative metaphors. They are aware that their attendance is voluntary and they are deriving something they want from the school. For individuals who consciously choose the school as a means to fulfill their academic goals—such as attending to fulfill lower-division general education requirements—they see their choice and the school's functionality as the college's dominant characteristics.

Metaphors of self-determination indicate to a listener that students see themselves as active managers of their experiences at the school. They shape the school to fit themselves, rather than being passive objects, forced to fit into an existing structure. They are aware of control mechanisms at the school but either reject them or find ways around them. These students see their success as being a direct result of their determination, strategic thinking, and patience. Users of metaphors of self-determination are not attempting to ignore the contradictory nature of the school. Rather, these students see the institutional contradictions as creating fissures in the system into which they are able to insert their own will or agenda.

These metaphors are positive, in that they point to a sort of infinite flexibility of the institution. Yet they would not be as applicable in an organization that was functioning efficiently and effectively. An institution that is so flexible that students can truly reshape it according to their needs is an amorphous and inconsistent place. It is, though, rich with the potential to be reworked by students. In much the fashion that electricity is neither good nor bad except for how it is used (electrocution versus operating a ventilator), this metaphor suggests that SIPI, too, is neither good nor bad. Rather, it implies that students have the ultimate decision in whether SIPI is a negative place or a positive one. Students who use metaphors of "SIPI is a resource for self-determination" make the school into a positive force in their lives; therefore, it is a positive place. It was pointed out to me that my example with electricity mirrors that of the explanation of the South Pacific concept of *mana*. In fact, I routinely use electricity as a metaphor to explain *mana* to introductory anthropology students. Perhaps SIPI has an inherent power, like *mana*, that can be used for good (getting an education) or bad (partying).

Many of the students who use these metaphors also speak of having, at the time of their first arrival, specific goals for their time at the school. They emphasize their *choice* to be there and their power to make that choice. Students using this discourse do also describe moments at SIPI in which they experienced institutional oppression. Their responses to this mistreatment, as narrated to me, are to assert their independence, willpower, and ingenuity. These students' narratives show that, when dealing with unfair or inappropriate treatment, they are able to manage the situation to their benefit, using their internal resources, rather than relying on other people. They resist institutional control in subtle or creative ways, and never in ways that would endanger their opportunity to get their education.

Darren Wingard is an example of a student doing SIPI his way. Darren conceptualizes SIPI as being infinitely malleable to his purposes. He entered the school with both educational and social goals. His stories share a theme of personalizing the school by working his way around obstacles. Making SIPI what he wants requires Darren to repeatedly reclaim and redefine his only private space on campus—his dormitory room. Central to this goal are his efforts to consciously and carefully build a social network with his space at the center. He intentionally outfitted his room to be comfortable and inviting. It became an informal lounge and social hub for students. He realized that his peers acknowledged the role of his room in the social life of the dormitory when he would find individuals that he did not know showing up to visit. Darren said that students are aware that his room is a social center, and he encourages everyone to come by and hang out.

> They start knocking on doors, asking me what I'm doing, what's going on. The next thing you know, I have a room full of friends. Watching TV, playing videogames, whatnot. I already have to tell them, "Get out! Get out! It's twelve o'clock. I need to sleep!" . . . People come by all the time, all the time [to] . . . see what's going on, you know? . . . I think a lot of times it's because I have food in my room, too! Yeah, "What's up? What have you got cooking?" or whatever. But generally I'm really friendly when it comes down to living here at the dorms. I don't discriminate against anybody. I think that's one of the reasons why they like me a lot here, especially at the dorms. I like to just socialize, you know. People I don't know come to my room with other friends and introduce themselves, and they may come the next night, without their friend, and just want to hang out. Interesting, huh? And sometimes we don't—we don't say anything. I just turn on the TV and watch, TV and they're sitting in the room watching TV with me.

Darren is invested in his education, certainly, but he is also invested in creating a socially and emotionally rewarding experience for himself while he is at the school. Darren is successful in making his dormitory room a social center, in part, by subverting the control mechanisms in the dormitory. He has had to resist efforts by the dormitory matrons to "unmake" his version of SIPI. Part of the process of claiming and personalizing his room in the dormitory required that Darren also remake his individual relationships with the dormitory staff. Unlike students who passively accept the controls and petty humiliations of living in the dormitories (and who might define SIPI as a prison or a boarding school), he finds subtle ways to influence or subvert dormitory control mechanisms. While his interactions with dormitory staff are respectful, he expects it to be a mutual respect—one adult working with another.

I suggested that perhaps the staff treated him respectfully simply because they knew he was older than his classmates. He soundly rejected this suggestion:

I don't think age has anything to do with it. No. The staff thinks I'm like twenty-one. I don't know if it's because I work [on campus], or because of the fact I'm really vocal about a lot of things. Because there's a lot of issues that have happened in the past that have affected my life. Personal. That I'm really vocal, and go up the appropriate chain of command. And I do write letters to follow up. I don't know if some of the staff might be intimidated by me, because I am very vocal and I will stand up. I think they just don't want to deal with me on that level. So, I think they kind of like don't want to run into this dude, you know? [AK: They let you operate in your space?] Yes, yeah, so—and then I leave them to operate in their space and "don't cross my path and I won't cross yours" kind of thing. It's on an understood level, even though it's never been said. If I do have a problem, I know to connect, and let them know what my problems are and what issues I have. A lot of the times, they don't respond but I do have to do a lot of following up on [things]—so, I think they kind of let me alone on that because I think they just don't want to deal with me.

Darren's remaking of SIPI in his own image is partially due to his ability to use the organization's own rules as tools for achieving his own ends. He describes a range of experiences he has had in the dormitories but insists that he is usually left alone by the dormitory staff. He asserts his right to protest the behavior of dormitory staff through official channels, by working up the chain of command and documenting his complaints every step of the way. Darren's strategy is effective because he operates within the existing grievance system. By complaining through official channels and in a way that is deemed appropriate, he does not fear retaliation. The same rules that make some students feel oppressed and imprisoned allow Darren flexibility in fulfilling his goal of creating a personally satisfying social space.

The bureaucratic wheels turn, albeit slowly. Darren's success in using the institution's own rules to his benefit, such as strictly following the chain of command or referencing the student handbook, runs counter to the experiences of several focus group students. One student told the group, "You know, you do what you're supposed to do, according to the handbook. Do what you're supposed to do, but nobody follows up. They just kind of forget about you." Darren acknowledges the tendency for administrators simply to ignore his efforts, but his self-determination motivates him to continue to protest. To minimize conflict, he has come to an unspoken mutual-avoidance policy with the matrons. He approaches his interactions with dormitory staff as a client, rather than as a ward. They are like apartment managers, not prison guards. Darren creates his own version of the school by resisting control mechanisms in the dormitories and making them moot.

Darren told a story during our interview that exemplifies his ability to subvert the power structures while preserving mutual respect with the dormitory staff. He did not engage in aggressive or obviously resistant behavior, as that would have undermined his goal of maintaining his dormitory room as a social hub. Instead, his response was to effectively parry the power dynamics and the mistrust he was confronted with. He gave an example of subtly reframing the context of his interaction with an intrusive matron, thereby changing the terms of the interaction.

> So, anyway, we're in my room. We're watching TV. We're watching the *Chappelle Show*—the Chappelle videos. That's just a hilarious comedy! Dave Chappelle. Oh, it's hilarious! So, we're in there laughing. Getting really out of hand, without liquor, if you can believe that! Anyways, the matron comes in, and he's all [gruff voice] "What's going on here? You guys are really loud." He said, "If you guys are drinking, I want you guys to . . . bust out with your liquor because you're not allowed to drink." And he's looking through the room, searching for liquor. And it's like, "There's no liquor here. We're just watching the Dave Chappelle show and eating pizza."
>
> He's all like, "Humph. Well, if I hear any more noise, I'm gonna come back." I was all like, "Okay, go ahead." I was like, "You want a pizza?" He was all like [using a hesitant tone], "Okay." So, he comes back ten minutes later, just to make sure everything was . . . cool. So, he went and ate his pizza, and came and checked up on us again, and everything was fine. He finally believed us. That there was no liquor involved, just having a good time.
>
> The next day he . . . asks me, "How come you have all those people in your room, all the time? How come there's so many people in your room all the time?" I was all, "I don't know!" [While thinking], "Because you guys don't provide entertainment! Something's wrong over here!"

Darren subtly subverted the power of the institution and its representative, the dorm matron, by effecting a subtle shift in his interaction with the matron. At the outset he was viewed as a potential threat to the order of the dormitories. By remaining calm and offering the matron food, he was redefined as a gracious host. The matron saw the shift happening, hence his hesitation before accepting the food. The matron did not know how to return to the previous power dynamics, although he tried when he insisted on returning to Darren's room a few minutes after his initial visit. At the same time, Darren's friends saw him maintain his high status by shutting down the dormitory matron's opposition and by implicating the matron in his own disempowerment by sending the matron off with the food provided by Darren. He shifted the dynamic from that of matron and student (with its parental connotations) to one of arriving guest (the matron) and affable host (Darren).

Darren entered the interaction with a sense of personal power—he was in his space, with his friends, watching his video, yet he appeared passive and accepting of the matron's institutionally supported power. The matron was redefined as a guest, and a guest needs the host to grant him the right to be present in the host's space. In return for accepting the host's hospitality, the guest is in social debt to the host. Darren maintained the appearance of passivity and friendliness. He did not let it appear that he was being forced to let the matron in the room, but cheerily invited the matron to enter. If the dynamic had become hostile, the difference in power would have been reasserted. Darren was able to remake the episode, maintain his personal space (which he clearly is open to sharing by invitation, as evidenced by the dorm matron's comments about how often people come to visit), and he was able to appear to still be following the rules.

Darren Wingard's story of his interaction with the suspicious matron shows that students can maintain or claim or even steal some personal power for themselves at the school by redefining the place as being their own, after a fashion. Darren was caught in a prototypical campus dilemma—of trying to not offend a campus authority figure while attempting to maintain his independence. The matron in this story entered Darren's dorm room, which most residential students argue is their most personal and private place on campus, and subtly accused him and his friends of violating SIPI policy. If they were in fact doing so, the matron would have the right to search the room and negate Darren's privacy, a huge personal violation that is constantly threatened within the context of the dormitories. In this narrative, Darren, rather than allowing his dorm room to be violated, and rather than viewing himself as helpless and depersonalized in the interaction, is instead able to diffuse the situation in his own favor. In fact, by feeding the matron some pizza, Darren makes the matron indebted to him for his hospitality. Darren's story shows that students can shape the dynamic between themselves and unhelpful staff in order to get the results that they want, regardless of institutional hurdles.

Where Do I Belong: Academic Placement

Undergoing placement testing is a common feature of entering college for the first time. SIPI students take a battery of placement tests for reading, writing, and math skills. Students are frustrated by the placement tests not so much because they are required to take them, but the sense they get that they are being held accountable to an unclear standard, one which even those individuals grading their tests do not understand.

Steven Tsosie complained that no matter how well a student did in their course work, if they tested poorly, they were sent to remediation. Another student, Chris Clerk, from an Alaskan tribe, described a similar experience when he first entered SIPI. To Chris, the rigid application of seemingly arbitrarily constructed rules undermines the potential for student success. He complained how seemingly inaccurate placement tests were used to the exclusion of any other assessment criteria when he was placed in his classes. Worse yet, school personnel did not seem to understand their own rules. His attempts to discuss the testing criteria were met with rigid resistance, as if he were attempting to subvert the very order of the school. When he raised his objection to his advisor:

> He replied that the test was concrete. He didn't say concrete per se. He said, "This is what the test says, this is what you do." It's kind of strange how I could go through all the details of it. We actually argued for a while. I asked him, "Well, I scored ninety-nine on the test, so I take it that's not out of a hundred. So what is this?" [H]e kind of sidestepped it for a while, and then finally he's like, "I don't know."
>
> I was like, "You know, just give me a straight answer here. I'm just wondering why I'm in English 100 [college preparatory English, focusing on essay writing]." I mean, here I was, I was reading *Brave New World* the other day. Do English 100 students normally do that? . . . It's not like I'm some genius or something, but come on! . . . [I]t didn't seem like he was really trying to look into my needs or anything. He just was . . . just following the rules . . . the SIPI "this is the way it is" mentality.

Chris's frustration with the placement process was exacerbated by the fact that he was being held to a standard that seemed arbitrary to him, and apparently, also to his advisor. The fact that there was seemingly no room for discussion, nor was he allowed to simply choose the most appropriate class for himself alienated Chris at the outset of his academic career at SIPI.

Lynae Archuleta, like Steve Tsosie and Chris Clerk, also spoke to me about her distaste for the standardized placement tests. She said her initial perception was that SIPI was like a high school because of the placement tests. "I'll never forget. We had to take these tests. Placement tests. That's what I referred to as high school. The Iowa test. The ITBS test. So, that's what I thought. That's what I didn't like." Her assumption was that if students all had to take high school–level exams upon arrival, the course content could not be college-level. She also described somewhat dismissive faculty behavior during her first class, and said, "The instructors are all . . . I don't know. I guess because we were incoming freshmen it was like, 'Oh, these kids!' We could see that. The way they just gave us our syllabus and stuff, and told us what we needed to do. Instead of having us think for ourselves. That's probably what [made me think] 'Oh, high school.'" She did add at the end of the interview that SIPI was academically enlightening and she was pushed to learn and grow, personally and intellectually. But her experience at the outset of her academic career, like Chris Clerk's, was uncomfortably familiar enough that she immediately mentally constructed SIPI as being like high school.

Conclusion

The academic opportunities offered by SIPI allow students to prepare for a career, matriculate to a four-year school, and gain confidence in their intellectual and academic abilities. As many of the students pointed out, to reap the benefits of the institution required a commitment from the students themselves. Arlene Padilla worried that many of her peers were too dependent on faculty to inform them of scholarships, deadlines, and assignments. Grace Nez thought students were undermining their education by not fulfilling course requirements, and undermining their peers by demanding that class time be used to cover material they should have studied on their own. Students spoke of incidents in which they chose to subtly resist the system, such as when Darren recast himself from being a ward of the dormitory staff to the role of affable host. Kira analyzed each administrative hurdle, then adroitly hopped right over. Students who saw the academic benefits of attending SIPI typically conceptualized it in terms of the opportunities that it provided or their belief that the school is what students choose to make of it. It serves as a conduit from one life to another. They are not fighting the institution because it offers them so much, but rather they find ways to make it fit their needs and serve their own purposes.

8
SIPI Is an Opportunity
Giving Students the Chance to Dream

What should we make of the Southwestern Indian Polytechnic Institute? As an institution, it has tremendous potential. Surely, even with its current flawed system, SIPI is an educational asset to the Native American community. Any institution that promotes and provides low-cost and easily accessible postsecondary education would be. Further, there is value in creating a place where Native American students can reach their full academic potential in an environment where they feel safe, accepted, and supported.

Creating a setting where Native American students can thrive is clearly necessary, as evidenced in the extensive, and not very reassuring, literature on Native American college students. Much of the research has been on Native students' transition into and retention in college, and their engagement with the school once they are there (AIHEC 2000a; Belgarde, M. 1992; Cole and Denzine 2002; Huffman 2008; Jackson and Smith 2001; Tierney 1992). The question of why Native students succeed or fail in school, and what education for Native American students should look like (and for that matter, if it should look any different than education for other groups in the United States), has created a half-century-long, and still raging, debate.

Are Native students—from preschool to college age—helped or hindered by their cultural background (Huffman et al. 1986; Huffman 2003, 2008; Tierney 1992; Willeto 1999)? Are low rates of college attendance and retention a result of: Cultural factors such as an emphasis on communality and low levels of competitiveness (Wax 1964; Willeto 1999)? Parental guidance or its lack (Willeto 1999)? Learning style? Brain hemisphere (Chrisjohn and Peters 1986; Stellern et al. 1986)? Any potential success criteria are essentially contradictory because they are proved wrong as often as they are right.

Cultural explanations are given for both academic failure and academic success: It was long assumed that a culturally based lack of emphasis on competition undermines Native student academic success. Yet the attention to detail and communal effort necessary for participation in traditional rituals might counterbalance the effects of noncompetitiveness (Willeto 1999:10). There was a slight correlation between commitment to traditional Navajo religious beliefs and cultural values and academic success (Willeto 1999:19). Research with Sioux students has shown that traditionalism, expressed by their participation in their tribe's rituals and cultural activities, benefited them academically, although this trait had been assumed to be counterproductive to student success (Huffman et al. 1986). Other research has proven statistically that virtually none of the "standard" factors for academic success, such as grade point average and parental educational achievement, affected Sioux student success in college. But equally telling is the fact that many of the assumptions about what motivates European American students were also proven incorrect (Huffman et al. 1986). The authors of the previous study note that the focus on empirical research ill serves the goal of describing and explaining Native American students' experiences in college, and they suggest that subjective research would be more effective (Huffman et al. 1986:37). I agree. Statistical answers are too varied, they require a standardizing of student experiences that strips out any individuality, they contradict each other, and ultimately they might be made moot as Native American students are pulled more and more into the American mainstream.

Rather than reducing Native American academic success or failure, institutional fit or alienation, to a set of easily quantified but ultimately inconclusive data sets, let us do as Huffman et al.(1986) suggest: Ask students about their educational experiences. Ask them about life at their college. What is worthy of comment? What do they elide? Ask them what worked for them and what did not. Ask them to fill in the blanks that statistics and grand educational theories do not seem to be resolving. Listen to the stories they tell, the narratives they use to sum up their experiences, the metaphors they craft to define the school. SIPI students have answers, and it is now up to the leadership at the school to listen.

Asking SIPI Students

The students at the Southwestern Indian Polytechnic Institute seek to succeed at an institution that is quite confusing, owing to its inherently conflicting institutional models and philosophies. While it was not a conscious process, students at SIPI make sense of the school and their experiences there through, among other things, the use of conceptual metaphors. They compared the college to analogous systems or institutions, which in turn allowed them to come to a functional understanding of the school and its operation.

Sometimes they define the school as a controlling institution, and label SIPI a high school, a prison, or a Bureau of Indian Affairs boarding school. They might see mistrust of students, unfairly applied power from school employees, and rules that regard them as willful children. Or they might instead view the school as a caring kin network in which they are supported, encouraged, and accepted. They might feel like a member of the larger Native American community for the first time in their lives. Or students might see SIPI as a functional device they use toward achieving their own ends by knowing what they want and outwitting the system. In this case, they might label the school a stepping-stone, opportunity, or whatever they choose to make it.

In cases where a student is unable to transcend the school's bureaucracy, there might be a context-driven shift to their use of other, more negative metaphors. Students who use metaphors of "SIPI is a resource for self-determination" are not immune to institutional frustration. Kira Thomas described the school as an oppressive government hand that held people down. Renee Verde, answering a question about her favorite campus location, declared that it was the campus road because "it can take me off campus" and away from her frustrations with the institution. Steve Tsosie was excited by the opportunity to experience the cultural diversity on the campus, which he saw not just among students, but in the instructional staff as well. Yet Steve felt infantilized and demeaned by the rigid application of placement testing. Cody Daniels worried at his own Pavlovian response of being hungry on cue, and worried further about his peers' willingness to become dependent on an institution that seemed to encourage dependence. Jonah Nesbitt spoke of feeling brainwashed by accepting unreasonably constraining rules and violations of his privacy as the price he paid for a free education. All of these successful students are telling us something important about their experiences at SIPI, and if we listen carefully, they also provide answers on how to remedy the situation.

Looking Back: Seeing SIPI in Their Rearview Mirror

Making sense and moving forward at the Southwestern Indian Polytechnic Institute requires looking in four directions: looking back at what students experienced at the school; looking forward to what they expect in the future;

looking outward to successful models of federally operated postsecondary educational institutions; and looking inward, at the suggestions and advice of those individuals at the school (students, faculty, and staff) who do not currently have a voice in its operation, yet are the reason for (students) and the backbone of (faculty, staff) the college.

Students who are close to completing their schooling at SIPI, or who have graduated, take the time to reflect on the role the school has played in their lives. Whatever frustrations they might have wrestled with in their time at SIPI, completion means moving on to a brighter future, and taking several nostalgic glances backward. The opportunity to complete two years of their college education in an all-Indian environment was valuable and life-changing, and as Kira Thomas said, it is hard to turn one's back on SIPI. Even the most frustrated student—like the bright, driven young Navajo woman who spent considerable time fighting against the school's bureaucracy and infantilizing rules (many of her complaints were well founded)—told me as she was preparing to leave SIPI after graduation that she knew she would be hit with a wave of longing virtually as soon as she reached the intersection just past the school's security gates.

An older man from a Midwestern tribe is a passionate proponent of the Southwestern Indian Polytechnic Institute. He had entered the school apprehensively, and been touched by the help and support he received. He knew some students focused on the negatives of the school: "I've seen a few students complaining." Their complaints, he felt, were less about the school and more about their own attitudes. He explained that SIPI alleviates many of the pressures of daily life for students by offering virtually free classes, housing, food, and textbooks. Students are liberated from mundane concerns, and can focus exclusively on their education. "To me, SIPI was a valuable place to go to school. All your needs were met . . . It gave students the chance to dream."

What do students value? Certainly they appreciate the chance to fulfill basic college credits, but also they appreciate their exposure to new ideas and, most importantly for some, the chance to explore their cultural identity, gain confidence, and as several students said, be heard.

After attending SIPI, Dallas Wicke found himself less interested in activities that did not help him move forward or grow. "I'm not as interested [in sports] as I get older. [I'm] trying to become more academic, wiser. And so I can really learn how to live in the world. And [by] living in the world, I think of just fighting the good fight. Just living my life. Just living it, you know? Yeah, not just passing time." Academics and education at SIPI offered him a chance to move far beyond simply killing time, and it made him realize that he had a larger and more satisfying role to play in the world. "There's a purpose. And I just want to fulfill my purpose and make sure my life is getting better and better every day . . . Not because I got older, I guess just because—just the way I see things and do things in my life has changed. I came here to SIPI and I want to get better. And I want to be outspoken. I'm tired of being isolated in an area where I'm not going nowhere." Exposure to new ideas and new people opened up the possibility of taking on a new worldview and approach, one in which he is willing to speak up. The Southwestern Indian Polytechnic Institute offered students these opportunities for growth, for change, and for safety.

Looking Forward: Students' and SIPI's Future

The future of the school, at least in the eyes of many students, is unclear. Students who answered a 2002 survey question about how they saw themselves, and SIPI, in five and twenty years were quite optimistic for themselves, but in describing the school they veered between truly optimistic, cautiously hopeful, and darkly pessimistic.

A typical response was that of a nineteen-year-old Navajo woman who had been raised on the reservation and was majoring in engineering. Her vision of her own future was quite positive, seeing herself going on to the University of New Mexico for a bachelor's degree, and eventually earning a Ph.D. in physics. Her vision for the school was more cautious, and she hoped that, at the twenty-year mark, SIPI would still exist.

SIPI offered one student a glimpse into the idealized American dream. A male student in his early twenties from an Oklahoma tribe described his life five years into the future as "having a good job and a house," and he saw himself in "twenty years, married with kids and a nice house with a dog in the back going 'roof, roof!'"

A twenty-year-old woman from a Central California tribe saw her own future and that of SIPI as equally positive. She had a very specific image of the improvements that would, or should, happen at SIPI. She wrote, "In five years I see SIPI expanding in building structures and students. In twenty years I see SIPI having a new dorm building to accommodate more students. The campus will be more advanced in different technical fields."

An Alaskan Native man in his twenties was neither hopeful nor concerned. When envisioning the nature of the Southwestern Indian Polytechnic Institute in twenty years, his pragmatic response was that the school would be, "Okay, I guess probably still the same. It's still the same for many that attended twenty years ago so I don't see it changing much twenty years into the future." SIPI would not move onward and upward, in his view, as much as it would keep inexorably moving forward in time, as it had before him, and it would do so after him. Several students described a rosy, short-term future for the school in their survey responses, while ultimately assuming that SIPI would not necessarily make it twenty years into the future. A Navajo man from Fort Defiance, Arizona, wrote that he envisioned the school in five years as, "going uphill, making advances toward a better college but in twenty years, this place will be gone."

A Navajo man from Albuquerque obliquely commented on SIPI's conflicted organizational model by laying out three goals for the college. He wrote, "More efficiently, hopefully. In twenty years it probably will be a bigger institution that might have a higher status and offer four year degrees. SIPI might also have twice or triple the student population. Hopefully the school will be more set up for Native Americans as far as curriculum based or offering subjects that deal with Native Americans like Native American history." This student offers an achievable set of institutional goals: efficiency, higher status, and class offerings more closely aligned with the curricular goals of a TCU.

At the time of the first survey, the new Science and Technology Building was on the horizon, but not yet built. For some of the survey respondents, the fact that the college's future held such a prestigious addition was a sign of better things to come. A twenty-one-year-old Ho-chunk woman wrote, "I actually see it improving. I hope to see that Natives will not drink as much as they do. In twenty years I hope that it will be larger and maybe turn into a four-year college. Therefore we can receive a bachelor's degree in whatever." A Navajo man majoring in computer science summed up the optimistic attitude best, perhaps, when he wrote, "In time, SIPI will truly rock."

Cody Daniels was not optimistic that the campus will improve in appearance (he suggested that if he were to visit in twenty years, he would see the "same old, olive green ceiling tiles!"). Regardless of appearances, his relationship with the school was so profound that he expected to have a lifelong connection to it. His commitment inspired him. He said:

[W]hen I get older, I hope that I can give back to SIPI somehow. I don't know if it's maybe some kind of scholarship, or just a donation. Or maybe, maybe teach something. I plan on getting my master's. At least a master's. I don't know about a Ph.D., a doctorate, anything like that, but you know, at least a master's. Maybe I can come back and teach. You know, I can see Indian students, Indian people where I was [in life]. Maybe the choices or the challenges of Indian people will be different by then. So, I hope to give back. I want to give back or I will be giving back, somehow, to this institution.

Students feel loyalty to SIPI; they see themselves as contributing to it in the future. It is up to the institution to find viable and productive avenues for graduates to contribute their effort, intellect, and understanding of the school.

Looking Outward: Models for the Future of SIPI

The Southwestern Indian Polytechnic Institute is clearly in need of profound rethinking or a fundamental shift in institutional philosophy. The organizational structure, corporate culture, and value system of the Southwestern Indian Polytechnic Institute are in constant opposition to each other. The school's halfhearted efforts to meld a college, a federal installation, a Bureau of Indian Affairs educational facility, and a tribally sensitive organization lead to considerable confusion for students attempting to function at the school.

It is not surprising that the college is such an inelegant amalgam, founded as it was at a time of significant change in federal policy toward Native Americans. SIPI was born at the tail end of the Bureau of Indian Affairs boarding school era, a time when federal schools for Native Americans were based on a model of control and forced assimilation. At the same time, the federal government was concluding the ill-conceived and poorly executed twin policies of tribal termination and government-funded relocation of rural Native Americans to cities, where they were expected to assimilate into European American culture. For all of its educational goals, the Southwestern Indian Polytechnic Institute is still a federal facility, and the rules and principles of operation for federal facilities are standardized to fit offices, not schools. Yet SIPI seeks to fit into its presumed sorority of sister institutions—the tribally controlled colleges and universities. Efforts to mesh these systems have led to significant institutional identity crises, internal conflicts, and lawsuits. This is the setting where students are expected to fit in and move forward. It is readily apparent to researchers and teachers at SIPI that the complexities and contradictions of the institution create problems for students and staff. As students' conceptual metaphors show, there is virtually no consensus on what type of institution the Southwestern Indian Polytechnic Institute is, or what type it should be. I suggest that lessons for resolving this dilemma—or rather, tools for at least minimizing some of the conflicts—are already in place, at other federally operated postsecondary educational institutions (such as the service academies), TCUs, and in the design of other, successful Native-serving institutions.

There are good models out there, but these models cannot simply be copied from whole cloth. Rather, SIPI needs to be fundamentally reconceived, from the absolute ground up, and "rebuilt" into a new, more functional, more cohesive organization. This requires a complete overhaul of the school's most central philosophies—a redrawing and redefining of its (pardon the reification) idea of itself. But simply saying "We are this" does not make it so, and any positive change requires looking beyond the institution to models of success, and to outsider input. And simply adopting practices that were successful elsewhere—such as the modified personnel system that makes it easier to hire and fire—without drastically and fundamentally changing the culture of the institution just leads to failure. SIPI does not need new rules; SIPI needs new thinking.

Looking Inward: Listening to the Silenced

The people who understand the Southwestern Indian Polytechnic Institute the best are those with the least voice in its operation. The lower links on the chain of command (including students, who are virtually off the chain) have no right to contribute because, as a federal installation, hierarchy is preeminent. Unfortunately, this silencing means that the people who can make the best contribution are effectively shut out of the conversation. It requires a seismic shift in institutional thinking at SIPI—soliciting and actively using the suggestions of the individuals who are most affected by administrative decisions. This means listening to suggestions the institution's representatives might not want to hear. Harder still, it means acting on those suggestions.

TCUs are shaped around the idea that faculty and staff have as much of a contribution to make at the school as their top administrators. SIPI does not operate this way, but I argue that it should. Who better to evaluate the policies in the dormitories than the students who live there? Who better to gauge if a policy is working for retention than faculty in the classroom? I am not arguing for the administration to simply throw their hands up and pass the keys over to the students. Certainly students whose goal it is to party and avoid classes are not the most reliable or productive analysts. Yet even the halfhearted students can offer a perspective on the school. And sadly, the most passionately motivated students are an invaluable asset, yet they fear speaking up.

How effectively will the institution retain the students who can be nurtured to succeed, but who feel distrusted and watched? Students recognize the institutional mistrust with which they are viewed. Some deserve it; many do not. Use legal recourse to punish those students who do break the rules, or worse, the law, but do not make good students feel as if the administration and security personnel are lying in wait, hoping to catch them out. Perhaps this means limiting enrollment. Or as several faculty members have suggested over the years, instituting basic admissions requirements. Unlike HINU, which requires minimum ACT and SAT scores for applicants, SIPI students need not even take these exams to apply for admission. Another faculty suggestion has been to treat attendance at the school as a type of fellowship—if a student maintains his grades and behaves appropriately, he maintains his fellowship (i.e., he keeps his tuition-free status). Only students who fail would be penalized by being charged for their future schooling.

SIPI is a tremendous asset to Native Americans who want a college education. Yet as its policies become more and more outdated, and its students remain as alienated as they have been over the course of almost forty years, there has to be some power sharing. The future of SIPI is by no means hopeless, but if the institutional leadership wants to transcend forty years of students feeling infantilized, and forty years of adversarial relations with the very people they are supposed to be serving, some dramatic and respectful changes must take place.

The Southwestern Indian Polytechnic Institute has attracted Native American people young, and older, to its doors for almost forty years. The school has a tremendous opportunity to contribute to the larger Native American community, to be a force for positive educational change in Indian Country. SIPI's students—smart, articulate, reflective, and striving—know where the school succeeds or fails. They are the residents of the school, the consumers of the classes, and ultimately the ones who outwit and overcome the contradictory and confusing system—perhaps it is time now to let them speak, so that, as the student wrote, "In time, SIPI will truly rock."

Appendix
Studying the Southwestern Indian Polytechnic Institute

The Southwestern Indian Polytechnic Institute underwent multiple changes during my time there, and the school continues to do so. The descriptions of the campus, the school's organizational structure, and the policies outlined in this book refer to what was in place for the majority of my time at the college. Changes, though, occurred throughout the campus and at all levels of the organization. Presidents came and went, departments were reorganized, student services offerings expanded and contracted again, fees were discussed and then imposed, parts of the physical plant were greatly improved while others aged ungracefully, and course offerings expanded and adjusted to changing student needs. My descriptions are true to what was the norm during the majority of my time at SIPI. Any specific changes enacted during the research period that affected student experiences are described as belonging to that period specifically or as being new. The institutional dilemmas of meshing organizational models still have not been resolved, nor am I aware of any institutional effort to recognize or address the issue.

Methodology and Data

My earliest research interest at SIPI was to examine its role as a national Native American community center. I had long been interested in the sustained impact of unrecognized genocides on the cultures of communities that had experienced them. This stemmed, in no small part, from my interest in the impact of genocide on Armenian-Americans, and I wondered about other small cultural groups. I began to think that SIPI served to nationally unite young Native Americans through bonds built at the school. In conversation, though, students quickly rejected the idea, with some telling me, "I won't be friends with these people after I leave here." Examining the issue more deeply, I began to see that students, even the most academically successful ones, typically have a conflicted relationship with the institution. I began to question the meaning of SIPI in general and its value as a place, both physically and conceptually. Students, I assumed, were making a personally and socially meaningful place for themselves at the school, whether it was a national community center or not. I began to ask questions designed to elicit responses about their views of and experiences at the school.

Instead of seeing students create ways to lay claim to the campus, I noticed two trends begin to emerge: First, a general view of the experience of attending SIPI began to take shape, and second, students were using a consistent set of metaphors to describe the school. These metaphors fell into one of three categories: metaphors of control, of kinship, and of self-determination. Student narratives created a type of story of SIPI—daily life, what they learned academically and about themselves, grappling with the school bureaucracy, the development of friendships and mentoring relationships, the way they experienced SIPI—and all of these were shot through with metaphorical descriptions of life at the school.

There are five components to the research for this book. Each component provides a different window into students' perceptions of the school and their experiences there. The first phase of research, which I undertook over the course of several years, was participant observation on campus, with a focus on important campus events and daily in-class or on-campus interactions. Conversations with students and impromptu in-class discussions raised my initial awareness of the range and usage of conceptual metaphors. I was a member of the SIPI community, not simply a clinically observing outsider. As a result, many of my insights are based on my long-standing presence and participation at the school.

Second, I analyzed institutionally produced texts for insight into how SIPI's leadership presented the school to potential students, local organizations, and Indian Country in general, and how it positioned itself in relation to other academic institutions. Much of SIPI's textual material was designed and printed in-house, until the Graphic Arts Program was shuttered. For most of the school's history, SIPI had an active print shop staffed by instructors and occupational technology students. The campus print shop provided printing services for the school, and many of the school's brochures, catalogs, and manuals were printed there. SIPI's textual self-representation must walk a fine line between acknowledging its nature as a federal Bureau of Indian Affairs institution while asserting its kinship with tribally controlled colleges and universities.

For the third portion of the research, I conducted two surveys, two years apart, with SIPI students on campus. The surveys helped me to shape my research questions. It was in the survey responses that student perceptions of the school began to become clear. The research goals of the two surveys were significantly different. Students who responded to the survey questionnaires hailed from more than fifty different tribes in the contiguous United States and Alaska.

I conducted the first survey in the spring trimester of 2002 as a preliminary look at student perceptions of the Southwestern Indian Polytechnic Institute and their choice to attend. The sample was intentionally small, as I was simply looking for a snapshot of student attitudes. Forty students participated in the 2002 survey. The questionnaire included questions on why students chose to attend SIPI specifically, where they saw themselves in five and twenty years, and how they envisioned the school in five and twenty years. Because, at the time of the first survey, I was curious whether SIPI acted as a sort of national inter-tribal community center by drawing students from all over the country, I also asked if attending SIPI had an impact on their identity as Native Americans, and if so, how it did so. The tribal statistics for the survey were fairly representative of the school's overall demographics. Twenty-one students listed themselves as Navajo, six were Pueblo, one was both Navajo and Pueblo, one was an Alaskan Native, seven were from Midwestern tribes, and four were from California–Pacific Northwest tribes. The gender ratio was fairly balanced, as twenty-two women and eighteen men responded. The average age of the participants was twenty-two years, with women averaging slightly below that and men a few months above.

The majority of students who responded to the 2002 survey questionnaire were majoring in liberal arts. This can be attributed in large part to the fact that I conducted these surveys in classes in the General Education Department. This was an intentional choice. The General Education Department serves students from all majors, including offering classes required for other majors. The Occupational Technologies and Business Technologies Departments rarely have non-majors in their classes. Twenty-five respondents to the first survey questionnaire described themselves as students in the Liberal Arts Department. Another five respondents named the majors they were planning to enter after matriculating to a four-year college, implying that they, too, were liberal arts students. Seven students were in a technical degree program, and one listed business administration as his major. One student gave an invalid response, and one did not list a major.

In 2004, I conducted another survey, with equal representation from liberal arts, adult developmental education, occupational technologies, and business technologies. The main research focus of the second survey questionnaire was the significance of SIPI as a place. Members of the SIPI community—students, faculty, staff—routinely use rhetoric of "this place" when talking about SIPI (typically when describing a negative aspect of the school). After the preliminary survey, and after speaking with a few students who roundly dismissed the concept of SIPI as a national community center, I began to question what meaning students were ascribing to the school.

One hundred and six students responded to the survey. The total number of tribal affiliations, though, exceeded that number as sixteen students overall listed themselves as belonging to two or more tribes. Federal rules require that an individual officially register with only one tribe, but political designation does not preclude Indian people from feeling culturally and socially affiliated with other tribes represented in their family tree. Navajo students made up the vast majority of respondents, as fifty students described themselves as entirely Navajo. Another five students described themselves as a mix of Navajo and another tribe (four of the five listed a local Pueblo as the other tribe). Twenty students named Pueblo tribes, with eight of those students describing themselves as having more than one tribal affiliation. Sixteen students came from Midwestern tribes, and fourteen of these students were Sioux. Surprisingly, only one student listed himself as Cherokee, although, this could reflect that the majority of Cherokee SIPI students are enrolled through Distance Education rather than attending classes on campus. Three students listed Alaskan tribal affiliations and four were from West Coast tribes. There were five students from Great Basin and Plateau region tribes (Colorado, Utah, and Wyoming).

Sixty respondents were female, forty-two were male, and four neglected to include gender information. Of the individuals who responded with both age and gender, the average age for the respondents was twenty-three years old, with men averaging a few months older than women. When asked which department they were enrolled in, unfortunately, twenty-four students left the answer blank. By looking at the class in which they participated in the survey (as some classes are specific to a major department), I was able to assign fifteen to a department. Twenty-one students were in the ADE Department. Twenty-seven were majoring in the Business Technologies Department. Nineteen were liberal arts majors. Thirty students were occupational technologies majors.

The fourth component of the research for this book was composed of intensive interviews with eight students in 2001 and eighteen students in 2004. I interviewed eleven men and fourteen women (I interviewed one individual twice, in 2001 and in 2004, for a broader view of the school—while that person was attending and in retrospect.) Three of the interview participants also participated in the focus group. One interview tape was so badly damaged that I got only very limited data from the interview. The interviews lasted at least an hour and focused around my request that they "tell me about SIPI." All students who participated in interviews and the focus group were academically successful by the standards of the institution: They maintained a grade point average (GPA) above that of probation levels (2.0), graduated within three years, or left prior to graduation in order to matriculate to a four-year institution. Nine of the students were exclusively commuters, sixteen were exclusively residents of the school, and three students (two women and one man) had lived both on and off campus while attending SIPI. Commuters were fairly evenly split along gender lines, with five women and four men. The students who participated in the interviews volunteered to do so and, I was told later, mentioned it to some of their peers who, in turn, allowed me to interview them. I noticed that students at SIPI were interested in talking about the school and having their opinions heard. Other than the student body president, there are no official channels for students to voice their opinions to the administration. One of SIPI's recent presidents did implement an open-door policy in which students were encouraged to drop by and express their concerns.

The students who participated in the interviews are all academically successful, but beyond that, their similarities stopped. Some lived exclusively on campus, others had never lived on campus, and yet others had moved on and off campus. There was more than a thirty-year age difference between the oldest and the youngest participants.

The students who participated in the research have all been assigned pseudonyms. Seven of the interview participants created their own pseudonyms. I used a random name generator for the others. Any similarity to an individual's real name, whether they are affiliated with SIPI or not, is purely accidental. I was playfully warned by a few people to watch out for a few Navajo pseudonyms that are actually punning, joke names. Indian Country is small, and SIPI is even smaller. For that reason, I have intentionally obscured their tribal affiliations for the majority of non-Navajo students. I have retained tribal designations for particularly large tribes (such as the Navajo Nation) or used a more general term that can specify several related tribes (such as the term "Pueblo" or "Sioux"). The more distant the tribe from the Southwestern United States, usually the fewer the students from that tribe. Ascribing specific tribal identities to interview participants, then, runs the risk of exposing the identities of students from small tribes. In cases where I have intentionally obscured a tribe, I have usually done so with general regional terms such as "a Midwestern tribe." This is meant to describe where a tribe is located in the current day, and makes no statement about historical locations. In some cases, in the quest for anonymity I have blurred an individual's personal history if that history is particularly unusual, as long as it does not change the meaning of their statements. My first concern has been to preserve the anonymity of the students who spoke with me. The ease with which members of small tribal communities can identify each other was made clear to me one day when a student showed me a dissertation he had checked out of a university library. The participants in that study had been given alphanumeric codes to replace their names. He pointed to the description of one individual and told me that this was a close relative, and that he had figured it out by piecing together the data supplied about the individual. Whether the student was accurate or not—and I believed that he was, in fact, correct—it made me quite conscious of the issue of anonymity in a community as small as the Southwestern Indian Polytechnic Institute.

The fifth and final component of the research for this book was a focus group that met early in 2005. There were six participants in all. Three members of the focus group had already participated in interviews, and the other three were new to the research. I asked focus group participants to comment on the discourses that arose during interviews and to raise any issues they found of interest. There were three men and three women, all of whom were close to completing their time at SIPI and all of whom lived on campus. The demographics of the focus group were fairly representative of the school, with two Navajo students, two Pueblo students, one student from a Midwestern tribe and one from a Western tribe. The students in the focus group were (pseudonyms) Brett Mann (Pueblo), Cecilia Ervin (Navajo), Jonah Nesbitt (Western tribe), Althea Running (Midwestern tribe), Renee Verde (Navajo), and Autumn McWright (Pueblo).

The peer-to-peer conversation in the focus group was helpful for understanding student perceptions of their experiences at the school. They were also helpful in their willingness to analyze discourses and metaphors commonly used by their peers. They also contributed a tremendous amount to the research, and provided insight to the school. The five phases of research provided me with an invaluable view into students' perceptions of the Southwestern Indian Polytechnic Institute and their experiences at the school.

Works Cited

Adams, David Wallace
1995   Education for Extinction: American Indians and the Boarding School Experience, 1875–1928. Lawrence, KS: University of Kansas Press.

Albuquerque Journal
1997   West Side Slashing Suspect Arrested. January 24: 1.
2001   Culture Shock 101 Not Required at SIPI. Editorial, Albuquerque Journal. June 21: A10.
2006   Man Charged with Sexual Assault. Journal Staff Report. September 26: 2.

American Indian Higher Education Consortium
1998   What Makes Tribal Colleges Unique? Prepared in conjunction with the Institute for Higher Education Policy and the Sallie Mae Education Institute. Alexandria, VA: AIHEC.
1999   Tribal Colleges: An Introduction. Prepared in conjunction with the Institute for Higher Education Policy and the Sallie Mae Education Institute. Alexandria, VA: AIHEC.
2000a   Creating Role Models for Change: A Survey of Tribal College Graduates. Prepared in conjunction with the Institute for Higher Education Policy and the Sallie Mae Education Institute. Alexandria, VA: AIHEC.
2000b   Tribal College Contributions to Local Economic Development. The Institute of Higher Education Policy. February 2000. Pp. 1–41. Alexandria, VA: AIHEC.
2001   Building Strong Communities: Tribal Colleges as Engaged Institutions. Prepared in conjunction with the Institute for Higher Education Policy. Alexandria, VA: AIHEC.

2002   The History Timeline. *In* Tribal College Journal of American Indian Higher Education. 14(2):43–44.
2005   AIHEC AIMS Fact Book Highlights 2005. Electronic document, http://www.aihec.org/resources/documents/AIHEC_AIMS_2005FactBook_Highlights.pdf, accessed February 23, 2009.

American Psychological Association
1999   APA Testimony on Suicide: Suicide: A Crisis Within the American Indian and Alaskan Native Community. APA Online Public Policy Office. Submitted to U.S. Senate Committee on Indian Affairs Hearing on Native American Youth Activity and Initiatives. Electronic document, http://www.apa.org/ppo/issues/psuicnat.html, accessed March 14, 2009.

Amnesty International
2008   Maze of Injustice: The Failure to Protect Indigenous Women from Sexual Violence in the U.S.A. Electronic document, http://www.amnestyusa.org/violence-against-women/maze-of-injustice/background-on-maze-of-injustice/page.do?id=1021170, accessed March 24, 2009.

Archuleta, Margaret, Brenda J. Child, and K. Tsianina Lomawaima
2000   Away from Home: American Indian Boarding School Experiences: 1879–2000. Phoenix: The Heard Museum.

Armijo, Barbara
2005a   Union: SIPI Layoffs Unfair. Albuquerque Journal West Side Edition. March 31: 1–2.
2005b   SIPI Driving Range Costly. Albuquerque Journal, April 2: 1–3.
2005c   SIPI Considered Partial Closure. Albuquerque Journal, April 5: 1–2.
2005d   SIPI Replies to Union on Layoffs. Albuquerque Journal, April 22: 1–2.

Asbury, C. H.
1916   Response to Letter from Malcolm McDowell. In the Ayer Collection at the Newberry Library, Chicago.

Associated Press
2000   American Indian Colleges Offer a Stepping Stone to Mainstream Schools. Community College Week. 13(2):17.

Barker, Debra K. S.
1998   Kill the Indian, Save the Child: Cultural Genocide and the Boarding School. *In* American Indian Studies: An Interdisciplinary Approach to Contemporary Issues. Dane Morrison, ed. Pp. 47–68. New York: Peter Lang.

Bauman, Kurt J., and Nikki L. Graf
2003   Educational Attainment: 2000 (Census 2000 Brief). August 2003. U.S. Department of Commerce. Economics and Statistics Administration.

U.S. Census Bureau. C2KBR-24. Electronic document, http://www.census2010.gov/prod/2003pubs/c2kbr-24.pdf, accessed February 24, 2009.

Belgarde, Mary Jiron
1992   The Performance and Persistence of American Indian Undergraduate Students at Stanford University. Unpublished dissertation, School of Education, Stanford University.

Belgarde, W. Larry
1993   Indian Control and the Management of Dependencies: The Case of Tribal Community Colleges. Unpublished dissertation, School of Education, Stanford University.

Bentham, Jeremy
1791   Panopticon, or, The inspection-house: containing the idea of a new principle of construction applicable to any sort of establishment, in which persons of any description are to be kept under inspection: and in particular to penitentiary-houses, prisons, houses of industry ... and schools: with a plan of management adapted to the principle. Dublin: T. Byrne.

Blanchard, Kendall
2001   American Indian Life and the 21st-Century University: The "Playful Worldview" and Its Lessons for Leadership in Higher Education. *In* Anthropologists and Indians in the New South. Rachel Bonney and J. Anthony Paredes, eds. Foreword by Raymond J. Fogelson. Pp.203–213. Tuscaloosa: University of Alabama Press.

Boyer, Ernest
2002   Defying the Odds: Tribal Colleges Conquer Skepticism but Still Face Persistent Challenges. Tribal College Journal. 14(2):13–18.

Briseno, Elaine
2003   SIPI Building Opens. Albuquerque Journal West Side edition, September 19: 1.

Brown, Donna
2002   The Perceptions of Selected Tribal College Transfer Students Attending the University of North Dakota. Unpublished dissertation, Department of Educational Leadership, University of North Dakota.

Carnegie Foundation for the Advancement of Teaching
1989   Tribal Colleges: Shaping the Future of Native America, A Special Report. With a Foreword by Ernest L. Boyer. Lawrenceville, NJ: Princeton University Press.

Carney, Cary Michael
1999   Native American Higher Education in the United States. New Brunswick, NJ: Transaction Publishers.

Chavis, Ben
1999   Off-Reservation Boarding High School Teachers: How Are They Perceived by Former American Indian Students? Social Science Journal. 36(1):33–45.

Child, Brenda
1998   Boarding School Seasons: American Indian Families, 1900–1940. Lincoln: University of Nebraska Press.

Chrisjohn, Roland D., and Michael Peters
1986   Right-Brained Indian: Fact or Fiction? Journal of American Indian Education. 25(2):1–7.

Cobb, Amanda J.
2000   Listening to Our Grandmothers' Stories: The Bloomfield Academy for Chickasaw Females, 1852–1949. Lincoln: University of Nebraska Press.

Coggeshall, C. T.
1916   Response to Letter from Malcolm McDowell. In the Ayer Collection at the Newberry Library, Chicago, IL.

Cole, James S., and Gypsy M. Denzine
2002   Comparing the Academic Engagement of American Indian and White College Students. Journal of American Indian Education. 41(1):19–34.

Community College Weekly
2000   American Indian Colleges Offer a Stepping Stone to Mainstream Schools. Community College Weekly. 13:2.

Cremin, Lawrence A.
1977   Traditions of American Education. New York: Basic Books.

Davis, Jerry
1998   From Termination to Self-Determination: American Indians and Alaska Natives in Higher Education. Unpublished dissertation, Department of History, University of New Mexico.

Dehyle, Donna
1992   Constructing Failure and Maintaining Cultural Identity: Navajo and Ute School Leavers. Journal of American Indian Education. 31(2):24–47.

Diné College
2001   General Catalog. Tsaile, New Mexico: Diné College.

Eubanks, Phillip
1999   The Story of Conceptual Metaphor: What Motivates Metaphoric Mapping? *In* Poetics Today. 20(3):419–442.
2000   A War of Words in the Discourse of Trade: The Rhetorical Constitution of Metaphor. Carbondale and Edwardsville: Southern Illinois University Press.

Fernandez, James
1974 The Mission of Metaphor in Expressive Culture. *In* Cultural Anthropology. 15(2):119–145.

Foucault, Michel
1977 Discipline and Punish: The Birth of the Prison. Translated from the French by Alan Sheridan. London: Penguin Books.

Garrod, Andrew, and Colleen Larimore
1997 First Person, First Peoples: Native American College Graduates Tell Their Life Stories. Foreword by Louise Erdrich. Ithaca: Cornell University Press.

Gilbert, W. Sakiestewa
2000 Bridging the Gap Between High School and College. Journal of American Indian Education. 39(3):36–58.

Harbert, Nancy
1996 Vocational School SIPI Marks 25th Year. Albuquerque Journal, September 13: B2.

Hoikkala, Paivi
1998 The Hearts of Nations: American Indian Woman in the Twentieth Century." *In* Indians in American History: An Introduction. Second edition. Frederick E. Hoxie and Peter Iverson, eds. Pp. 253–276. Wheeling, IL: Harland Davidson, Inc.

Horne, Essie Burnett, and Sally McBeth
1998 Essie's Story: The Life and Legacy of a Shoshone Teacher. Lincoln: University of Nebraska Press.

Hoxie, Frederick E.
1998 The Curious Story of Reformers and American Indians. *In* Indians in American History: An Introduction. Second edition. Frederick E. Hoxie and Peter Iverson, eds. Pp. 177–197. Wheeling, IL: Harland Davidson, Inc.

Huffman, Terry
2003 A Comparison of Personal Assessments of the College Experience Among Reservation and Nonreservation American Indian Students. Journal of American Indian Education. 42(2):1–16.
2008 American Indian Higher Educational Experiences: Cultural Visions and Personal Journeys. Peter Lang: New York.

Huffman, Terry, Maurice L. Sill, and Martin Brokenleg
1986 College Achievement Among Sioux and White South Dakota Students. Journal of American Indian Education. 25(2):32–38.

Hurd, Hilary
2000 Staying Power: Colleges Work to Improve Retention Rates. *In* Black Issues in Higher Education. 17(18):42.

Institute of American Indian Arts
2007   President's Report. Electronic document, http://www.iaia.edu/documents/PresReportFY07Final.pdf, accessed March 20, 2009.

Jackson, Aaron P., and Steven A. Smith
2001   Postsecondary Transitions Among Navajo Indians. Journal of American Indian Education. 40(2):28–47.

Jones, Jeff
1998   SIPI Student Assaulted: Two Women Arrested in Dorm Beating. Albuquerque Journal. April 3: C2.

Juneau, Stan
2001   Indian Education for All: A History and Foundation of American Indian Education Policy. Montana Office of Public Instruction. Feb. 2001. Electronic document http://www.opi.mt.gov/pdf/indianed/Resources/indpolicyhistory.pdf, accessed February 17, 2009.

Khachadoorian, Angelle A.
2005   Boarding School, Family and Opportunity: Student Discourses as Adaptive Strategies at the Southwestern Indian Polytechnic Institute. Unpublished dissertation, Department of Anthropology, University of New Mexico.

Koch, Susan, and Stanley Deetz
1981   Metaphor Analysis of Social Reality in Organizations. The Journal of Applied Communication Research. 9(1):1–15.

Kovecses, Zoltan
2005   Metaphor in Culture: Universality and Variation. Cambridge: Cambridge University Press.

Lakoff, George, and Mark Johnson
1980   Metaphors We Live By. New Afterword, 2003. Chicago: The University of Chicago Press.

Logan, Paul
2005   Indian Education. Albuquerque Journal, Special Section, April 10: 76.

Lomawaima, K. Tsianina
1994   They Called It Prairie Light: The Story of Chilocco Indian School. Lincoln: University of Nebraska Press.

Lomawaima, K. Tsianina, and Teresa L. McCarty
2006   To Remain an Indian: Lessons in Democracy from a Century of Native American Education. Multicultural Education Series, Ed. James A. Banks. New York: Teachers College Press.

Lovell, John P.
1979   Neither Athens nor Sparta?: The American Service Academies in Transition. Bloomington: Indiana University Press.

Machamer, Ann Marie
   2000   Along the Red Road: Tribally Controlled Colleges and Student Development. Unpublished dissertation, Department of Education, University of California, Los Angeles.

Makuakane-Dreschel, Teresa, and Linda Serra Hagedorn
   2000   Correlates of Retention Among Asian Pacific Americans in Community Colleges: The Case for Hawaiian Students. Community College Journal of Research and Practice 24(8):639.

Manifold, Carol, and Betty Rambur
   2001   Predictors of Attrition in American Indian Nursing Students. Journal of Nursing Education 40(6):279–281.

Manzo, Kathleen Kennedy
   1994   Breaking Point: Tribal Colleges Overcome Neglect, Lack of Resources. How Much Longer Can They Persevere? Black Issues in Higher Education 11(16):34.

Marquand, Barbara
   2006   Fighting the Meth Addiction Epidemic in Indian Country. Minority Nurse. Fall. Electronic document, http://www.minoritynurse.com/American-indian-native-American/fighting-meth-addiction-epidemic-indian-country, accessed March 24, 2009.

McCall, William
   2005   American Indian Students Protest Fence. Associated Press, February 19.

McCarty, Teresa L.
   2002   A Place to Be Navajo: Rough Rock and the Struggle for Self-Determination in Indigenous Schooling. Mahwah, New Jersey: Lawrence Erlbaum Associates, Publishers.

McClellan, George S., Mary Jo Tippeconnic Fox, and Shelly C. Lowe
   2005   Where We Have Been: A History of Native American Higher Education. *In* Serving Native American Students. New Directions in Student Services. 109 (Spring). San Francisco: Wiley Periodicals.

McDowell, Malcolm
   1916   Letter to Superintendents of Indian Agencies. Copy in the Ayer Collection at the Newberry Library, Chicago, IL.

McReynolds, Mary Jane
   1997   "Hitting the Mountain": Educational Success Among Native American Women in Albuquerque, New Mexico. Unpublished dissertation, Department of Anthropology, University of New Mexico.

Merten, Don, and Gary Schwartz
   1982   Metaphor and Self: Symbolic Process in Everyday Life. American Anthropologist 84(4):796–810.

Monette, Gerald Carty
1997 Tribal Colleges: Tradition, Heritage, and Community. ERIC Review 5(3):24–225.

Nagel, Joane
1997 American Indian Ethnic Renewal: Red Power and the Resurgence of Identity and Culture. New York: Oxford University Press.

National Congress of the American Indian
2006 Methamphetamines in Indian Country: An American Problem Uniquely Affecting Indian Country. Electronic document, http://www.ncai.org/ncai/Meth/Meth_in_Indian_Country_Fact_Sheet.pdf, accessed March 24, 2009. Pp.1–7.

National Diabetes Education Program. National Institute of Health
2008 The Diabetes Epidemic Among American Indians and Alaska Natives. August. Electronic document, http://www.ndep.nih.gov/diabetes/pubs/FS_AmIndian.pdf, accessed March 24, 2009.

Office of Indian Affairs. Department of the Interior
1906 Teaching the Rudiments of Cooking in the Class Room: Primary Methods and Outlines for the Use of Teachers in the Indian Schools. Washington, D.C.: Government Printing Office.
1913 Tentative Course of Study for United States Indian Schools. Preface by Cato Sells, Commissioner of Indian Education. Washington, DC: Government Printing Office.

Ogunwole, Stella U.
2006 We The People: American Indians and Alaska Natives in the United States. Census 2000 Special Reports. Issued February 2006. CENSR-28. Electronic document, http://www.census.gov/prod/2006pubs/censr-28.pdf, accessed March 19, 2009. Pp.1–23.

Olson, James S., and Raymond Wilson
1984 Native Americans in the Twentieth Century. University of Illinois Press.

Oppelt, Norman T.
1990 The Tribally Controlled Indian Colleges: The Beginnings of Self Determination in American Indian Education. Tsaile, AZ: Navajo Community College Press.

Pavel, D. Michael
1992 American Indians in Higher Education: The Community College Experience. ERIC Digest. Los Angeles: ERIC Clearinghouse for Junior Colleges.

Pavel, D. Michael, Thomas R. Curtin, Bruce Christenson, and Blair A. Rudes
1995 Characteristics of American Indian and Alaska Native Education: Results from the 1990–91 Schools and Staffing Survey. U.S. Depart-

ment of Educational Research and Improvement. National Center for Education Statistics. Washington, DC: Government Printing Office. NCES 95-735.

Pavel, D. Michael, and Ella Inglebret
2007 The American Indian and Alaska Native Student's Guide to College Success. Westport, CT: Greenwood Press.

Pavel, D. Michael, Ella Inglebret, and Susan Rae Banks
2001 Tribal Colleges and Universities in an Era of Dynamic Development. Peabody Journal of Education 76(1):50-72.

Peterson's Online
2008 Southwestern Indian Polytechnic Institute. Electronic document, http://www.petersons.com/UGChannel/code/InstVC.asp?inunid=8764&sponsor=13, accessed February 11, 2009.

Pevar, Stephen L.
1992 The Rights of Indians and Tribes: The Basic ACLU Guide to Indian and Tribal Rights. Second edition. An American Civil Liberties Handbook. Carbondale: Southern Illinois University Press.

Phillips, John L.
2003 A Tribal College Land Grant Perspective: Changing the Conversation. Journal of American Indian Education 42(1):22-35.

Relph, Edward C.
1976 Place and Placelessness. London: Pion.

Reyhner, Jon, and Jeanne Eder
1989 A History of Indian Education. Eastern Montana College Printing Services.
2004 American Indian Education: A History. Norman, Oklahoma: University of Oklahoma Press.

Ridgeway, Michael
1998 Overcoming Reservations About Leaving the Reservation. Community College Week 10(5):11.

Rosenfelt, Daniel M.
1974 Legal Obligations to Provide Educational Services for Indians. Journal of American Indian Education 13(2):4-8. Electronic document, http://jaie.asu.edu/v13/V13S21eg.html, accessed February 16, 2009.

Rousey, Annmaria, and Erich Longie
2001 The Tribal College as Family Support System. American Behavioral Scientist 44(9):1492-1504.

Soldier, Lydia Whirlwind
1997 Inventing New Approaches to Tribal Education. Tribal College Journal of American Indian Higher Education 8(4):38.

Southwestern Indian Polytechnic Institute
1998   Student Handbook 1998–99. Albuquerque, New Mexico: Publisher Unknown.
1999   Catalog 1999–2001. Albuquerque, New Mexico: Publisher Unknown.
2000   Southwestern Indian Polytechnic Institute Employees Handbook, January 10, 2000. Albuquerque, New Mexico: Publisher Unknown.
2001   Student Handbook 2001–2002. Albuquerque, New Mexico: Publisher Unknown.
2003   Catalog Supplement. Albuquerque, New Mexico: Southwestern Indian Polytechnic Institute Graphic Arts Program.
2004   Registration Data. Southwestern Indian Polytechnic Institute's Registrar's Office. Unpublished.
2008   "Conference Presentation Slides." Office of Indian Education. July 8–10, 2008. Partnerships for Indian Education. Electronic document, http://www.indianeducation.org/userfiles/files/SIPI%20BIE.pdf, accessed October 28, 2008.

Standing Bear, Luther, Earl Alonzo Brininstool and Richard N. Ellis (Interpreter)
2006   My People the Sioux, 2nd ed. With a new introduction by Virginia Driving Hawk Sneve. Lincoln: University of Nebraska Press.

Stein, Wayne J.
1988   A History of the Tribally Controlled Community Colleges: 1968–1978. Unpublished dissertation, Department of Educational Administration and Supervision, Washington State College.
1998   American Indian Education. *In* American Indian Studies: An Interdisciplinary Approach to Contemporary Issues, Dane Morrison, ed. Pp. 73–92. New York: Peter Lang.

Stellern, John, Jim Collins, Bob Gutierrez, and Elaine Patterson
1986   Hemispheric Dominance of Native American Indian Students. Journal of American Indian Education 25(2):8–17.

Swentzell, Rina
1997   Conflicting Landscape Values: The Santa Clara Pueblo and Day School. *In* Understanding Ordinary Landscapes, Groth, Paul Erling, and Todd W. Bressi, eds. Pp.56–66. New Haven: Yale University Press.

Swisher, Karen, and Michelle Hoisch
1992   Dropping Out Among American Indians and Alaska Natives: A Review of Studies. Journal of American Indian Education 31(2):3–23.

Szasz, Margaret Connell
1988   Indian Education in the American Colonies, 1607–1783. Albuquerque, New Mexico: University of New Mexico Press.
1999   Education and the American Indian: The Road to Self-Determination

Since 1928. 3rd ed. Albuquerque, New Mexico: University of New Mexico Press.

Tierney, William G.
1992   Official Encouragement, Institutional Discouragement: Minorities in Academe—The Native American Experience. Norwood, New Jersey: Ablex Publishing Company.
1998   Power, Identity and the Dilemma of College Student Departure: Preparing Learners for College. Reprint of papers from "Embracing the Vision Conference: April 19–21, 1998." Flagstaff: Northern Arizona University.
1999   Models of Minority College-Going and Retention: Cultural Integrity versus Cultural Suicide. The Journal of Negro Education 68(1).

Trennert, Robert A. Jr.
1988   The Phoenix Indian School: Forced Assimilation in Arizona, 1891–1935. Norman: University of Oklahoma Press.

Turtle Mountain Community College
2002   Catalog. Chicago, IL: Turtle Mountain Community College.

United Nations Economic and Social Council
2003   Prevention of Discrimination and Protection of Indigenous People, Preliminary Report of the Special Rapporteur, Erica-Irene A. Daes, submitted in accordance with Sub-Commission resolution 2002/15. E/CN.4/Sub.2/2003/20.

United States Department of Education, National Center for Education Statistics.
1998   American Indians and Alaska Natives in Postsecondary Education. NCES 98-291, by D. Michael Pavel, Rebecca Skinner, Elizabeth Farris, Margaret Cahalan, John Tippeconnic, and Wayne Stein. Project Officers, Bernard Greene and Martha Hollins. Washington, DC: 1998.
2008   Status and Trends in the Education of American Indians and Alaska Natives: 2008. Institute of Education Sciences. September 2008. NCES 2008-084. Electronic document, http://nces.ed.gov/pubs2008/nativetrends/ind_6_2.asp, accessed February 24, 2009.

United States Department of Health and Human Services
2007   Tuberculosis. Minority Women's Health. Electronic document, http://www.4woman.gov/minority/Americanindian/tb.cfm, accessed March 24, 2009.

United States House of Representatives
1997   "Haskell Indian Nations University and Southwestern Indian Polytechnic Institute Administrative Systems Act of 1997." 105th Congress, 1st Session. Electronic document, http://bulk.resource.org/gpo.gov/bills/105/h1337ih.txt, accessed February 23, 2009.

United States Indian Service. Department of the Interior.
1913   Rules for the Indian School Service. Washington, DC: Government Printing Office.

Uyteebrouk, Oliver
2001   Tribal College Gets High Grades in Student Retention. Community College Week 13(25):2.

Wax, Murray L., Rosalie H. Wax, and Robert V. Dumont Jr.
1964   Formal Education in an American Indian Community. Atlanta: Emory University. With the assistance of Roselyn Holyrock and Gerald Onefeather. Social Problems: Official Journal of the Society for the Study of Social Problems. Cooperative research project no. 1361.

Wilkins, David E.
2002   American Indian Politics and the American Political System. Boulder, CO: Rowan and Littlefield.

Wilkins, David E., and K. Tsianina Lomawaima
2001   Uneven Ground: American Indian Sovereignty and Federal Law. Norman: University of Oklahoma Press.

Willeto, Angela A. A.
1999   Navajo Culture and Family Influences on Academic Success: Traditionalism Is Not a Significant Predictor of Achievements Among Young Navajos. Journal of American Indian Education 38(2):1–24.

Woodcock, Don B., and Osman Alawiye
2001   The Antecedents of Failure and Emerging Hope: American Indians and Public Higher Education. Education 121(4).

Zitkala-Sa
2005   American Indian Stories. New York: Barnes and Noble Books.

Index

ADE. *See* Adult Developmental Education
Adult Developmental Education, 14, 23, 185, 223
AIHEC. *See* American Indian Higher Education Consortium
Albuquerque Indian School, 1, 24, 65
Albuquerque Journal, 104
American Indian Higher Education Consortium, 10, 11, 75, 76, 77, 81, 191, 198
Asbury, C. H., 65

Bacone College, 54
Barker, Debra K. S., 43
Bentham, Jeremy, 66, 67, 69, 152, 153
BIA. *See* Bureau of Indian Affairs
BIE. *See* Bureau of Indian Education
boarding schools, 3, 5, 33, 34, 43, 56–62, 65–70, 72, 145, 150, 151, 182, 217; curriculum, 61, 62–63. *See also* Bureau of Indian Affairs, Indian schools
Bureau of Indian Affairs, 1–7, 9, 16–17, 31, 33, 34, 42, 43, 49–52, 55–59, 63–65, 69–74, 76–80, 83, 100–102, 117, 127, 144, 150–52, 167–68, 178, 182, 217, 222. *See also* boarding schools, Bureau of Indian Education, day schools, Indian schools
Bureau of Indian Education, 3, 4, 16–17, 22

Cankdeska Cikana Community College, 181, 182
Carlisle Indian School, 59, 60, 61, 63, 66–68
Carnegie Foundation for the Advancement of Teaching, 79, 81
CCCNM. *See* Community College of Central New Mexico
Certificate of Degree of Indian Blood, 85, 89, 161
CIB. *See* Certificate of Degree of Indian Blood
"Civilization Fund," 55
Coggeshall, C. T., 65
Community College of Central New Mexico, 24, 100, 118, 187

Davis, Jerry, 8
day schools, 57–58. *See also* Bureau of Indian Affairs, Indian schools
Department of the Interior, 3, 5
Diné College, 3, 74, 75, 79, 81
distance education, 10, 11, 15, 162, 224
dormitories, 94, 97, 99, 102, 109–13, 120, 132, 138–48, 152, 186, 200, 204–208; "details" and student housekeeping duties, 62, 63, 67, 108, 112, 138, 139–40, 144–48, 209; gender differences, 141–42; roommates 111–13, 140, 151, 164, 191, 203
D-Q University, 75

drug and alcohol issues at SIPI. *See* Southwestern Indian Polytechnic Institute: drug and alcohol issues, zero-tolerance policy

faculty at SIPI. *See* Southwetern Indian Polytechnic Institute: faculty
Foucault, Michel, 153
Four Winds Lodge. *See* dormitories

Garrod, Andrew, 36
GED. *See* General Equivalency Degree
General Equivalency Degree, 14, 15
Golden Eagle Lodge. *See* dormitories

Hampton Institute, 60
Haskell Indian Nations University, 1, 4–6, 8, 17, 19–20, 30, 49, 76, 85, 86, 182, 219
HBCU. *See* Historically Black Colleges and Universities
Head Start, 15, 84
HINU. *See* Haskell Indian Nations University
Historically Black Colleges and Universities, 36, 81
Hogan, the, 29, 83, 132, 135–38
Horne, Essie Burnett, 182
House Concurrent Resolution 108, 73–74
Huffman, Terry, 36, 38, 181

IAIA. *See* Institute of American Indian Arts
in loco parentis, 32–34, 49, 117–19, 123, 138–44, 195–202
Indian schools, 50–52, 54–59, 61–62, 64–69, 117. *See also* boarding schools, Bureau of Indian Affairs
Institute of American Indian Arts, 4, 5, 17, 76

land grant institutions, 75, 78, 128
Lomawaima, K. Tsianina, 191
Lodges. *See* dormitories
Lovell, John P., 49

Machamer, Ann Marie, 8
matron: at historic Indian schools 62, 70;
SIPI dormitory aides, 69, 110, 121, 130, 131, 139, 141, 143, 146–48, 205–208
McDowell, Malcolm, 64, 65
McReynolds, Mary Jane, 8
Meriam report, 65,
metaphor: 40–45; "SIPI is a network of support," 39, 42, 44, 86–89, 108, 155–61, 168–79, 180–84, 192; "SIPI is a resource for self-determination," 1, 43, 44, 89, 105, 116, 131, 163, 185, 199–208, 211; "SIPI is a system of control," 42, 43, 93, 95, 98, 102, 108, 116–31, 132, 142, 147, 151, 153–54, 185, 187, 189–90, 197, 203, 210, 213
Miss SIPI, 113
Morgan, Lewis Henry, 55
Ms. Frybread, 114

Native American college students, 7, 8, 10, 14, 20, 36–40, 49, 51, 77–78, 80, 211
Navajo Community College. *See* Diné College

Office of Indian Affairs, 51, 62, 64
Office of Indian Education Programs, 3, 17, 22
OIEP. *See* Office of Indian Education Programs
Oppelt, Norman T., 80

Panopticon, 66–67, 69, 152, 153
"partying" and "party school" reputation. *See* Southwestern Indian Polytechnic Institute: drug and alcohol issues, zero-tolerance policy
Pevar, Stephen L., 84
Phillips, John L., 78, 169
placement testing, 13, 14, 209, 210, 213
powwows, 113, 125, 175
Pratt, Richard Henry, 34, 59–60, 64, 66

Reyhner, Jon, 181
Rio Grande River, 1, 23, 24, 25, 119, 131, 133, 137, 171
Roessel, Robert, 71, 72,
Rough Rock Demonstration School, 63, 71, 72, 77
Rousey, Annmaria, 182

Santa Clara Pueblo, 57–58, 152
Sinte Gleska University, 85
SIPI. *See* Southwestern Indian Polytechnic Institute
Southwestern Indian Polytechnic Institute: accreditation as community college, 6, 13, 31, 186; adjunct instructors, 13, 21, 45, 46, 186, 187, 188; assemblies, student resistance to, 123–26; board of regents, 12, 13, 18, 20, 22, 34, 99; budget, 4, 6, 20, 21, 22, 28, 217; campus layout and description, 23–30, 170; campus security services, 32–33, 119, 126–32, 147, 219; campus violence, 95, 96, 97, 174, 203; drug and alcohol abuse, 95–101, 117, 121, 122, 128–29, 133, 147–48, 156, 174, 176, 179, 203, 204, 207; employee layoffs, 6, 22–23; faculty, 94, 103, 124–25, 175, 179, 181, 188–91, 192–99, 210; family ties on campus, 86–93, 96, 97, 156, 176, 180, 182–84, 188, 203; institutional models, 6, 30–35, 49, 116, 187, 212; and metaphor (*see* metaphor); organizational structure and academic departments, 11–17; student activities, 21, 26, 101, 113–16, 126, 139, 202; student demographics, 10–11, 223, 226; student protests, 138, 139; Student Senate, 18, 118, 188; zero-tolerance policy, 95, 99, 103, 120–22, 128–29, 133, 140, 147–49, 190. *See also* specific buildings or programs
Standing Bear, Luther, 63, 64, 67, 68
Student Union Building, 27, 88, 114, 115, 116
SUB. *See* Student Union Building
Swentzell, Rina, 57, 58

TCU. *See* tribally controlled colleges and universities
Technical Vocational Institute (Albuquerque). *See* Community College of Central New Mexico
Termination. *See* House Concurrent Resolution 108.
Tierney, William G., 7, 30, 37, 187, 192
Tinto, Vincent, 37, 38
treaty obligations: and education, 20–21, 54, 85
tribally controlled colleges and universities, 3–7, 10, 14, 17, 31, 34, 36–39, 42, 49, 50, 53–54, 57, 63, 72, 73–85, 93–94, 135, 153, 162–63, 168, 173, 181–82, 186, 187–88, 191, 192–93, 216–18, 222
Tribally Controlled Community College Act of 1978, 75
Turtle Mountain Community College, 81
TVI. *See* Community College of Central New Mexico

United States Air Force Academy, 5, 45, 47–49
United Nations Economic and Social Council, 51
United States House of Representatives, 19–20
University of New Mexico, 13, 14, 24, 27, 73, 100, 117, 118, 186, 187, 188, 193, 215
UNM. *See* University of New Mexico
USAFA. *See* United States Air Force Academy

Wax, Murray L. and Rosalie H., 36

Zitkala-Sa, 68–69